LEFT BRAIN RIGHT STUFF

HOW LEADERS MAKE WINNING DECISIONS

PHIL ROSENZWEIG

PublicAffairs
New York

Copyright © 2014 by Phil Rosenzweig.

Published in the United States by PublicAffairs™,
a Member of the Perseus Books Group.

PublicAffairs books are available at special discounts for bulk
purchases in the U.S. by corporations, institutions, and other
organizations. For more information, please contact the
Special Markets Department at the Perseus Books Group,
2300 Chestnut Street, Suite 200, Philadelphia, PA 19103,
call (800) 810-4145, ext. 5000, or e-mail special.markets@
perseusbooks.com.

Book Design by Pauline Brown
Typeset in Goudy Old Style Std by the Perseus Books Group

Library of Congress Cataloging-in-Publication Data

Rosenzweig, Philip M., 1955–
    Left brain, right stuff : how leaders make
winning decisions / Phil Rosenzweig.—First edition.
        pages cm
    Includes bibliographical references and index.
    ISBN 978-1-61039-307-2 (hardcover)—
    ISBN 978-1-61039-308-9 (e-book)
    1. Decision making. 2. Decision making—
Psychological aspects. 3. Leadership—Psychological aspects.
    I. Title.
HD30.23.R6725   2013
658.4'03—dc23
2013031990

First Edition

10 9 8 7 6 5 4 3 2 1

For the home team

Laura, Tom, and Caroline

CONTENTS

CRUNCH TIME ON A HOT AUGUST NIGHT

COMPARED WITH MANAGING, TRADING WAS ADMIRABLY DIRECT.
YOU MADE YOUR BETS AND EITHER YOU WON OR YOU LOST.

MICHAEL LEWIS, *LIAR'S POKER*, 1989

It was a billion-dollar decision, give or take a few million.

On the night of August 12, 2010, Bill Flemming, president of Skanska USA Building, faced a tough choice. Get it right, and the upside could be very lucrative. Get it wrong, and the results could be disastrous.

The story began a year earlier, when the National Security Agency (NSA) announced plans to build a computer facility for the security information it gathers around the world. The Utah Data Center (UDC) would be fully self-contained, with its own power plant and water supply, and would come equipped with anti-terrorism defenses. The site for this sprawling complex was the abandoned airfield at Camp Williams, a National Guard base in a lonesome canyon south of Salt Lake City. A forbidding location, but ideal for this purpose. It was vast, remote, and very secure.

Skanska USA Building was a division of the Swedish-based company, Skanska, and a leader in the North American construction industry. It had a strong record of large and successful projects. The company had recently completed the MetLife Stadium in New Jersey, home of the football Giants and Jets, a state-of-the-art marvel that could hold eighty-two thousand fans. It was currently at work on dozens of projects, from the renovation of the United Nations building on Manhattan's East Side to the World Trade Center Transportation Hub, the network of train and subway stations under Ground Zero.

The UDC was doubly attractive to Flemming. It was a "design/ build" project, meaning that the contractor handled both design and construction. Flemming explained: "If you can come in with a better design—more efficient and smarter functionality—and if you have methods to build the facility faster, then you might beat the other bidders."[1]

But Skanska wouldn't be bidding alone. Several other top construction companies were just as eager to win the deal.

The first step was to answer the NSA's Request for Qualifications, which asked for a list of relevant experience and resources. Skanska USA Building, working with a partner, Okland Construction Company, was one of twelve bidders to submit an RFQ in February 2010. Two months later, the NSA eliminated seven and invited just five—Skanska and four others—to submit formal bids. They were given sixty days.

Over the next weeks, Flemming and his top aides worked with a team of subcontractors to prepare the bid. The NSA was explicit about the layout and capacity it wanted and also defined the technical standards. Although no price was stated, it was rumored that Congress had appropriated more than $1 billion. For prospective bidders the message was clear: it was more important to provide the best performance than to meet a specific price.

On June 16 Skanska USA Building submitted a bid for the Utah Data Center with a price tag of $1.475 billion. And then it waited.

In mid-July the NSA issued its reply. All five bids had come in between $1.4 billion and $1.8 billion, substantially more than the government wanted to spend. Now the NSA narrowed the scope of the project, keeping the key elements but eliminating a few redundancies. Technical performance was just as important, and the schedule was unchanged. For the first time the NSA specified a target price: $1.212 billion. Now price was a crucial element. A bid in excess of that amount would be rejected for noncompliance.

The same five companies were invited to submit new bids, with Best and Final Offers due on August 13, just six weeks away.

Now it was game on. At Skanska USA Building's head offices in Parsippany, New Jersey, a large conference room was dedicated to the UDC bid. Only approved personnel were allowed inside, their access limited by swipe cards. A team of twenty-five pored over every aspect of the project, looking for ways to lower the cost. Removing some redundancies helped, but there was still a long way to go. Everyone was focused on a single goal: how to get to *one-point-two-one-two*.

For the next six weeks, during the hottest summer on record, Flemming's team looked for ways to drive down costs.[2] They worked with their subcontractors to streamline the procurement process, buying in bulk or working directly with suppliers to cut out middlemen. They looked closely at the contingency for risk, a standard part of any bid. After concluding that certain inputs were unlikely to rise over the next three years, they were able to reduce the contingency. They also reviewed the provision for management fees, in effect what they would earn. By committing to working more quickly and efficiently, they were able to lower the bid still further.

By early August Skanska USA Building's bid stood at $1.26 billion, now tantalizingly close to the target of $1.212 billion. Could Skanska take out even more and eliminate that $48 million gap, producing a bid that was low enough to win but high enough to earn a profit? Or would going lower expose Skanska to serious losses?

As he pondered the way forward, Flemming considered several factors. The UDC would take three years to build, during which time it should be possible to find additional savings. The question was how much. Skanska had reason to be optimistic. In an industry known for cost overruns, Skanska USA Building had often done better than budget. It had won the MetLife Stadium contract with a bid of $998 million, well below its nearest rival, and still found a way to earn greater profits than expected.[3] The World Trade Center Transportation Hub was currently running ahead of schedule and also below cost. Surely further savings would be possible for the UDC as well. Flemming commented: "The experience that I've had over the years is typically, you can get someplace between another 3 percent and 4 percent out." Taking out 3 percent would bring Skanska from $1.26 billion to $1.222 billion, still short of the goal. Reaching $1.212 billion would require lowering the bid by 3.8 percent, which was very ambitious but not impossible.

The problem was that coming in exactly at the target might not be enough. Skanska was up against four large, experienced contenders. Although none was likely to "take a flier"—the industry phrase for a lowball bid designed to win at any price—the chances were good that at least one would come in below the threshold. If Skanska did no better than meet the target, it would lose to a more aggressive rival. To win would call for going even lower.

Flemming also considered the policies of his parent company. Skanska's headquarters in Stockholm had an edict known as the Five Zeros. All construction projects were to be safe (zero accidents), ethical (zero ethical breaches), of high quality (zero defects), and green (zero environmental incidents). Above all, they had to be profitable (zero loss making). There was good reason to stress profit in the construction industry. Even at the best of times, most projects earned only small margins, so that one loser could wipe out the profits of several good ones. Losing money on a large project was unacceptable, and Flemming knew it.

Yet playing it safe and missing out on a large, high-profile project was also unthinkable. As president, Flemming was concerned about questions of reputation. What would the joint venture partner think if, after months of hard work, the project fell through because Skanska had been unwilling to make a big bet? Would it ever work with Skanska again? As for rival companies, would they conclude that Skanska lacked nerve? And what about Flemming's staff, the people he worked with day in and day out? If he wasn't willing to go the extra mile, would they see him as prudent and wise, or would they wonder if he was overly cautious and risk averse? As for the parent company, it wanted to avoid losses, but also wanted to win big deals. Successful managers didn't just walk away from big-ticket projects; they found ways to win contracts *and* make them succeed. Of course, never far away was the specter of failure. The worst outcome of all would be to win the bid, but lose money.

The Best and Final Offer was due at four o'clock the next afternoon at Army Corps of Engineers offices in Baltimore. As night fell, Bill Flemming agonized: "I'm staring at a number that's about $50 million too high, and I know I could be disqualified if I don't get to the government's number. Fifty million out of $1.26 billion isn't that much. Do we risk going in with a bid that's over the limit, and maybe not get it? Or do we take a lower amount and trust that we can find some innovation?"

Eventually Flemming made the call: Skanska would enter a bid of $1.2107 billion, placing the company $1.3 million under the target. How it would earn a profit wasn't entirely clear. Flemming explained: "We'll take the chance that somewhere along the line we can become even more productive—by improving our scheduling, or finding ways to work faster, or discovering ways to reduce our costs."

With that, the meeting broke up. The bid team worked through the night, finalizing stacks of documents and assembling binders. The next afternoon, the final bid was delivered to ACE offices on South Howard Street in Baltimore barely an hour before the deadline.

Back at Skanska the mood was positive. Flemming recalled: "We were optimistic. We had been struggling to get to the number, but we did it. We felt good."

THINKING ABOUT DECISIONS

Not many of us will have to make a decision quite like the one that Bill Flemming faced on that hot August night. We won't have to submit a bid worth more than a billion dollars, with hundreds of jobs at stake and with the clock ticking down. But in other respects, Flemming's decision was typical of thorny decisions we face in many walks of life, not just business but also politics, sports, and the military. These decisions are complex, consequential, and laden with uncertainty. Learning to make better decisions—smarter, wiser, and more likely to lead to success—is a high priority.

In recent years a large number of books have been written about decision making. Many draw on the findings of research in cognitive psychology. Human beings, we have learned, are not the rational creatures we read about in economics textbooks. They make predictable errors, or biases, which often undermine their decisions.

By now we're familiar with many of these errors, including the following:

- People are said to be overconfident, too sure of themselves and unrealistically optimistic about the future.
- People look for information that will confirm what they want to believe, rather than seeking information that might challenge their hopes.
- People labor under the illusion of control, imagining they have more influence over events than they really do.
- People are fooled by random events, seeing patterns where none exist.
- People are not good intuitive statisticians, preferring a coherent picture to what makes sense according to the laws of probability.
- People suffer from a hindsight bias, believing that they were right all along.

The standard advice for making better decisions is to be aware of our tendency for common biases and to find ways to avoid them. That makes sense for many kinds of decisions. But as we'll see, it's not sufficient for others, including many of great importance.

THE VIEW FROM THE 32ND FLOOR

A few months after the events described here, I met with Bill Flemming and two of his colleagues at Skanska's US corporate offices on the 32nd floor of the Empire State Building in New York City. It was one of those stunning winter days when you can see for miles in every direction and the world seems crystal clear. Our conference room, bordering Fifth Avenue, offered a dazzling view. Straight ahead, looking east, was the broad expanse of Queens and Brooklyn. To the left the skyscrapers of midtown Manhattan were arrayed against a deep blue sky; looking right, the towers of lower Manhattan stood out in a silvery silhouette against the winter sun.

As the Skanska executives described how they had determined what to bid, I listened for evidence of common errors. Had their bid been shaped by biases? Or had they managed to steer clear of biases and make a sound bid? Neither view was quite right.

I asked about the weeks leading up to August 12, as they tried to bring a bid of $1.475 billion down to the target of $1.212 billion. Had they searched for evidence that would help them win the bid, an error known as the confirmation trap? They answered without hesitation. *Of course* they had looked for confirmatory evidence! Anyone can find reasons *not* to do something, they said. If you don't push yourself to go ahead, you'll never be successful. That didn't mean they had disregarded potential problems. But in this sort of competition, finding ways to lower the bid was essential.

I also looked for signs of overconfidence. The final bid was based on finding another $50 million in savings; had they committed to more than could be justified? *Definitely*, they agreed. But they didn't see that as excessive confidence at all. Betting that they could find further improvements was entirely reasonable. Moreover, in the context of competitive bidding, it was necessary. Anyone *not* willing to bet they could find further savings would have no chance. What seemed excessive by one definition was essential by another.

I also inquired about something called the winner's curse. Were they aware that in a competitive bid, the winner often goes too far and ends up a loser? *Yes*, they said. As industry veterans, each one was acutely aware of the danger of runaway bids. The last thing they wanted to do was make a foolish bid. Yet they also knew that if they were too cautious, they would have no chance of winning. Worry too much about the winner's curse, and you'll have a different kind of problem: you will *never* win.

As I listened to the Skanska executives, the standard lessons of decision research—to be alert to common errors and to guard against them—didn't do justice to the complexities they faced.

DECISIONS IN LABORATORIES AND IN THE REAL WORLD

Over the past several decades we have learned a great deal about decision making, thanks in large part to finely crafted experiments. One important stream of research looked at the way people make choices under conditions of risk. An experiment asked: "Would you rather have $90 for sure, or a gamble that provided a 90 percent chance of getting $100 and a 10 percent chance of getting nothing?" From a strict mathematical perspective, the two options are identical. Both have what economists call an *expected value* of $90. But people do not see them as the same. Most would much rather have $90 for sure than run a 10 percent risk of winding up with nothing at all. (Many of us would even prefer $80 for sure rather than take the gamble offered, even though on average it would give one $90.)

A separate line of research set aside the question of risk and examined the way our choices can be affected by how options are framed. Recently I have used an example in my executive education class based on an experiment devised by Amos Tversky and Itamar Simonson, which goes like this: imagine you're shopping for a camera and are offered two options. Which would you prefer?[4]

- Minolta S1 priced at $269.99, rated 6 out of 10 by *Consumer Reports*
- Minolta S2 priced at $539.99, rated 8 out of 10 by *Consumer Reports*

When I asked this question of a group of managers not long ago, most picked the S1. A large majority said they would rather spend less for a good camera, whereas only a minority said they'd be willing to spend twice as much for the better camera. In parallel, a different set of managers was offered a choice that included these two options, but added a third:

- Minolta S1 priced at $269.99, rated 6 out of 10 by *Consumer Reports*
- Minolta S2 priced at $539.99, rated 8 out of 10 by *Consumer Reports*
- Minolta S3 priced at $839.99, rated 7 out of 10 by *Consumer Reports*

Faced with this choice, very few selected the S3, but the preference for the other two was reversed. Now a large majority preferred the S2, and fewer went for the S1.[5] Merely by adding the very expensive S3, the S2 appeared to be the moderate middle option and offered the best combination of price and quality. According to economic theory, such a shift seems irrational. If customers prefer the S1 to the S2, they shouldn't switch to the S2 just because a third option is added. But that's what happens. How decisions are framed can shape our choices.

Crucially, these experiments are designed so you can choose the option you want, but you can't alter the options. In the first example, you can either take the $90 or accept a gamble, but you can't change the terms. You can't improve the odds of winning $100 to something better than 90 percent, nor can you boost the amount you stand to win from $100 to, say, $120. In the second example, you can pick one camera or another, but you can't alter the choices. You can't do anything to make the cameras better, perhaps by adding features, nor can you bargain the prices down, nor can you ask to see a Canon or a Nikon. You respond to the choices presented, period.

There's a good reason that experiments about choice are designed this way. If you *could* alter the options, it would be much more difficult to compare answers. We would wind up with many different answers to a wide range of options, rather than a neatly comparable set of data. The way to learn about choice is to present people with a limited number of options, then compare their responses.

A separate line of research examined the way people make judgments under uncertainty. A well-known example asks people to make guesses about such things as the length of the Nile, or the year Mozart was born, or the weight of a Boeing 747. Asked to provide a range that they are 90 percent certain contains the correct answer, people routinely provide ranges that are far too narrow, leading to the conclusion that they are overconfident.

Here again, people are asked to make judgments about things they cannot influence. Your guess may be accurate or far off, but either way you won't change the length of the Nile, or the year Mozart was born, or the weight of a Boeing 747. Again, there's a good reason that experiments about judgment ask about things we cannot influence. If we *could* influence what we evaluate, responses would reflect our different abilities, or at least our perceptions of those abilities. Ask two people to make a judgment about a simple task—how far they can throw a ball, for example—and their replies will differ based on their abilities. The best way to learn about judgment is precisely the approach researchers have followed: make sure everyone has the same ability to influence outcomes—that is, none at all.

Most experiments about judgment and choice also have a few other features. They typically ask you to make the decision that's best for you, without considering anyone else. There is no competitive dimension. You don't have to think about what someone else might do. They also usually involve decisions that are made quickly and have outcomes that are known right away. That's helpful to make sure everyone faces the exact same circumstances, so answers can be compared without worrying about intervening factors. Finally, these experiments ask participants to make their decisions alone, as individuals, not as members of a group. They don't have to worry about how they will be perceived by a subordinate, or whether their decisions today are consistent with those they made last week, or whether people will think they're bold and decisive as opposed to wishy-washy.

Thanks to carefully crafted laboratory experiments, we know a great deal about the way people make judgments and choices. As psychologist Dan Ariely explains: "For social scientists, experiments are like microscopes or strobe lights, magnifying and illuminating the complex, multiple forces that simultaneously exert their influences on us. They help us slow human behavior to a frame-by-frame narration of events, isolate individual factors, and examine them carefully and in more detail."[6]

Experiments about judgment and choice have made important contributions to many fields.[7] In consumer behavior, we have a much better understanding of how people make purchasing decisions.[8] For marketing managers, eager to entice buying behavior, it's immensely valuable to understand how small changes in pricing or in the presentation of options can lead customers to open their wallets. For consumers, also, it's useful to understand the forces that shape our choices, so we can see through marketing ploys and try to avoid being manipulated. These experiments typically involve individuals acting alone, making choices from fixed options, without regard to any competitive forces.

In public policy, we have learned a great deal about the way people save for retirement, how (or if) they purchase health insurance, and even how drivers respond to traffic signals on busy roads. Armed with a sharper understanding of the way people make decisions, government agencies can design services in a more cost-effective manner.[9] Once more, these decisions involve individuals responding to options they cannot alter, without any competitive pressure.

In finance, too, we have learned a lot about the way people make investment decisions. We know they make predictable errors when managing their portfolios, often buying and selling at the wrong time. They neglect the natural tendency of regression toward the mean and succumb to the fixed cost fallacy.[10] Once again, most investment decisions involve the purchase or sale of assets the performance of which cannot be affected directly. Traders place their bets and either win or lose, but can't influence the outcome. Similarly, as a private investor you can buy a share of IBM or a share of Google, but you can't improve the performance of either one after you buy it. You can't inspire a newly acquired share to rise faster, or encourage it to outperform the market, nor will you hurt its feelings and cause it to fall if you sell. As Adam Smith (the pen name of George Goodman) wisely observed in his classic, *The Money Game*, "*The stock doesn't know you own it.*"[11] There's no place for optimism or wishful thinking. Furthermore, most of us manage our investments to do well, but not as part of a competition in which we try to amass more wealth than someone else.[12]

Yet for all we know about these sorts of decisions, we know less about others.

First, many decisions involve much more than choosing from options we cannot influence or evaluations of things we cannot affect. When he decided what to bid for the UDC, Bill Flemming wasn't making a choice from options he could not alter. If Skanska USA Building won the contract, Flemming and his team would spend the next few years carrying out the project. By applying their skill and energy, by communicating goals and mobilizing employees, they would be able to influence outcomes—maybe by a little, maybe a lot.

Second, many decisions have a competitive dimension. We not only seek to do well, but to do better than our rivals. Flemming didn't just have to meet the government's price of $1.212 billion; he had to come in below the others. For that, he had to size up his rivals and consider what they might bid. That's the essence of strategy: to outperform rivals, who are trying to do better than us.

Third, many decisions take a long time before we know the results. Large construction projects like the UDC take place over years, meaning that feedback is slow and imperfect. They're nothing like decisions in which results are known right away and feedback from one can be used to make adjustments to the next.

Fourth, many decisions are made by leaders of organizations. As president of Skanska USA Building, Flemming had a range of roles and responsibilities. He had to consider Skanska's relationship with its partners and its reputation in the industry, as well as what his colleagues would think of him. Matters of perception and credibility were important.

In sum, experiments have been very effective to isolate the processes of judgment and choice, but we should be careful when applying their findings to very different circumstances. As psychologist Philip Tetlock puts it, "Much mischief can be wrought by transplanting this hypothesis-testing logic, which flourishes in controlled lab settings, into the hurly-burly of real-world settings where ceteris paribus never is, and never can be, satisfied."[13] We have learned a lot about decisions in many fields—consumer choice, public policy, and financial investments—but much less about complex decisions in the real world.

THE KEY TO GREAT DECISIONS: LEFT BRAIN, RIGHT STUFF

In *Thinking, Fast and Slow*, psychologist and recipient of the 2002 Nobel Prize in economics, Daniel Kahneman, describes two systems of thought. Our intuitive mind follows the very rapid System 1, which is often effective but frequently leads to common errors. Our reflective mind uses the slower but more deliberate System 2. Kahneman advises: "The way to block errors that originate in System 1 is simple in principle: recognize the signs that you are in a cognitive minefield, slow down, and ask for reinforcement from System 2."[14]

That's good advice, provided we have educated our System 2 to provide the right kinds of reinforcement. The aim of this book is to describe what some of those reinforcements might look like. Its goal is to identify specific ways we should think about real-world decisions—not the sorts of judgments and choices commonly studied in the lab, but more complex decisions we often encounter in the real world.

The central idea in this book is that winning decisions combine two very different skills. I call them *left brain, right stuff.*

Left brain is shorthand for a deliberate and analytical approach to problem solving. It's a bit of a misnomer, of course, because both of the brain's hemispheres are used in many tasks. Problem solving isn't purely a left brain function, any more than artists rely exclusively on their right brains. But to the extent that the left brain is more strongly associated with logical reasoning, the term is apt. Great decisions call for clear analysis and dispassionate reasoning. Using the left brain means:

- knowing the difference between what we can control and what we cannot, between action and prediction
- knowing the difference between absolute and relative performance, between times when we need to do well and when we must do better than others
- sensing whether it's better to err on the side of taking action and failing, or better not to act; that is, between what we call Type I and Type II errors
- determining whether we are acting as lone individuals or as leaders in an organizational setting and inspiring others to achieve high performance
- recognizing when models can help us make better decisions, but also being aware of their limits

All these factors are important, but they're not enough. Great decisions also demand a willingness to take risks, to push boundaries and to go beyond what has been done before. They call for something we call the right stuff. The phrase comes from Tom

Wolfe's 1979 book about the US manned space effort, and was meant to sum up those intangible qualities that set the best pilots apart from the rest. As Wolfe put it, the right stuff wasn't just a willingness to risk one's neck. Any fool could do that. Rather, it meant "to have the ability to go up in a hurtling piece of machinery and put his hide on the line and have the moxie, the reflexes, the experience, the coolness, to pull it back at the last yawning moment."[15] The right stuff was about the intelligent management of risk.

Having the right stuff means:

- summoning high levels of confidence, even levels that might seem excessive, but that are useful to achieve high performance
- going beyond past performance and pushing the envelope to seek levels that are unprecedented
- instilling in others the willingness to take appropriate risks.

Left brain and right stuff may seem like opposites, but they're complementary. For many decisions they're both essential. They are what Bill Flemming had to call upon when deciding what to bid for the UDC, and they're required in many other situations as well. Great decisions call for a capacity for considered and careful reasoning, and also a willingness to take outsize risks.

THE PRACTICE OF WINNING DECISIONS

The ideas in this book are based on my experience in the business world, first in industry and then as a business school professor. For the past decade I have worked mainly in the field of executive education. I interact on a daily basis with managers from a wide range of industries and from all over the world. My starting point is the world of practice, not theory. My aim is to help people think more clearly, to exercise their capacity for critical thinking, and to make better decisions.

This goal led me to write *The Halo Effect*, in which I pointed out some of the mistakes that undermine the way we think about company performance. I wasn't shy about exposing flaws in several well-known studies, some of which, despite lots of data and apparently rigorous scientific research, are little more than feel-good fables. This book also aims to help managers think for themselves, but this time the focus is on decision making. The central idea in this book—that real-world decisions demand the combination of left brain analysis and right stuff ambition—is based on my work with practicing managers.

A recent classroom episode brought home this point. Not long ago I attended a lecture during which a prominent business school professor, an expert in risk management, declared to a group of executives that a major cause of bad decisions was overconfidence. Research has shown, he said, that people suffer from a pervasive bias of overconfidence. To demonstrate, he conducted the experiment mentioned previously, in which members of the audience were given a series of questions of general knowledge, including such things as the length of the Nile and the year Mozart was born, and were asked to state a range that they were 90 percent confident contained the correct answer. As the professor revealed the right answers, it turned out that participants had been wrong at least four times out of ten, and some even more. Their ranges had been far too narrow. The professor declared: "You see? You're overconfident!" And by implication: "You should avoid overconfidence to make better business decisions."

Glancing around the room, I saw a variety of expressions. Some of the executives wore sheepish smiles, as if to say, "Yes, I guess that's right. I suppose I am overconfident." But others seemed puzzled: "Okay, I was off by a bit. But does that really mean I'm overconfident when it comes to other kinds of decisions?" There were even some expressions of doubt: "Isn't a high level of confidence a good thing? How can I be successful if I'm not willing to take chances?" These executives seemed to know intuitively what academic researchers sometimes do not: that when it comes to managerial decisions, what seems excessive by one definition can be useful, or even necessary by another. They understood intuitively that not only left brain logic is needed—so is the right stuff.

THE ROAD AHEAD

Throughout this book I examine a number of elements one at a time, then bring them together. Chapters Two through Nine cover many of the elements associated with the left brain. Chapter Two makes the fundamental distinction between decisions for which we cannot control outcomes and those for which we can. For the former, there is little benefit to wishful thinking or optimism, but when we can shape outcomes, positive thinking can be powerful. Chapter Three introduces the dimension of relative performance, in which it's not enough to do well, but essential to do better than one's rivals. Many studies of judgment and choice omit any competitive dimension, but when we have to do better than others, the need to think strategically is crucial. Chapter Four combines these first two dimensions, showing what happens when an ability to influence outcomes and the need to outperform others are both present. Far from being a rare or special case, such situations are very common. When it comes to strategic management, they might even be considered the norm.

From there, I offer different ways of thinking about two well-known biases. Chapter Five examines perhaps the most widely cited of all errors, overconfidence, and presents a radically different interpretation. On closer inspection, what seems like a simple idea—that people are prone to overconfidence—turns out to be much more complex. In competitive situations, not only is a very high level of confidence often useful, but it can be essential. Chapter Six looks at another well-known error, the base rate bias. The basic finding—that people tend to overlook population base rates—is correct, but the common advice—that we should heed base rates—is incomplete. There are instances when not only can we go beyond what has been done before, but competitive circumstances dictate that we must. Far from being reckless, however, we can find ways of limiting risk, using the left brain in service of the right stuff.

Chapter Seven adds the temporal dimension and makes the vital distinction between decisions for which feedback is rapid and tangible, and those for which it is slow. For the former it may be possible to learn through deliberate practice, but for the latter it is more important to get the decision right the first time. Chapter Eight moves beyond decisions made by individuals acting alone to consider decisions by leaders in organizations. Now it may be essential to inspire others to go beyond what might seem justified, which forces us to take a fresh look at concepts like transparency, authenticity, and sincerity. Chapter Nine focuses on decision models, a topic of current interest given the rise of Big Data. Models can be very powerful and often provide remarkably accurate predictions. Yet in our embrace of decision models, we have sometimes applied them incorrectly. Knowing when models are useful, but respecting their limitations, is also vital.

From there I take up two comprehensive examples. Chapter Ten explores competitive bidding and takes a fresh look at another well-known error, the winner's curse. Chapter Eleven addresses entrepreneurship and new venture creation, once again replacing current ideas about decision biases with a more realistic and nuanced understanding of how people can and should make decisions in the real world.

Finally, Chapter Twelve summarizes the key lessons for making great decisions, not in routine settings of consumer choice or investments—for which we neither can influence outcomes nor need to outperform rivals—but in complex real-world settings, like the one facing Bill Flemming.

Throughout, an important theme involves critical thinking. One of the people I admire most, the physicist Richard Feynman, once gave a lecture about science and religion in society. Feynman was no believer in miracles or divine intervention, but he saw no value in telling other people what they should believe. More important was that they think for themselves and learn to ask questions.

Speaking about the holy site of Lourdes in southwestern France, where in 1858 a young girl claimed to have seen an apparition of the Virgin Mary and which now attracts millions of pilgrims every year, Feynman observed: "It might be true that you can be cured by the miracle of Lourdes. But if it is true then it ought to be investigated. Why? To improve it."

If our aim is to cure people, we should investigate the best way to do that. We might ask whether a person has to enter the grotto at Lourdes to get the full effect of its healing powers, or whether it is good enough to come close. If so, how close is close enough? If hundreds of people gather outside the grotto, is the healing effect as strong in the back row as it is in the first row? At what point does it diminish, and by how much? Is it good enough for a few drops of the spring water to be sprinkled on your forehead, or do you have to immerse yourself to get the full effect? Do people have to visit in person, or can they be cured by touching someone else who made the pilgrimage to Lourdes? Feynman concluded: "You may laugh, but if you believe in the power of the healing, then you are responsible to investigate it, to improve its efficiency."[16]

The same applies here. For all the advances of recent years, we have not yet grasped the nature of many important and complex decisions. That's why our duty is to investigate. So we can make winning decisions.

THE QUESTION OF CONTROL

THE DIFFERENCE BETWEEN PILOT AND PASSENGER IN ANY FLYING
CRAFT CAME DOWN TO ONE POINT: CONTROL.

TOM WOLFE, *THE RIGHT STUFF,* 1979

The first key to making great decisions seems simple: Are you making a decision about something you cannot influence, or can you exert control?

Let's start with an easy example. We'll look at golf—not because I'm an avid golfer (I have played just enough to know how devilishly difficult the sport really is), but because it illustrates how people influence outcomes. Playing a round of golf isn't about predicting something over which we have no control. It's about taking action.

What does it take to excel at golf? For starters, it's important to have good technique. Begin with a balanced stance with proper weight distribution. Put your hand, wrist, and elbow in the correct position, and keep your head down and steady. Draw the club in a smooth backswing and then bring it forward in a strong downward stroke. Rotate your hips so the club head strikes the ball at the best angle, and make a full follow-through. Physical conditioning matters, of course. You need strength, stamina, and agility. Choose your equipment wisely: not just clubs but also gloves, shoes, and comfortably fitting clothing. Practice is vital, ideally under the watchful eye of a coach who can point out flaws, so you can make improvements and try again.

All of these are essential, but they're not sufficient. Also crucial is a positive mind-set. If there's one theme that runs through the vast literature about golf, it's this: *Golf is a game of confidence*. Instructional books and coaches all stress the need to believe that you can—that you *will*—successfully make the shot.

Many of the best golfers are known as much for their mental approach as for their physical skills. One of today's leading pros, Ian Poulter, explains: "There's a very fine line between being very confident and being arrogant. . . . I genuinely think I can pull things off, if I set my mind to it, whether it's holing out from the fairway or sinking a 40-foot putt."[1] He adds: "Very few people at the top of this wonderful game lack self-belief. Mine is often mistaken for arrogance—but if you don't think you'll be good, you won't be." Or as Mark O'Meara once said about the Masters, golf's premier tournament, which he won in 1989: "You can't win this tournament if you're standing over a six foot putt *hoping* to make it."[2] Hoping isn't enough. You have to *believe* it will go in. Dave Stockton, a star golfer of the 1970s, described his attitude this way: "I think I *deserve* to get the ball in the hole every time I stand over a putt."[3]

It shouldn't come as a surprise that golfers are often a bit off when it comes to their self-assessments. Some years ago the Professional Golfers' Association (PGA) examined all the putts in a full year of professional tournaments, 11,600 in all, focusing on six-footers, not so close as to be easy tap-ins, but not so long as to be very low-probability shots. Most pros estimated they could sink at least 70 percent of their six-foot putts, and some were much more optimistic. One said: "If you aren't making at least 85 percent of your six footers, you aren't making any money."[4] The facts told a different story. Only 54.8 percent of all six-foot putts, or slightly more than half, were successful. When they were told this figure, many golfers were surprised, but on reflection it makes sense. Most believed they could do better for a good reason. *Thinking* they can sink a six-foot putt increases the chances that they *will*.

The effect of perception on performance in golf was recently demonstrated in a laboratory experiment every bit as rigorous as studies about judgment and choice. Dr. Jessica Witt of Purdue University recruited thirty-six people to putt golf balls from a distance of 1.7 meters, or a bit less than 6 feet, at a standard sized golf hole, 5 centimeters in diameter.[5] Above the hole a downward-facing projector beamed a ring of circles, creating an Ebbinghaus illusion, named after the nineteenth-century German psychologist who pioneered studies of cognition and memory. For half of the participants the projector created a ring of eleven small circles, called a "little surround"; for the other half it beamed five large circles, creating a "big surround," as shown in Figure 2.1. Although the holes were identical in size, the mind perceived the one on the left, surrounded by large circles, to be smaller than the one on the right.

The research question was simple: Would the two groups differ in their ability to sink a putt? The answer turned out to be a clear "Yes." Those who faced the "little surround" sank almost twice as many putts as those facing the "big surround." Simply by shaping

FIGURE 2.1 SHAPING PERCEPTIONS AND CHANGING PERFORMANCE

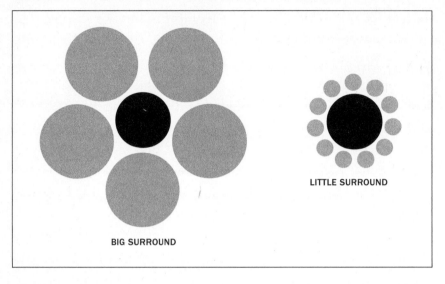

LITTLE SURROUND

BIG SURROUND

perceptions, Dr. Witt was able to produce better performance. Thinking the hole was larger led to more accurate putts.

Now, before you go out and buy a projector, let me give you the bad news: not many golf courses will let you play a round of golf with a projector in tow. They won't let you shine small circles to make the hole look bigger. But you *can* do the next best thing, which is to use techniques of visualization to help perceive the hole as large and inviting, not small and forbidding. And that's exactly what coaches teach. By adopting a positive mind-set, even by holding a view that is somewhat exaggerated, you can often improve results.

These findings take us in a very different direction than what has often been written about decision making. Conventional thinking urges us to avoid biases. We should ward off optimism and unrealistic self-evaluations. That makes good sense when we're asked to make a judgment about something we cannot influence. There's no reason to be anything other than accurate.

But when it's up to us to make something happen—such as knocking a ball into a hole—the story changes.

YOU MAKE WHAT'S GOING TO HAPPEN

Golf isn't the only activity in which a positive mind-set can improve performance. Dr. Kevin Thompson, director of sport and exercise science at the University of Northumbria in England, recruited nine male athletes, averaging age thirty, to take part in an experiment using stationary bicycles. On the first day the men were instructed to pedal as fast as they could for the equivalent of 4 kilometers, or about 2.4 miles. The research staff gave the men standardized verbal encouragement—things like "Keep it up" and "You're doing fine"—and informed them of the distance they had covered so far, while a variety of instruments measured oxygen intake and energy exertion. Their times on this first day served as a baseline of maximum effort.

Over the following days each man undertook two more sessions, now pedaling in front of a computer screen that displayed images of two cyclists, called avatars. One of the avatars showed the cyclist's present effort, and the other was said to move at the cyclist's baseline speed, recorded on the first trial. Unknown to the athletes, in one of the two sessions (assigned randomly) the baseline avatar was programmed to go 2 percent *faster* than the true baseline speed.

The research question was: Would cyclists watching the "deceiving avatar" be able to match or even surpass that speed? Once again the results were a clear "Yes." When watching the deceiving avatar, eight of the nine cyclists were able to go even faster than their previous best. Dr. Thompson concluded that they were able to surpass what they believed was a maximal effort by drawing on a metabolic reserve. He concluded (in the language of scientific research) that "surreptitiously augmented feedback derived from a previous performance reduces time taken for cyclists to accomplish a time trial of known duration." In plain English, *thinking they could go faster helped them do so.* Not without limits, of course. In subsequent studies Dr. Thompson found that speeding up the avatar by 5 percent was too much, and athletes weren't able to boost their performance to keep up. But for eight of the nine athletes, a 2 percent boost was achievable.[6]

These results didn't surprise athletes or sports psychologists. They confirmed what has long been understood. Athletic performance is shaped by many factors, from proper technique to good conditioning to smart nutrition, but a positive mind-set is also vital. Roger Bannister, the first man to break the four-minute mile and also a physician, once remarked: "It is the brain, not the heart or lungs that is the critical organ. It's the brain."[7] When you *think* you can go faster, you often can.

Baseball is another sport in which mind-set is crucial. Batters need to adopt a proper stance, watch the pitcher's point of release, then rotate their hips and make contact with a level swing. This is all very important, but not sufficient. According to Karl Kuehl, a veteran baseball coach: "Consistent success is built upon a player's belief that he can perform successfully every time he steps onto a field. Only players with the highest level of confidence will have the mental toughness to emerge on top when they are challenged. . . . Confidence is the basic internal belief that a person can and will succeed. A pitcher must believe he *can* and *will* throw that two-seamer on the outside corner; a hitter must believe he *can* and *will* drive the inside pitch."[8]

Of course, a hitter *won't* always drive the inside pitch, any more than a pitcher will always spot the ball perfectly on the outside corner. But maintaining confidence is essential. Former San Francisco Giants relief pitcher Brian Wilson, an intimidating presence on the mound, put it this way: "You can't go in there with doubts. You can't accept failure, and you certainly can't go into a situation thinking, 'Oh, gosh, what's going to happen?' You make what's going to happen. . . . This game isn't for negative emotions, or being scared."[9]

Perhaps no one in baseball stressed positive thinking as much as former Los Angeles Dodgers manager Tommy Lasorda. Over the course of a long career, Lasorda was known for encouraging young players to achieve their very best. He summed up his approach this way: "I believe in the power of positive thought. It is something I have seen work numerous times, and it is something I try to teach my players." His catch phrases were relentlessly positive: "If you believe it, you can achieve it. Success begins with confidence. It comes in cans, not in can'ts. Really believing you can do something is the beginning of doing it. Doubts just get in the way."[10]

Lasorda recalled the advice he offered to one of his players, a good but not excellent hitter who was keen to improve. The missing ingredient was mind-set. To succeed against the great pitchers of the day, he needed to bolster his confidence. Lasorda told him:

> When you're going up against a pitcher the next day, you
> have to picture yourself mentally and physically ready to hit
> that pitcher. You got to step into the batter's box *believing* that
> there isn't a man alive who can get you out. You have to want
> to live for the day you can drive in the big run for the Dodgers.
> You've got to *believe* that you are the best with the bat. The
> night before you're going to hit against Juan Marichal or Bob
> Gibson or Bob Veale you have to picture yourself hitting
> them, you have to know you can hit them. . . .

You must never even think, "I can't hit this guy." What you've got to be saying is "This guy can't get me out." You have to really *believe* you are the best hitter in baseball. I want you to repeat, over and over, every day, "I believe I am the best hitter in baseball."[11]

That was good advice at the time, and it's still useful today. Hitting a small sphere traveling at a speed greater than 90 miles per hour is sometimes thought to be the most difficult task in sports. Positive thinking—even having self-belief that is, objectively speaking, somewhat exaggerated—is crucial to success.

WHEN ILLUSIONS CAN BE HEALTHY

Sports is a good setting in which to appreciate the impact of mind-set on performance, because we can observe a discrete action—striking a ball or turning a wheel—in a clear and objectively measureable way. But the lessons of positive thinking are not limited to sports. People have long understood that a positive mind-set can improve all kinds of performance. That's why we read our children stories like *The Little Engine That Could,* about the humble blue train that huffed and puffed its way over the mountain by repeating, "I think I can, I think I can." We hope that optimism and tenacity will rub off on young minds. Before that, Norman Vincent Peale's *The Power of Positive Thinking* found a responsive audience. And long before that, one of the keenest observers of human nature, Goethe, observed: "To achieve all he can, a man must think he is more capable than he is." Not *far* more capable, of course; we're not suggesting that delusions of grandeur are healthy. But for many activities, in which we don't just make predictions about things we cannot influence but have a hand in shaping outcomes, positive thinking matters.

The implication is profound. Traditionally, mental health has been defined as seeing the world as it is. We assume that healthy individuals are able to perceive things clearly, free of bias. To see things as they are *not* is to suffer from delusions or distortions. That's why so much of decision theory has been aimed at warning people to avoid common biases.

But when we *can* influence outcomes, the story changes. Psychologists Shelley Taylor and Jonathan Brown found that *positive illusions*—thinking we're better than we really are, thanks to what they referred to as "unrealistically positive self-evaluations, exaggerated perceptions of control or mastery, and unrealistic optimism"— often bring a variety of benefits.[12] Positive illusions lead people to take the initiative rather than accept the status quo. They help us cope with adversity and survive tough times. They make us more resilient and less willing to concede defeat. Positive thinking stimulates people to be more creative, to look for new ways of doing things, and to persevere in the face of competition.

Taylor and Brown also found that people who display positive illusions tend to have more friends and create stronger social bonds, both of which are important ingredients of happiness. They concluded that healthy people—those who are socially well adjusted and functional, not depressed or neurotic—habitually exhibit three kinds of distortions: they have unrealistically positive self-perceptions, they exaggerate their level of personal control, and they tend to have unrealistic optimism about the future. In sum, a healthy person is *not* someone who always sees things as they are, but one who has the "enviable capacity to distort reality."[13] It's the *absence* of these illusions that we associate with depression and unhappiness.[14]

None of this should let us conclude that a positive attitude can overcome any obstacle, or surmount all odds, or any other such

New Age motivational nonsense. For things that we cannot influence, there's not much to be gained from positive thinking. As Dr. Thompson's cycling experiment showed, improvements are demonstrable but hardly unlimited. Yet the general rule holds. When we can influence outcomes, positive thinking—even holding views that are somewhat exaggerated—can be beneficial.

THE ILLUSION OF CONTROL, RECONSIDERED

The need to distinguish between what we can control and what we cannot is summarized in what has come to be known as the Serenity Prayer: "God grant me the serenity to accept the things I cannot change, courage to change the things I can, and wisdom always to know the difference."[15] These words are widely quoted, sometimes to the point of cliché. But there's really nothing trite about the Serenity Prayer. It was penned in the 1930s by the theologian, Reinhold Niebuhr, and makes a simple yet profound distinction: trying to change what we cannot leads to frustration and stress, but failing to change what is within our power can breed fatalism and helplessness. To know the difference is a sign of wisdom.[16] When there's no way to exert control, the best approach is usually sober and detached judgment. It's smart to identify and ward off common biases. But when we *can* get things done—when we can influence outcomes—positive thinking is highly useful.

Saying that people should try to distinguish between what they can and cannot control leads to more questions: How well do most people know the difference? Do they accurately assess their ability to influence events, or are they often wrong?

On this point, decision research offers a clear answer: people display an exaggerated sense of control. The best-known studies were conducted in the 1970s by Ellen Langer, a psychologist at Harvard University. Imagine you're going to play the lottery. Would you rather pick the number yourself, or would you be just as happy if someone else picked it for you? Presumably you shouldn't care, because the winning numbers will be drawn at random, and any numbers are as good as any other. But people *do* care, even to the point of being willing to pay for the privilege of selecting the numbers.[17] Another experiment involved cutting cards. Once again people acted as if they could influence outcomes, even when it should have been clear they could not. Langer called this phenomenon the *illusion of control*.[18] Since her initial findings were published in 1975, they have been replicated many times, with very consistent findings. People often act as if they can control events when they cannot.

For a real-world example, consider the dice game known as craps. (The word comes from the French, *crapaud*, for toad; imagine bettors crouching as they roll dice on the ground, and you get the picture.) At casinos, craps is played at a table where one person tosses the dice while others place bets. There are strict rules for the shooter, all meant to ensure a fair throw. You can shake the dice, but always with your palm upward so the dice are visible at all times; concealing the dice is forbidden. You have to throw the dice so they strike the far end of the table, where they will hit a green cushion with an indented diamond pattern to ensure a random bounce. As long as these rules are obeyed, gamblers can—and do—try all sorts of things to improve their luck. They shake the dice, or blow on them, or even talk to them. Some throw them gently when they want a low number and throw them hard for a high number. Some gamblers are even willing to pay for dice-throwing "lessons." Surfing the Internet, I found one course that charges $179 for a two-hour session that teaches various techniques, such as grips with names like "ice tong" or "two fingers," as well as wrist action for backspin or corkscrew twists, all meant to improve your throws. It's never exactly promised that you will be able to *control* the dice, only that you can improve your throws enough to make the difference between losing and winning. (Exactly how it all works is never spelled out, but if enough people are willing to part with $179, it may not really matter.) The inevitable conclusion when we see these sorts of gimmicks? That dice players suffer from an *illusion of control.*

The illusion of control is widely recognized as a pervasive error of judgment. It is frequently included on lists of common biases. As a result, people are urged to temper or rein in the belief that they can shape events. They're advised: *You can control less than you think.*

All of this makes a good story and reinforces the notion that people exhibit common biases. There's just one problem: it's not entirely correct.

Take another look at the examples in Langer's experiments. What do picking lottery numbers, cutting cards, and throwing dice have in common? In every instance, the event is entirely random. There's no ability whatsoever to influence the outcome. That may seem like the ideal setting to observe the illusion of control, but it's not. To the extent that people misperceive their ability to control outcomes, they will *inevitably* be on the high side. Any error *has* to be in the direction of exaggerating control, which means we have no way to distinguish between random error and systematic error, which is another word for bias.

If we want to see whether people have a pervasive bias toward overestimating control, we need to take a different approach. We have to study a variety of situations, some of which afford low control and others high control, and then compare the results.

Recently a team of researchers at Carnegie Mellon University, led by psychologist Don Moore, did just that. They recruited a group of volunteers, working individually, to perform a series of tasks at a computer screen. Partway through the task the screen changed from the usual appearance—black letters on a white background—to an annoying shade of violet. A small notice on the screen indicated that the click of a mouse could change that screen back to white. People were randomly assigned to one of four conditions, from high control (in which clicking the mouse turned the screen white 85 percent of the time), to moderate control (effective 50 percent of the time), to low control (effective just 15 percent), and finally to no control (clicking the mouse had no effect at all). After the test was over, the subjects were asked how effective they thought their clicks had been at changing the screen back to white. Those in the no control and low control groups thought they had a greater ability to change the screen color, a result that was consistent with Langer's findings about the illusion of control. But for the high control and moderate control groups, the results were in the *opposite* direction. They *underestimated* their level of control, and often by a substantial amount. Far from suffering from an illusion of excessive control, they didn't realize how much control they really had.[19]

Moore and his colleagues ran several other versions of this study, all of which pointed to the same conclusion: people do *not* consistently overestimate their level of control. A simpler explanation is that people have an imperfect understanding of how much control they can exert. When control is low they tend to overestimate, but when it's high they tend to underestimate.

This finding is highly significant. For decades researchers have told us that people have a pervasive tendency to overestimate control. We have been admonished to recognize that we can control less than we imagine. But that's not a fair conclusion. By running experiments that only looked at instances of low or no control (like throwing dice or choosing lottery numbers), researchers could only observe the tendency to overestimate control, not the reverse. If there is an error here, it's in the way researchers have conducted their experiments. (Moore and his colleagues called this *the illusion of illusion of control!*) For the past decades we have favored a dramatic conclusion—that people suffer from an illusion of control—rather than a less surprising but more accurate one: that people can and do err in *both* directions.

WHICH ERROR IS MORE COMMON, AND WHICH IS MORE SERIOUS?

Noting that people can underestimate as well as overestimate control leads to another question: Which of these errors is more likely in our daily lives? For things over which we have no control—whether tomorrow will be sunny or rainy, the fortunes of our favorite sports team, or the movements of the S&P 500 on a given day—any error will naturally be on the side of exaggerating control. For these sorts of things, it's wise to recognize, lucky charms and magic spells notwithstanding, that we can't influence outcomes.

But many activities *are* largely within our control—not just playing golf or pedaling a bicycle, but how we do our jobs, or how well we perform on an exam, cook a meal, or play a musical instrument. All of these depend very much on the actions we take. They depend on our skills and talent, on our ability to excel under pressure, and also very much on our mind-set. Here the more common error is not an illusion of excessive control, but the reverse: a failure to recognize how much control we really have. Whereas decision research has warned us against the illusion of excessive control, for many activities the more important lesson is exactly the opposite: we should try not to *underestimate* our control.

The distinction between what we can and cannot control may seem simple, but it's often not an easy one to make. Doctor and author Atul Gawande offered this reflection after years as a practicing surgeon: "I used to think that the hardest struggle of doctoring is learning the skills. But it is not, although just when you begin to feel confident that you know what you are doing, a failure knocks you down. It is not the strain of the work, either, though sometimes you are worn to your ragged edge. No, the hardest part of being a doctor, I have found, is to know what you have power over and what you don't."[20]

Gawande is correct: in medicine, distinguishing between what we can and cannot control is crucial. Unfortunately the distinction is often overlooked. In *How Doctors Think*, Dr. Jerome Groopman draws on research in cognitive psychology to show how common biases can distort the way physicians make diagnoses.[21] He mentions many errors and biases that by now are well known. The *availability heuristic*, a mental shortcut whereby people place too much importance on information that is readily available, causes doctors to mistakenly diagnose diseases that come easily to mind while overlooking diseases that are less common. The *confirmation bias*, a tendency to look for evidence that supports an initial hunch, prevents doctors from probing thoroughly for evidence that might contradict that hunch. The *anchoring effect* is also important, as initial data become an anchor that's usually not modified sufficiently by subsequent information. For each bias, Groopman provides vivid examples of how cognitive biases can lead to serious mistakes, and he urges doctors to be on their guard.

All of that makes good sense for the *diagnosis* of disease, which involves judgments about things we cannot influence. But many doctors, apart perhaps from specialists like pathologists, think about much more than simply making an accurate diagnosis. They are also in the business of helping patients recover, and in that they *can* influence outcomes. The power of a positive mind-set to improve recovery from many illnesses is well established. A recent article in the *Annals of Behavioral Medicine* summarized eighty-three studies that examined illnesses ranging from cancer to cardiovascular disease, and found a strong relationship between patient optimism and good health.[22] In turn, a patient's attitude is in part guided by what he or she hears from the doctor. No wonder a recent survey of doctors found that almost half admitted to shading the truth in their communications with patients. The reason isn't dishonesty or an unwillingness to face reality, but awareness that maintaining a positive attitude can have a powerful impact on eventual recovery. (Jerome Groopman is no stranger to the subject, having written *The Anatomy of Hope*, which dealt with the topic of hope and health.)[23]

Of course it would be absurd to go to the other extreme and imply that all diseases can be cured by positive thinking. Doctors aren't primarily in the business of spreading optimism. Barbara Ehrenreich's *Bright-Sided: How Positive Thinking Is Undermining America* offers an incisive exposé of foolish optimism.[24] She includes several examples from health care in which charlatans insist upon the power of positive thinking even in the face of a grim prognosis. But if we dismiss all benefits of positive thinking in health care, we will be arguing against the weight of considerable evidence. Positive thinking matters, for patient and physician.

Doctors need to recognize how situations differ and develop the skills to respond to each with the appropriate behavior. When in contact with patients, even as they retain objectivity and a sense of perspective, doctors may often convey optimism and seek to impart hope, not to deceive or create false expectations, but to improve patient health. They need the ability to make dispassionate judgments about things that cannot be influenced and strive to improve what can be changed. Both actions require wisdom as well as courage. The need to exhibit versatility, to think simultaneously in a dispassionate and unbiased way while conveying optimism and positive thinking when outcomes can be influenced, is one reason health care is such a demanding profession.

FROM MEDICINE TO MANAGEMENT

How should we think about control when it comes to managerial decisions? A clue comes from the word itself. *Manage* comes from the Italian *maneggiare*, to handle, and before that from the Latin *manus*, for hand. Anytime you lend a hand, literally or figuratively, to get something done, you're managing. *Manage* is a cousin of another word with the same root, *manipulate*. Managers don't just make choices they cannot influence, like a shopper buying one product or another, or an investor buying or selling a share of stock. (You might manage your shopping list, but you choose a product; you manage your portfolio, but you buy or sell an asset.) Nor do managers merely place bets, akin to buying a lottery ticket or throwing dice. The essence of management is to exercise control and influence events.

Of course managers don't have complete control over outcomes, any more than a doctor has total control over patient health. They are buffeted by events outside their control: macroeconomic factors, changes in technology, actions of rivals, and so forth. Yet it's a mistake to conclude that managers suffer from a pervasive illusion of control. The greater danger is the opposite: that they will underestimate the extent of control they truly have.

Compared to striking a ball or turning a pedal, however, managerial decisions are more complex. They may not often have as much at stake as Bill Flemming's bid for the UDC, but they involve an ability to mobilize people and resources and to actively shape outcomes. For Flemming some elements were surely outside his control, including the performance of subcontractors, possible delays in delivery, the effect of local competition on construction wage rates, and the weather in Utah, which can be prone to severe winters. But Flemming knew there would be ways to improve performance, even if he didn't know precisely what they were. (Recall his words: "We'll take the chance that somewhere along the line we can become even more productive—by improving our scheduling, or finding ways to work faster, or discovering ways to reduce our costs.")

In this regard Flemming was typical. In an extensive study of managerial risk taking, Zur Shapira of New York University found that managers don't see themselves simply as making choices or judgments, but as actively using their skill to exert control.[25] Further, they see their actions as part of an ongoing process, not like placing a bet on a horse at the racetrack or choosing a number at the roulette table, where nothing can be done to improve outcomes. As one manager put it: "[G]ambling contains elements of uncertainty and positive or negative outcomes. Managerial decision making is (hopefully) based on an educated guess of what is most likely to happen and what can be done to remedy a negative outcome. That is, decision making is a continuous process in which each decision is dependent on previous decisions. Gambling has only two outcomes—win or lose, and each decision and outcome is independent of others." Another manager commented: "Decision theory puts all the emphasis on the analysis leading to the moment of choice. While it is definitely important, my experience taught me that my ability to influence whatever goes on after the moment of choice is perhaps even more important."[26]

These managers understood intuitively that, unlike players of games of dice or purchasers of lottery tickets, they have an ability to exert control and influence outcomes. Far from suffering from an illusion of control, managers are more likely to underestimate their ability to influence outcomes. They often can achieve more, influence more, and bring about more change than they imagine.

WISDOM, PART 2: ON WHICH SIDE SHOULD WE ERR?

Of course we'd all like to have the wisdom to know the difference between what we can change and what we can't, but often we don't. That leads to more questions: When we don't know for sure, is it better to err on one side or the other? Is it better to imagine we have more control than we really do, or better to be mistaken in the other direction?

FIGURE 2.2 CONTROL, BELIEF AND REALITY

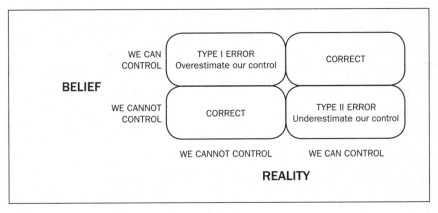

Figure 2.2 shows four possible combinations of belief and reality about control. If we believe we can control outcomes and we truly can, we're in the upper right quadrant. If we believe we cannot control outcomes and in fact we cannot, we're in the lower left. In both cases our beliefs are correct. But what about the other two

quadrants? In the upper left, we believe we have control when we really don't. We overestimate our control. That's a Type I error, or a false positive. The result is an error of commission; we go ahead with some action when we shouldn't. In the lower right, we don't believe we can influence outcomes when in fact we can. Here we underestimate our control. That's a Type II error, or a false negative. We fail to act when we should.[27]

Of course we would like to minimize the chance of error, and often gather information to improve the accuracy of our beliefs. But even so, some uncertainty remains. That's why we still need to consider the consequences of error. Is it better to act as if we have control (and run the risk of a Type I error), or is it better to assume we don't have control (and run the risk of Type II error)? By thinking about the consequences of each, we can try to avoid the more serious of the two.

Suppose a disease sweeps through a remote village. Children, the elderly, and the weak succumb in great numbers. Current remedies are ineffective. One option is to keep seeking a treatment for the disease. The downside if we're wrong and commit a Type I error is wasted resources, perhaps, but not much more. The other option is to conclude that we have no way to halt the disease, perhaps regarding it as fate or God's will. The downside in the event we're wrong and commit a Type II error is additional deaths. By structuring the decision in this way and comparing the consequences of Type I and Type II errors, we might conclude that it's wise to keep searching for a cure.

Now think about everyday activities that are less dramatic than a deadly disease. When you have no ability to control events—such as tomorrow's weather or the outcome of next week's football game—any error will be on the side of exaggerated control. The way to avoid error is to be sure not to make a Type I error. But for activities in which you *can* influence outcomes—which include preparing for an exam or launching a new product—the more likely error will be in the direction of *underestimating* control. Type II errors—the failure to take action when we can effect change—can be very serious.

Decision research has often warned us against the illusion of excessive control, but has overlooked an even more important lesson: for activities in which we can influence outcomes, we should be sure not to underestimate control. As a rule of thumb, it's better to err on the side of thinking we can get things done rather than assuming we cannot. The upside is greater and the downside less.

THINKING ABOUT CONTROL

A first key to making good decisions calls for us to understand whether we can control outcomes. Are we making a choice among options we can't change or a judgment about something we can't improve? Or are we able to exert control and make improvements? Unfortunately, many laboratory experiments set aside entirely the ability to shape outcomes. That's fine if the aim is to isolate the mechanisms of judgment and choice in a single frame. But in the real world we often *can* influence outcomes, and positive thinking *can* improve performance. Believing we can achieve something, even holding a belief that is somewhat exaggerated, can lead to better performance.

Furthermore, contrary to what has become accepted wisdom, people do *not* suffer from a pervasive illusion of control. Yes, they exaggerate control when none is possible, because any error will be on the high side. When they *can* influence outcomes, however, errors will often be in the opposite direction. Given that so much of our daily lives involves things that we can influence, the greater tendency isn't to exaggerate control but precisely the opposite. We're more apt to *underestimate* our ability to influence outcomes.

Beyond the wisdom to know what we can change and what we cannot, a second kind of wisdom speaks to the better way to err. So often the emphasis in decision research has been on avoiding Type I errors and not thinking we can do more than we truly can. But if we can take action to influence outcomes, the more serious mistakes may be Type II errors. We should make every effort to influence what we can.

PERFORMANCE, ABSOLUTE AND RELATIVE

WE'RE ADDING A LITTLE SOMETHING TO THIS MONTH'S SALES CON-
TEST. AS YOU ALL KNOW, FIRST PRIZE IS A CADILLAC ELDORADO.
ANYBODY WANT TO SEE SECOND PRIZE? SECOND PRIZE IS A SET OF
STEAK KNIVES. THIRD PRIZE IS YOU'RE FIRED.

DAVID MAMET, *GLENGARRY GLEN ROSS*, 1983

The second key to making great decisions is to know if we're trying to do well, or if we need to do better than rivals.

Consider for a moment your personal finances. You want to save enough each month and earn enough from your investments to meet your objectives. Perhaps you're trying to save for your children's education, or have enough to buy a home, or build a nest egg for retirement. Of course you want to earn as much as possible, but you're not in competition with anyone else. You're not going to make investment decisions—buying this stock or selling that one—with an eye to outperforming rivals.

When it comes to managing your finances, decision research offers many useful lessons. For starters, you should bear in mind that stocks move in random patterns, and that several days of gains neither mean the next day will bring another uptick, nor that a correction is due. Don't monitor your portfolio every day, because people feel losses more acutely than gains, so the fluctuations of the market will only add to your anxiety. And don't try to time the market, looking for the exact moment to jump in or cash out, because no one can time the market with accuracy. Rather, you should periodically review the allocation of your assets and make adjustments. Invest for the long term and follow a strategy of buy-and-hold, with index funds that track the market while charging low expenses. Do all these things, and you'll very likely generate solid long-term gains.[1]

Now consider a very different kind of investment decision. The National MBA Stock Market Competition is held among colleges and universities across Canada. The contest begins in September, with each team being given a fictitious endowment of C$100,000. Over the next ten weeks the students manage their portfolios, "buying" and "selling" as often as they wish. At the end of November the team with the most valuable portfolio claims a C$5,000 prize for its school, and the rest get nothing. Now the aim isn't just to do well, but to do better than others.

In one recent year more than fifty teams took part in the National MBA Stock Market Competition.[2] The winner was a trio of students from the University of Alberta Business School, whose portfolio almost doubled in ten weeks to a whopping C$199,368, which works out to a return of more than 1600 percent on an annualized basis. How did they do so well? By following what they acknowledged was an "aggressive and sometimes extremely risky strategy." One of the students explained, "You can do all the long-term planning you want, but it's really the short-term speculation that's driving this."

The best approach had not been obvious from the start. When the competition began, the Albertans put together a portfolio of nine stocks, each team member picking three. It was the sort of portfolio you might devise if you were investing for the long term, balanced and prudent. After three weeks the team had earned a return of 9 percent, which would normally be excellent, but in this particular bull market didn't even place them in the top ten. An update from the tournament organizers revealed that the leading team had already racked up a return of 22 percent! At that point reality hit home. One of the students recalled, "We realized for the sake of the competition a diversified portfolio was not necessarily the way to go, so our strategy shifted to being a lot more speculative. If we were going to win, we had to try to pick the short-term winners."

Now diversification went out the window, and the students began to load their eggs into a single basket. First they piled their assets into a pharmaceutical company that, lucky for them, showed a quick profit. After three days they pocketed their gains and put everything into a little-known fiber optics company. As if on cue, the stock surged. Soon they cashed out of fiber optics and invested in a broadband wireless company. Again their timing was impeccable, and the shares rose briskly.

From there they moved all their assets into a biotech company. This time, to their horror, the stock began to plunge. Rather than watch their dreams of winning vanish, the students took their riskiest gamble of all. They switched from a long position to a short position, betting everything on a further decline. Selling short isn't for the faint of heart, but extreme measures were needed. The students knew they had to finish ahead of all the other teams, every one of which was trying to finish ahead of *them*. Luckily for the

Albertans, the biotech stock continued to drop, and the value of their portfolio shot through the roof.

At the end of ten weeks they were crowned champions of Canada. The University of Alberta student newspaper was full of praise: "The team members say they've learned a lot from their foray into high finance, and they hope the win will help them when they hit the job market in about a year. They can't help feeling a little cocky about their chances playing the market for real, but they're trying to remain level-headed."[3] That's one lesson, perhaps.

A better lesson might be that when there is a C$5,000 prize for first place and nothing for anyone else, and when you don't have to absorb any losses, the only sensible strategy is to take huge risks. Great fun? Sure. Good training for the investment world? Maybe not. As one student observed, "It's a little different than playing with real money, because you want to win, and only first place wins." For this sort of competition, the smart approach was to go for broke.[4]

Two examples of financial management, but calling for entirely different decisions. Managing your personal investment portfolio is a matter of *absolute performance*. You keep what you earn, regardless of what anyone else does. There's no element of competition. The National MBA Stock Market Competition is purely about *relative performance*. It's not enough to do well; all that matters is doing better than the rest.

THE ART OF OUTDOING AN ADVERSARY

A great deal of decision research has asked us to make judgments and choices that suit us best, never mind anyone else. There are no rivals to worry about. That's fine if our aim is to isolate cognitive mechanisms. Adding a competitive dimension isn't necessary; in fact it makes matters more complicated than they need to be.

But we have to be careful when taking those findings and applying them to situations that involve competition.

Now we move into the realm of strategic thinking, defined by Avinash Dixit of Princeton and Barry Nalebuff of Yale as "the art of outdoing an adversary, knowing that the adversary is trying to do the same to you."[5] Strategic thinking is vital, they note, when "[s]uccess is determined by relative rather than absolute performance."[6]

The National MBA Stock Market Competition is one of many situations in which success demands that we outthink our adversaries. Some years ago, I took part in an office pool that involved (very small) bets on the outcome of NFL playoff games. Twenty of us put in $5, for a total pot of $100, to be paid to the one who picked the most winners of the upcoming playoff games: two wild card games, four divisional playoff games, two conference championships, and the Super Bowl. (In the event of a tie, the prize would be shared.) The maximum possible score was nine, and the minimum was zero. Here was the catch: we had to predict who would win each of the nine games *before the first one was played*. That made things difficult, because we didn't know which teams would win their first games and advance to the next round. You might think the Steelers were a good candidate to win the Super Bowl, and you might therefore pick them to win all their games, but if they lost in the first round and went home, too bad for you.

At the time I was living in Northern California, and both of our local teams, the 49ers and the Raiders, were in the playoffs. Many of us bet with our hearts and picked them both to advance far in the playoffs.[7] As it happened, the 49ers had a great year and won the Super Bowl, but the Raiders lost their first game, a tough 13–7 defeat to the Seahawks, which hurt many of us who had bet on them to do well.[8]

The eventual winner of the pool, an accounting manager named Steve, had picked the Seahawks to win against the Raiders, and that made all the difference. "How did you know the Seahawks would win?" I later asked him. Steve replied that in fact he had thought the *Raiders* were more likely to win, but correctly figured that just about everyone else would pick the Raiders. Given that there were twenty contestants and the payoff was winner-take-all, there was little to be gained by going along with the majority, but potentially a lot to be gained if he picked the Seahawks and they won. That was a smart strategic move, made with an understanding of the likely actions of rivals. Steve knew the name of the game wasn't just to do well, but to do better than the rest of us, and he made his bets accordingly.

PAYOFFS AND END POINTS

Knowing whether performance is relative or absolute is a good start, but a further point is crucial: the distribution of payoffs. Competitions vary in the way they allocate payoffs.

When the top performer wins a bit more than others, but the distribution is fairly even across competitors, skew is low. In Figure 3.1A, the top competitor wins more than others, but not a great deal more. Benefits are fairly evenly distributed. There isn't a great need to finish at the top; most players can do well. In Figure 3.1B, payoffs are moderately skewed. Now it's fairly important to do well in relative terms, because benefits drop off more steeply. This distribution might be found in industries where the leading company—

FIGURE 3.1 DISTRIBUTION OF PAYOFFS AND EXAMPLES OF SKEW

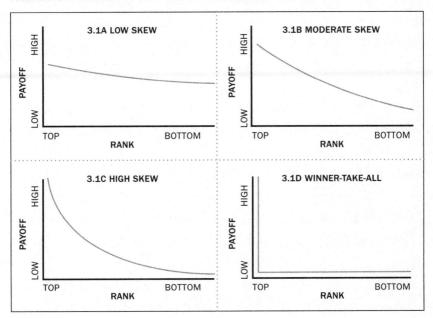

whether the one with the lowest costs or with the highest quality products—earns higher profits than the rest.

When payoffs are highly skewed, as in Figure 3.1C, it becomes very important to do better than rivals. The top competitor does very well, but benefits fall off sharply for the rest. Now we'll expect to see intense rivalry, with competitors—be they companies or athletes or game show contestants—trying very hard to come out on top. The most extreme distribution of payoffs, in Figure 3.1D, is winner-take-all. All the benefits go to the single top finisher; the rest get nothing. Now we need to go for broke.

Not only did the National MBA Stock Market Competition involve relative performance, but it had the most extreme distribution of payoffs possible: winner-take-all. Here, to quote Sean Connery in *Indiana Jones and the Last Crusade*, "There's no silver medal for second place." The smart move is to act very aggressively, which is precisely why the University of Alberta came out on top. Same for the NFL football pool, in which the single highest score took the entire pot. It was winner-take-all; there was no reward for finishing second.

If, on the other hand, the National MBA Stock Market Competition gave prizes to more than just the top team, then the payoff distribution would have been less highly skewed. Suppose it awarded prizes to the top three teams, similar to awarding gold, silver, and bronze medals. That's not as extreme as winner-take-all, but with more than fifty teams taking part in the competition, it would still make sense to take high risks to finish in the top three.

But what if instead of C$5,000 for the top team, all teams finishing in the top quartile received a prize of C$400? Performance would still be relative, in the sense that any prize would depend on how they stacked up against the other competitors, but now the payoffs would be much less skewed. Contestants would very likely make less risky investments, because they would no longer have the pressure to finish at the very top.[9] As a rule, the greater the skew, the more important it is to outperform rivals—and the more extreme chances you're likely to take.

The National MBA Stock Market Competition was notable for another reason: there was a definite end point. Contestants knew that a single winner would be declared at the end of exactly ten weeks. It was the same for the NFL pool: once the Super Bowl was played, the contest was over and the winner was declared. Coming close didn't give you a head start in next year's pool; this was a one-time, winner-take-all competition.

The combination of highly skewed payoffs and a clear end point makes for highly dramatic competitions. Consider the television game show *Jeopardy!* Only the first-place contestant gets to keep the prize money and may return to play again, while the others go home with a handshake and a consolation prize. No wonder so much is riding on the last question, known as "Final Jeopardy." It all comes down to the final question, and the contestants know it.

Or consider a golf tournament like the Masters, played each April at the Augusta National Golf Club in Georgia. Financial payoffs are highly skewed. The winner receives about twice as much in prize money as the runner up, and from there the payoffs decrease further. In 2013, Masters champion Adam Scott collected $1.44 million, compared to $864,000 for Angel Cabrera in second place, and $544,000 for Jason Day in third. Scott and Cabrera were tied at the end of four rounds, and decided the championship in a sudden-death playoff. A single stroke between the first two was worth $780,000. But financial payoffs aren't the only thing at stake. The champion gets the Green Jacket and a lifetime invitation to the tournament; the second place finisher gets neither. Winning the Masters is *much* better than coming in second. There's also a precise end point, with the championship decided after exactly seventy-two holes played over four days, and in the event of a tie, a playoff. No wonder the final round at Augusta offers such high drama. Four days of competition can come down to a single excruciating hole.

The monthly sales contest in David Mamet's play *Glengarry Glen Ross* is an example of relative performance aimed at getting all participants to do their very best (or worst, as you may believe). The hard-nosed boss, played memorably in the movie by Alec Baldwin, presents the payoffs: a car, a set of knives, or a pink slip. Absolute performance means nothing; all that matters is doing better than the others. Past performance is irrelevant, and promises about future sales are worthless. All that counts is performance *this* month. Set up a game with this payoff, and don't be surprised at the desperate tactics that are employed.

In many competitive settings performance is relative, but the nature of the payoffs isn't clear. There are no clearly stated rules with payoffs that are known to all, no standings posted in clear view so all can see how they are doing, and no game show host to read the questions and immediately judge the replies. There may not even be a clear end point, making it difficult to know how much to bet. Competition is complex and fraught with uncertainties.

Or there may be multiple end points, with rivals aiming at somewhat different objectives. We normally think of an election as an instance of relative performance (the absolute number of votes doesn't matter; whether you get more votes than your opponent is what counts), with highly skewed payoffs (the winner is elected; the loser goes home) and a very clear end point (when the polls close on election day). But not always.

In 2008 Mitt Romney spent millions on an unsuccessful campaign for the Republican presidential nomination. After a series of second-place finishes in Iowa, New Hampshire, Massachusetts, and Michigan, he ended his campaign and pledged to support the Republican nominee, John McCain. By one measure Romney had lost a winner-take-all contest. He was done for 2008. But Romney was playing a different game, one with more than a single end point. By standing aside in 2008, he improved his chances to win the Republican nomination four years later, in 2012. Two candidates were competing for the same votes, but playing different games, with two different prizes in mind.

PERFORMANCE IN THE BUSINESS WORLD

Game shows, sporting events, and elections are designed to produce dramatic tension, with highly skewed payoffs and clear end points.

In other kinds of competition, however, there's neither a clear end point nor an explicit payoff distribution.

Consider the business world. Performance is relative, in the sense that the fortunes of one company are linked to the performance of others in the same industry. (That's the definition of an industry: a group of companies that compete against one another, like airlines, or automobiles, or the makers of smartphones.) Even if performance is relative, however, it's rarely winner-take-all. Often it is not even highly skewed. Think of restaurants in the city where you live. They compete in the sense that on any given night, a diner who goes to one won't eat at another, so the fortunes of one are affected by the fortunes of others. But there's no precise distribution of payoffs among restaurants, and many can be profitable and prosper year after year.

In other industries direct competition can be so intense that there's room for only a few successful companies. Any that are too small to enjoy economies of scale or that fail to gain sufficient market share may fail. In some cases the lion's share of profits may accrue to just a few companies. That was the basis for Jack Welch's famous dictum, upon taking charge of General Electric in 1981, that all of GE's units should be Number 1 or Number 2 in their respective segments, or they would be fixed, sold, or closed. Welch understood that profits were significantly higher for the largest players and were often very small or even nonexistent for the rest. There wasn't much point in devoting resources, whether financial or managerial, to units that were unlikely to gain a leading market share.

As for end points, competition in business is typically ongoing and open ended. There may be some instances of a clear end point, such as the deadline for bidding on the UDC project, but even that referred to a single project rather than the survival of the entire company. Companies are known as *going concerns* because they compete with one another on an ongoing basis. There's rarely a precise end point at which one is declared the winner and others go out of business.

Of course companies seek to outperform their rivals, and often compete aggressively. But rarely is competition so intense that it's necessary to be the single best performer on a given date. Success is often a matter of achieving high performance over the long term. Here again, industries differ a great deal. In some, company performance can remain relatively steady over years and even decades. The candy bars that were on sale when I was a boy are pretty much the same ones that we find today: Snickers, M&Ms, Hershey's, Milky Way, Baby Ruth, and more. The same is true for consumer staples like razor blades, a market in which Gillette and Schick have held dominant positions for years. Despite other companies' continuing efforts to improve their products and get a leg up on competitors, the market leaders remain the same. Competition is relatively stable. Contrast that with industries in which technology shifts rapidly, and with it the fortunes of leading companies. In mobile phone handsets, what was state of the art ten years ago has been surpassed by at least three generations of new technology. The fortunes of Nokia, Motorola, Ericsson, and BlackBerry have risen and fallen, with success in one year no guarantee of success in another year.

For such highly dynamic industries, a new phrase has entered the lexicon: Red Queen competition. The idea comes from Lewis Carroll's *Through the Looking-Glass*, in which the Red Queen explains to Alice that in her country, "it takes all the running you can do, to keep in the same place." In Red Queen competition, companies are constantly under pressure to outdo one another—to introduce new and improved products, to find new ways to bring value to customers, and to experiment with new business models—all to gain an advantage over rivals. Red Queen competition means that a company can run faster but fall further behind at the same time.[10] Recent empirical research suggests that in many industries competitive advantage is difficult to maintain, and that the speed of regression toward the mean is becoming faster.[11] The reasons are clear. Technology change accelerates. Customers can easily find alternatives. Rivals imitate leaders. Consulting firms spread best practices. Employees move from one firm to another, leveling advantages. All of this means that companies cannot afford to stand pat, because those that do face an inevitable erosion of performance.

For business executives, devising a successful strategy requires more than knowing the end point, understanding the distribution of payoffs, and deciding how much risk to take. The first task is to assess the nature of performance. How intense is the rivalry? How skewed are the payoffs, both at present and over time? There may be moments when it's important to be among the very few top players, because otherwise we stand a good chance of going out of business in a process known as shakeout, when many companies lose out and only a few remain.

In the face of this uncertainty, managers often rely on a rule of thumb that involves two points: the *aspiration point* and the *survival point*. The *aspiration point* asks: What's the best I can do? Can I make a bold move that, if successful, will place me at the top of the pack, at least for a while? Is it worth making a risky bet that could bring great benefits? The *survival point* asks: What's the least I need to do in order to stay alive? What must I do to avoid being eliminated, so that at a minimum I can live to fight another day? Managers often make decisions with an eye to these two points, hoping to reach the aspiration point but at least making sure they pass the survival point.[12]

WISDOM TO KNOW THE DIFFERENCE—
ABOUT PERFORMANCE

In Chapter Two we quoted Reinhold Niebuhr's Serenity Prayer. To know the difference between what we can change and what we cannot is a profound kind of wisdom. Now we can add another kind of wisdom: to recognize the dynamics of competition.

In some situations the rules of the game are clearly stated. We're deluding ourselves if we don't recognize that performance is relative and highly skewed—perhaps not as ruthless as in *Glengarry Glen Ross*, but tending in that direction.

In much of life, however, there's no such clarity. It's up to us to determine how we wish to think about performance. How competitive are you when it comes to, say, your achievements at work, in athletics, or in leisure activities? Is your sense of satisfaction and well-being based on an absolute standard of achievement, or does it depend on doing better than others? In *The Happiness Hypothesis*, psychologist Jonathan Haidt explains that people who engage more actively in social comparisons—that is, whose sense of well-being is based on how well they do relative to others—tend to achieve more, but enjoy those achievements less.[13] It's a paradox: the pressures that propel us to do well in an *absolute* sense may deprive us of enjoyment in a *relative* sense. The poem *Desiderata*, by Max Ehrmann, expresses the thought: "If you compare yourself with others, you may become vain and bitter; / for always there will be greater and lesser persons than yourself." We may lead a more contented life if we can resist unnecessary comparisons. Why let the achievements of others make us feel worse (in relative terms) when we can feel satisfied by focusing on our (absolute) achievements? A great deal of grief comes from people thinking in relative terms—"keeping up with the Joneses" is the common phrase—when they would be better off focusing on absolute well-being.

As simple as the distinction may seem, in practice people often confuse absolute and relative performance. Returning to an earlier example, performance in medicine is best understood as absolute. Doctors make the best diagnoses they can for each patient, never mind what another doctor might do. They're not (at least we hope!) trying to outperform others to finish at the top of some competition among doctors, in the way that Steve picked the Seahawks with an eye to finishing ahead of rivals to win $100. Patient care, too, is a matter of absolute performance, in the sense that one patient's recovery doesn't prevent another patient from recovering. Quite the contrary: if we have a ward full of people suffering from a mysterious ailment, we hope to find a treatment that cures them all.[14]

A few years ago David Sackett, Gordon Guyatt, and their colleagues at McMaster University developed what they called *evidence-based medicine*, which aimed to replace received wisdom and rules of thumb with sound data-driven analysis. The results were impressive, leading to a growing acceptance of fact-based decisions in medicine. Recently two professors of clinical epidemiology at the University of California, San Francisco, wrote a book titled *Evidence-Based Diagnosis* designed to teach medical students about effective diagnostic, screening, and prognostic tests.[15] All of that makes good sense in the world of medicine.

It didn't take long for the success of evidence-based medicine to catch the attention of other fields. The US Office of Management and Budget recently announced that it would rely on data analysis to assess the effectiveness of public agencies, a move that was dubbed "evidence-based public policy."[16] That makes good sense, too, as the delivery of public services is a matter of absolute performance: the aim is to deliver services effectively and efficiently, not for one department to outperform others.

Soon the business world took note as well, and we began to hear about "evidence-based management."[17] The idea was that managers, much like doctors, should base their decisions on empirical data. That might make good sense for business decisions that don't involve competition with rivals—how to manage inventory, or reduce defects, are good examples—but the strategic management of a company calls for much more than thinking like a doctor. The success of a company calls for *relative performance*. When companies compete, the performance of one is related to the success of others, and often with highly skewed payoffs.

Failure to appreciate this essential difference is at the crux of a story about Thomas Watson Jr., the legendary president of IBM. In 1956, Watson was asked by a colleague whether IBM should share its pricing information with John Burns, IBM's chief adviser at the consulting firm Booz Allen Hamilton. Watson immediately replied in the affirmative: "Sure, it's like your doctor. You have to tell them everything." A few months later, Burns called to say that he had been offered the job as president of RCA, one of IBM's biggest competitors at the time, and wanted to know if Watson had any objections to him taking the job. Watson was furious: "I said, 'I most certainly do, John!' because we had entrusted him with detailed knowledge of our organization and methods and plans."[18] The idea that a consultant who knew the inner workings of IBM's pricing strategy would head a rival company was appalling. It was completely unacceptable.

As John Gapper of the *Financial Times* later wrote, Watson had been wrong: "A consultant is not like a doctor because a patient is at worst indifferent to whether a physician uses the knowledge gained from treating him to cure someone else, and is usually happy to help others. A company wants a consultant to help it not only to become better but to hurt its competitors." You wouldn't mind if your doctor shared information about your medical history to help other patients. Your recovery is unrelated to theirs. If anything, you'd probably be glad to help out. Business is entirely different. Firm performance—whether measured in terms of market share, revenues, or profits—is not only relative but often highly skewed, such that the success of one company often comes at the expense of others. In these circumstances it's not just irresponsible to share information, but dangerous. What is sensible when performance is absolute may be suicidal when performance is relative and payoffs are highly skewed.

ABOUT PERFORMANCE:
ON WHICH SIDE SHOULD WE ERR?

We can now pose a question like the one in Chapter Two: When it comes to absolute and relative performance, on which side would you rather err? Of course, you want to know when performance is relative and payoffs highly skewed so that you can take appropriate actions, much like the University of Alberta students. You'll also want to know when performance is absolute and payoffs have low skew so you can act accordingly.

FIGURE 3.2 PAYOFFS, BELIEF AND REALITY

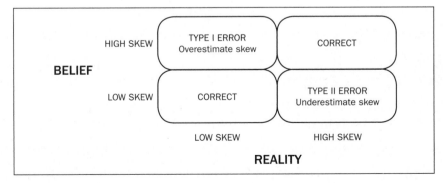

But if you're not sure, which sort of error is best? There are unpleasant consequences in either direction, of course. If you believe there's an intense pressure to outperform rivals when that's not the case, you might prefer a Type I error. You might take action sooner than necessary or act more aggressively when the better approach would be to wait and observe. The risks can be considerable, but perhaps not fatal. On the other hand, if performance is not only relative but payoffs are highly skewed, and you don't make every effort to outperform rivals, you'll make a Type II error. Here the consequences can be much more severe. Fail now, and you may never get another chance to succeed. By this logic, the greater error is to underestimate the intensity of competition. It's to be too passive in the face of what could be a mortal threat. When in doubt, the smart move is to err on the side of taking strong action.

THINKING ABOUT PERFORMANCE

Decision making has often been studied without any regard to competition. We ask people to make judgments and choices without having to worry about the actions of others. Implicitly, at least, performance is absolute.

In many fields, however, performance is best understood as relative. In business, politics, sports, and more, many of the most important decisions are made with an eye to rivalry. The aim isn't to just do well, but to do better than others.[19] Sometimes the distribution of payoffs is clearly stated, but often the intensity of rivalry, the nature of payoffs, and whether competition is open or closed ended, is unknown. Very often we have to make crucial decisions without all the information we need.

It has sometimes been suggested that business executives often ignore the findings of decision research. They seem not to heed lessons about common errors and biases. It's ironic: the very people who face some of the most complex decisions appear unwilling to embrace techniques that can lead to better results. Perhaps they're in denial, or maybe their past successes have made them stubborn and unwilling to learn.

This chapter and the previous one point to a different explanation. The most consequential managerial decisions are fundamentally different from those that have often been studied, and in two crucial ways. Not only can managers often exert control over outcomes, but they also have to outperform rivals. And as the next chapter will show, when these two factors are combined, some conventional ideas about decision making are turned on their heads.

WHAT IT TAKES TO WIN

4

IN TIMES OF CHANGE, MANAGERS ALMOST ALWAYS KNOW WHICH
DIRECTION THEY SHOULD GO IN, BUT USUALLY ACT TOO LATE AND
DO TOO LITTLE. CORRECT FOR THIS TENDENCY: ADVANCE THE PACE
OF YOUR ACTIONS AND INCREASE THEIR MAGNITUDE. YOU'LL FIND
THAT YOU'RE MORE LIKELY TO BE CLOSE TO RIGHT.

ANDY GROVE, *ONLY THE PARANOID SURVIVE*, 1995

Combine the ability to exert control with the need to outperform rivals, and what happens? Now it's not just possible to influence outcomes, but often necessary.

For a stark example, let's look at the world of professional cycling. The Tour de France has been held every year since 1903, aside from a few interruptions during wartime. It's a grueling race with twenty-one stages over three weeks, some long and flat, winding through fields and villages, and others rising over steep mountain passes in the Alps and the Pyrénées. Going fast is a matter of strong technique and stamina as well as positive thinking. As for performance, not only is it relative—the cyclist with the lowest total time is crowned champion and wears the *maillot jaune*—but payoffs are highly skewed, with a huge prize and massive prestige for the winning cyclist and his team, and lesser rewards for others. (Several other prizes are awarded—best sprinter, best climber—as well as for members of the winning team.) There is also a clear end point to each stage and a culmination on the last Sunday with the final sprint on the Champs Elysées in Paris.

In this context, cyclists naturally do all they can to improve their performance. There's constant pressure for innovation in equipment, training, nutrition, and so forth. Not surprisingly, the temptation to find less ethical ways to go faster is also present.

The use of illicit drugs was already common in the 1960s and 1970s, with amphetamines and other stimulants in vogue. But in the 1990s, with the advent of erythropoietin, better known as EPO, the game changed completely. EPO stimulates the production of red blood cells, crucial to carrying oxygen to muscles in a long and arduous race, and can significantly improve racing times. American cyclist Tyler Hamilton estimated that EPO could boost performance by about 5 percent. That may not seem like much, but at the very highest levels of competitive racing, where everyone is fit, talented, and works hard, a 5 percent gain is massive. It was roughly the difference between finishing in first place and being stuck in the middle of the pack.[1]

For a few years in the mid-1990s, as EPO found its way into the *peleton*, reporters noted that there seemed to be two groups of cyclists: those who continued to race at standard times, and a small but growing number who were noticeably faster, their legs and lungs able to tap what appeared to be an extra reserve of energy. The cyclists were running at two speeds, *a deux vitesses*. *Sports Illustrated*'s Austin Murphy wrote: "Rampant EPO use had transformed middling talents into supermen. Teams riding *pan y agua*—bread and water—had no chance."[2] No wonder so many professional cyclists resorted to doping. The performance difference was so clear that those who resisted had no chance of winning. Many of them quit altogether.

From 1999 through 2005, while Lance Armstrong was winning the Tour de France an unprecedented seven years in a row, there were persistent rumors of doping. Suspicion was widespread but nothing was proven. By 2008, thanks to persistent investigations, evidence of doping began to emerge. One of the first American cyclists to admit wrongdoing, Kayle Leogrande, was asked if he thought Armstrong had taken performance-enhancing drugs. To Leogrande there could be little doubt: "He's racing in these barbaric cycling races in Europe. If you were a rider at that level, what would you do?"[3]

When Armstrong finally admitted in 2013 that he had used performance-enhancing drugs, he acknowledged the full menu. EPO? "Yes." Blood doping? "Yes." Testosterone? "Yes." Asked if he could have won the Tour de France without resorting to these measures, Armstrong said "No." There would have been no way to win such a competitive race without using all means at his disposal. The sad fact is that Armstrong was probably correct, although by doping he exacerbated the problem, making it impossible for others to ride clean.[4]

None of this is meant to justify the use of illegal drugs, of course. Many cyclists refused to dope, and their careers suffered as a consequence. We should condemn both the cyclists who used drugs and the officials who were slow to insist on stronger controls. The advent of a biological passport, which establishes a baseline for each athlete and permits the detection of deviations in key markers, is an encouraging step forward.

For our purposes, the example illustrates something else: that even a small improvement in absolute performance can make an outsize difference in relative performance, in effect between winning and losing.

ABSOLUTE IMPROVEMENT AND RELATIVE SUCCESS

To illustrate how improvements in (absolute) performance can affect (relative) success, let's return to the example in Chapter Two, when people were asked to putt toward a hole. (We'll skip the projector and the circles that made the hole appear larger or smaller.)

Let's suppose that a group of novice golfers, shooting from a distance of six feet, have a 30 percent chance of sinking each putt. If we ask them to take 10 shots each (and if we assume each shot is independent, meaning there is no improvement from one shot to the next) they'll produce the distribution on Figure 4.1. A very few (2.8 percent of the golfers) will miss all ten shots, while 12.1 percent will sink one putt, 23.3 percent will make two, and 26.7 percent (the most common result) will sink three putts. From there the distribution ramps down, with 20 percent sinking four putts, 10.3 percent making five, and 3.7 percent making six. Fewer than one percent will sink seven putts out of ten, and doing even better than that is not impossible but less and less probable.

FIGURE 4.1 NOVICE GROUP, 30% SUCCESS RATE

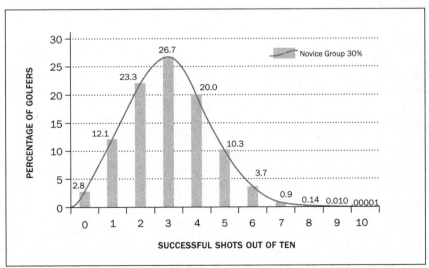

Suppose we assemble another group and provide them with putting lessons. We train them to make a smooth swing with a good follow-through. We teach them to focus their minds and to derive the benefits of positive thinking. Let's assume that members of the Trained group have a 40 percent success rate, a considerable improvement over the 30 percent rate for Novices but still far short of the 54.8 percent for professionals golfers mentioned in Chapter Two. If members of this group take 10 shots each, they'll produce the distribution in Figure 4.2. Now almost none will miss all ten, 4 percent will sink just one, 12.1 percent will make two, 21.5 percent will sink three, 25.1 percent will make four, and so on.

If we bring together the Novice and Trained golfers, as shown in Figure 4.3, we see quite a bit of overlap between the two groups. In any given competition, some Novice golfers will do better than Trained golfers.

FIGURE 4.2 TRAINED GROUP: 40% SUCCESS RATE

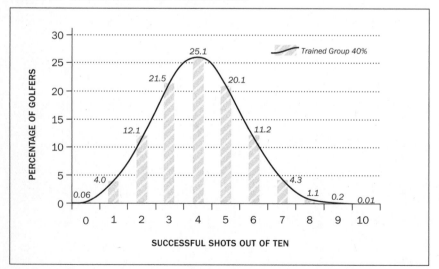

FIGURE 4.3 NOVICE 30% AND TRAINED 40% GROUPS, COMBINED

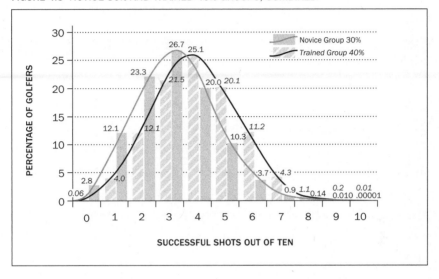

Here's the question: If we hold a contest between Novice and Trained golfers—let's say, 30 Novice and 30 Trained golfers each taking 20 shots—what's the chance that a member of one or the other group will finish in first place out of all 60 contestants? Of course it's more likely a Trained golfer will win, but just how likely? Is there a good chance that a Novice will come out on top, or only a slim one?

To find out, I used a Monte Carlo simulation, a technique developed in the 1940s when scientists at the Manhattan Project needed to predict the outcome of nuclear chain reactions. The physics of chain reactions is so complicated that a precise calculation of what would happen in a given instance was impossible. A better method was to calculate what would happen in many trials, and then aggregate the results to get a sense of the distribution of possible outcomes. The scientists, John von Neumann and Stanislas Ulam, named their method after the Monte Carlo casino in Monaco, with its famous roulette wheel. Any single spin of a roulette wheel will land the ball in just one slot, which won't tell us a great deal. Spin the roulette wheel a thousand times, however, and you'll get a very good picture of what can happen.[5]

To examine the impact of a change in absolute performance on relative performance, I devised a Monte Carlo simulation to conduct one thousand trials of a competition where 30 Novice golfers and 30 Trained golfers take 20 shots each. The results showed that 86.5 percent of the time—865 out of 1,000 trials—the winner came from the Trained group. There was a tie between a Trained and a Novice golfer 9.1 percent of the time, and only 4.4 percent of the time—just 44 times out of 1,000 trials—did the top score come from the Novice group. The Trained group's *absolute* advantage, a 40 percent success rate versus 30 percent, gave its members an almost insurmountable *relative* advantage. Less than one time in twenty would the top Novice finish ahead of all 30 Trained golfers.

What if the gain from training was much smaller—say, from a success rate of 30 percent to just 33 percent? Now the Trained group would have a distribution as shown in Figure 4.4, and there would be much more overlap with the Novice group, in Figure 4.5. The chance that a Novice might win should go up, and that's what we find. Even so, the Monte Carlo simulation showed that in a competition where 30 members of each group take 20 shots, a member of the Novice group would finish first 19.9 percent of the time (199 out of 1,000 trials). A member of the Trained group would win 55.5 percent of the time (555 out of 1,000), with 24.6 percent resulting in a tie. Even with a relatively small improvement, from 30 percent to 33 percent, the winner would be more than twice as likely to come from Trained group.

FIGURE 4.4 TRAINED GROUP: 33% SUCCESS RATE

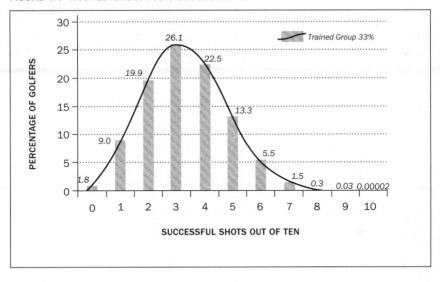

FIGURE 4.5 NOVICE 30% AND TRAINED 33% GROUPS, COMBINED

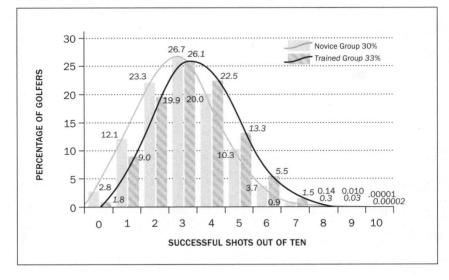

The lesson is clear: in a competitive setting, even a modest improvement in absolute performance can have a huge impact on relative performance. And conversely, failing to use all possible advantages to improve absolute performance has a crippling effect on the likelihood of winning. Under these circumstances, finding a way to do better isn't just nice to have. For all intents and purposes, it's essential.*

BETTER PERFORMANCE IN THE BUSINESS WORLD

The examples of EPO in cycling and the Monte Carlo golf simulation point to the same conclusion: even small improvements in absolute performance can have an outsize effect on relative performance. Still, we should be careful not to generalize too broadly. Surely the "barbaric" pressures of competitive cycling are unusual, and though a simulated putting tournament is illustrative, it's nevertheless contrived. It's therefore open to question whether we would find quite the same impact of modest absolute gains in real-world decisions.

For a point of comparison, let's look at the business world. It's very different from a bicycle race or putting competition, of course.

---

* The improvements in these examples, from 30 to 40 percent (an increase of 33 percent) or from 30 to 33 percent (an increase of 10 percent) were greater than the gain attributed to EPO, which was estimated to boost performance by 5 percent. Does it follow that the overlap between the two groups in cycling would be greater, therefore weakening the claim that the winner very likely would have doped? The answer is no, because there's another variable to consider. In my simulated golf competition, each participant putted twenty times. Had I asked for, say, one hundred putts, the overlap between the populations would have been much less, and the chance that a member of the Novice group would have outperformed members of the Trained group would have been far lower. Given that the Tour de France is a multistage bicycle race held over several thousand kilometers, the chance that a lower performer can beat a higher performer is very small. All else being equal, a 5 percent improvement, whether due to EPO or some other enhancement, would produce an almost insurmountable competitive advantage.

The distribution of payoffs in business is rarely stated explicitly, with fixed prizes for first, second, and third place. Nor is there usually a precise end point when a company needs to be among the leaders or face elimination. Nor is there anything quite like EPO, a powerful drug that, all else being equal, can raise performance by 5 percent. Companies can't pop a pill to become 5 percent more efficient or 5 percent more innovative.

Yet for all these differences, business nevertheless shares many of the same competitive dynamics. Although there may not be a clearly defined payoff structure, payoffs in business *are* often highly skewed, with a great disparity between top and low performers. There may be no precise end point, but that's not necessarily a source of comfort, because the threat of elimination can be constant. Furthermore, unlike sports, in which the rules are known to all and the standings are clear for all to see, competition in business has many sources of uncertainty. Technologies can change suddenly and dramatically, new competitors can enter the fray at any time, consumer preferences can shift from one week to the next, and rivals can merge or form alliances. If anything, competition in business is *more* dynamic and less forgiving than in sports. Not surprisingly, there is incessant pressure to find ways of doing better, whether through innovative technology, new products and services, or simply better execution. Only by taking chances, by pushing the envelope, can companies hope to stay ahead of rivals. Michael Raynor of Deloitte Consulting calls this "the strategy paradox": that strategies with the greatest possibility of success also run the greatest chance of failure. "Behaviorally, at least," Raynor observes, "the opposite of success isn't failure, but mediocrity. . . . Who dares wins . . . or loses."[6] A commitment to bold action may not be sufficient to guarantee success, but when performance is relative and payoffs are highly skewed, one thing is assured: playing it safe will almost guarantee failure. You're bound to be overtaken by rivals who are willing to take big risks to come out ahead.

The importance of taking action in business—who dares wins—isn't a new idea. Already in 1982, the first principle of success in Tom Peters and Robert Waterman's *In Search of Excellence* was "a bias for action," which they defined as "a preference for doing something—anything—rather than sending a question through cycles and cycles of analyses and committee reports."[7] One of Stanford professor Robert Sutton's rules for innovation is to "reward success and failure, punish inaction."[8] The failure to act is a greater sin than taking action and failing, because action brings at least a possibility of success, whereas inaction brings none. Virgin founder Richard Branson titled one of his books *Screw It, Let's Do It*—a provocative title, and surely not meant as an ironclad rule, but nevertheless conveying a crucial insight. In the highly competitive industries in which Branson operated, such as retail and airlines, the willingness to take bold action was a necessity. Standing pat would inevitably lead to failure. Heike Bruch and Sumantra Ghoshal, in *A Bias for Action*, took this thinking one step further: "While experimentation and flexibility are important for companies, in our observation the most critical challenge for companies is exactly the opposite: determined, persistent, and relentless action-taking to achieve a purpose, against all odds."[9] Why "against all odds"? Because in a competitive game with skewed payoffs, only those who are willing to defy the odds will be in a position to win.

The use of *bias* by Peters and Waterman and by Bruch and Ghoshal is worthy of note. A great deal of decision research has been concerned with guarding *against* biases. Why, then, does bias seem to be discussed here in a favorable way?

For that, we have to come back to the word itself. Decision research has often been concerned with cognitive biases, which are mental shortcuts that sometimes lead people to make incorrect judgments. Cognitive biases are unconscious. Once we're aware of them, we can try (although often with difficulty) to correct for them. In everyday speech, however, a bias isn't just an unconscious cognitive error. It refers more generally to a preference or predisposition and can even be deliberate. You might have a tendency to, say, vote for incumbents, perhaps on the theory that they have valuable experience that shouldn't be lost. (Or maybe, given the gridlock in Washington, your bias is in the opposite direction—to throw the rascals out.) Or you might have a preference for aisle seats on airplanes, because you like to get up and walk around during flights. These are *biases* in the sense that they reflect a consistent preference or inclination. They're programmed responses that let you act quickly and efficiently, without having to think carefully each time the question comes up. They're rules of thumb. If your predisposition is to choose an aisle seat, you can be said to have a bias, although such a bias is neither unconscious nor dangerous.

In strategic management, a bias for action simply means a preference for action over inaction. Such a preference arises from the recognition that when performance is relative and payoffs are highly skewed, only those who take outsize risks will be in a position to win. The University of Alberta team displayed a bias for risk taking when it pursued what it admitted was "aggressive and sometimes extremely risky strategy." They weren't wrong. Their bias for taking risks reflected an astute understanding of the competitive context.

WHY IT'S OFTEN BETTER TO ACT

In Chapter Two we saw that contrary to popular thinking, it's not true that people suffer from a pervasive illusion of control. The more serious error may be a Type II error, the failure to understand how much control they have. Similarly, in Chapter Three we saw that when it comes to understanding performance, the more serious error may be Type II, the failure to recognize the extent to which payoffs are skewed.

Put them together, and not only *can* we improve outcomes by taking action, but given the nature of competitive forces we're much better off erring on the side of action. That's what Intel chairman Andy Grove meant by the title of his book, *Only the Paranoid Survive*. Grove didn't say that *all* who are paranoid will be sure to survive. He made no claim that paranoia leads predictably to survival. His point was merely that in the highly competitive industry he knew best—semiconductors—only companies that push themselves to be among the very best and are willing to take risks will have a chance of living to see another day. The choice of words was deliberate. Grove knew from experience that paranoia may not ensure success, but any companies that survive will have exhibited something resembling paranoia.

Is Grove's dictum applicable to all industries? Not to the same extent as to semiconductors. It might not make sense for, say, running a restaurant or a law firm, or a company in whose industry the pace of change and the distribution of payoffs is more forgiving. There's no need for the makers of candy bars or razor blades, products where technology is relatively stable and consumer tastes don't change much, to gamble everything on a risky new approach. But high-tech companies, like makers of smartphones, absolutely need to. In fact, in many industries the intensity of competition, coupled with an acceleration in technological change, means that the need to outperform rivals is more intense than even a few years ago.[10] As a rule, preferring to risk a Type I error rather than a Type II error makes more sense. As Grove remarked in the quote at the start of this chapter, the natural tendency of many managers is to act too late and to do too little. We should, he urged, correct this mistake. The best course of action is not only faster but to do more. True, you may not always win, but at least you will improve your chances. That was a good rule of thumb in the 1990s, when Grove took a gamble on moving into microprocessors, and it's still true today. In 2013 Intel was under pressure as its position in microprocessors for PCs was fading because of the growing popularity of tablets, smartphones, and cloud computing. Chief executive Paul Ottelini announced that he was stepping down three years short of the company retirement age, citing the need for new leadership. Meanwhile, Intel chairman Andy Bryant told employees to prepare for major change. Past success didn't guarantee future profits, he reminded them. Bryant pointed out that customers had changed, and that Intel had to change as well. Where revenues come from today is not where they will in the future.[11] Once again, the greater mistake would be to err on the side of complacency. That way extinction lies.

WHICH ONE IS THE SPECIAL CASE?

If we want to understand the mechanisms of judgment and choice, it makes good sense to design experiments that remove the ability to influence outcomes and the need to outperform rivals. That way, to use Dan Ariely's metaphor, we can create the equivalent of a strobe light to capture a single frame.

Thanks to the abundance of such experiments and the insights they have given us about judgment and choice, it's easy to imagine that such decisions represent a sort of baseline or norm. Decisions for which we can influence outcomes and for which we have to outperform rivals might be thought of as a special case, worth noting but hardly representative of most decisions.

But we could just as easily turn this logic on its head. In the real world, the combination of these two features—an ability to exert control over outcomes and the need to outperform rivals—isn't a special case at all. In many domains it's the norm. If anything, those carefully designed experiments that remove control and competition are more accurately seen as the special case. True, their findings can be applied to many real world decisions, including consumer behavior, in which people make discrete choices from explicit options, and financial investing, in which we cannot easily influence the value of an asset. But they should not be thought to capture the dynamics of many real-world decisions.

Unfortunately, in our desire to conduct careful research that conforms to the norms of social science, with its rigorous controls, we have sometimes generalized findings to situations that are markedly different. As an example, a recent study in *Strategic Management Journal*, a leading academic publication, contended that better strategic decisions could result from a technique called *similarity-based forecasting*.[12] To demonstrate the effectiveness of this approach, it tested the accuracy of predictions about the success of Hollywood movies. A model that looked at the past performance of similar movies, rather than relying on hunches or anecdotes, produced better predictions of box office success. Decision models can be enormously powerful tools (as we'll see in Chapter Nine), and predicting movie success is surely one kind of real-world decision. Yet predicting the success of *The Matrix* or *The War of the Worlds* calls for an accurate judgment, period. It's a mistake to equate the prediction of an event we cannot influence with the broader field of strategic management, which not only affords the change to influence outcomes but also involves a competitive dimension. In our desire to devise predictive models, we sometimes overlook the stuff of management.

I recently observed a similar oversight at my institute, IMD. One of our most successful programs, "Advanced Strategic Management," attracts a range of senior executives who seek to boost company performance. Their desire, as the program title suggests, is to achieve better strategic management of their companies. In recent years two of my colleagues have added sessions about decision making. The finance professor showed how financial decisions are often distorted by cognitive biases, and the marketing professor did the same for consumer choices. That's not a bad thing. Executives are surely better off knowing about common errors, and no doubt they enjoyed the sessions. But understanding decisions in finance and marketing does not adequately capture what is distinctive about *strategic* decisions. For a program about strategic management, we should consider situations in which executives can influence outcomes, and in which performance is not only relative but highly skewed.

Once we do that, we have to look at decision making very differently. In the next chapter we take a fresh look at a topic that's widely mentioned but poorly understood: *overconfidence*.

CONFIDENCE . . . AND OVERCONFIDENCE

5

Of all the errors and biases that undermine our judgment, the most frequently cited is overconfidence. Already in 1995, summarizing research from the previous two decades, behavioral economist Richard Thaler observed, "Perhaps the most robust finding in the psychology of judgment and choice is that people are overconfident."[1] Around the same time, psychologist Scott Plous reached a similar conclusion: "No problem in judgment and decision making is more prevalent and more potentially catastrophic than overconfidence."[2]

Since then the notion that people suffer from overconfidence has been repeated over and over, to the point where it has become accepted as fact. A few quotes from recent years are representative:

- Joseph Hallinan, Pulitzer Prize–winning business journalist, in *Why We Make Mistakes*: "[M]ost of us tend to be overconfident, and overconfidence is a leading cause of human error."[3]
- David Brooks, *New York Times* columnist, in *The Social Animal*: "The human mind is an overconfidence machine."[4]
- Ken Fisher, president of Fisher Investments: Investors make mistakes due to an "innate tendency toward overconfidence."[5]
- Nate Silver, in *The Signal and the Noise*: "[O]f the various cognitive biases that investors suffer from, overconfidence is the most pernicious. Perhaps the central finding of behavioral economics is that most of us are overconfident when we make predictions."[6]

And so, given this widespread problem, we are advised to beware. We're urged to acknowledge our natural tendency to be overconfident and to guard against it.

At first glance all this makes good sense. Look in any dictionary, and *overconfidence* is defined as "excessive confidence" or "greater confidence than circumstances warrant." The adjective *overconfident* means "too confident" or "excessively confident." These definitions are reasonable, because the prefix *over* denotes excess. Naturally we should want to avoid excessive confidence. Who wouldn't?

Yet in Chapter Two we also saw that positive illusions can improve performance. Shouldn't it follow that a very high degree of confidence is a good thing? Why must it be "potentially catastrophic"? Furthermore, as we saw in Chapter Three, when performance is relative and we need to do better than rivals, a very high level of confidence can be more than useful and even necessary. We need to ask: If *overconfident* means *too confident*, too confident compared to what? If *overconfidence* means *greater confidence than circumstances warrant*, which circumstances are we talking about? Very soon, what seems like a simple idea becomes much more complicated.

In an essay published in 1947, "Politics and the English Language," George Orwell wrote: "A man may take to drink because he feels himself to be a failure, and then fail all the more completely because he drinks. It is rather the same thing that is happening to the English language. It becomes ugly and inaccurate because our thoughts are foolish, but the slovenliness of our language makes it easier for us to have foolish thoughts."[7] That's a good summary of the current state of affairs regarding overconfidence. Foolish thinking has led to inaccurate language, and slovenly language has made it easy to have foolish thoughts. To help make great decisions, we need to take a new look at what we mean by *confidence* . . . and what we mean by *overconfidence*.

OVERCONFIDENCE IN OUR DAILY CONVERSATION

In everyday speech, overconfidence is typically applied after the fact to explain why something went wrong. Examples abound in all walks of life.

In November 2012, after a long and closely fought campaign, President Barack Obama was reelected by a small margin of the popular vote and a decisive majority of electoral votes. Soon reporters declared that his opponent, Mitt Romney, had suffered from overconfidence. Their evidence? Rather than working to get out the vote on election day, Romney spent his time drawing up a list of White House appointments, while $25,000 worth of fireworks sat nearby for a victory party that never took place. A senior aide explained: "It was overconfidence based on inaccurate assumptions and flawed data."[8] Curiously, no one had accused Romney of overconfidence during the campaign, when he worked long hours, going from state to state and speaking at rallies from morning to night. But when the votes were counted and he fell short, it was irresistible to claim he had been overconfident.

Four years earlier, the same label had been pinned on a different losing candidate. In June 2008, when Hillary Clinton ended her long quest for the Democratic nomination, the *New York Times* explained that her campaign had been "suffused in overconfidence, riven by acrimony and weighted by emotional baggage."[9] By *overconfidence* the article meant that the Clinton campaign had been complacent, perhaps imagining the nomination was in the bag, which led to serious errors and eventually to defeat. In fact, a closer look showed that Clinton had worked tirelessly and campaigned relentlessly, which is hardly the stuff of complacency. What had gone wrong? The race was decided during a few weeks in February, when Barack Obama sprinted ahead in delegate count thanks to a shrewd focus on small states, gaining a lead that he never lost.[10] True, the Clinton campaign made a crucial strategic error by overlooking small states, but that by itself doesn't justify a charge of overconfidence (unless of course we attribute any bad outcome, after the fact, to overconfidence, which is often what happens). As for Barack Obama, he was described as having *gaudy confidence* and *outsize confidence*, but never *overconfidence*, and for an obvious reason: he was the eventual winner. His confidence, no matter how great it may have been, turned out to be justified. But on reflection, who had displayed unwarranted confidence: a prominent senator backed by an impressive political machine, or a first-term senator with little national experience?

These examples are typical. Overconfidence is a common explanation any time something turns out badly, and not just in politics.

When the Fukushima nuclear reactor was damaged in March 2011 by a tsunami, spilling radioactivity into the air and sea along the Japanese coast, a civil engineer pointed to three separate instances of overconfidence: a poor understanding of earthquakes when the reactor was designed, reliance on simplistic failure models regarding plant reliability, and an emphasis on the reactor vessel rather than on spent fuel storage after the tsunami struck. Similarly, when Hurricane Katrina devastated New Orleans in 2005, FEMA director Michael Brown charged that the Bush administration had failed to take precautionary measures because it had been "overconfident" that it could handle the crisis.[11]

We know that athletes understand the importance of confidence. Quite naturally, when they're victorious they give credit to their high confidence, and when they're defeated are quick to blame overconfidence. In December 2012, before his fight with José Manuel Marquez, a smiling boxer Manny Pacquiao was described as relaxed and composed, "his face filled with confidence."[12] Hours later, after a stunning right cross had knocked him cold, Pacquiao saw it differently: "I just got overconfident in this fight."[13] Well, at least that's how it seemed after the fact. And by that logic, Pacquiao may believe that if he just watches out for overconfidence, he should be able to win the next time they meet.

Perhaps nowhere is failure blamed on overconfidence as often as in the business world. In July 2011 Netflix, the enormously successful movie rental company, announced that it would split its rental business from a new video streaming business and charge customers extra if they wanted both. Customers were outraged, and after three weeks, chief executive Reed Hastings was forced to apologize and reverse his decision. The damage was severe: Netflix lost 800,000 subscribers, and its stock price fell by more than 25 percent. In

October Hastings showed contrition and admitted that he had been guilty of overconfidence.[14] As he explained, he had been too sure of himself and failed to take note of customer concerns. In the future, he promised, Netflix would slow its decision making to make sure there was room for debate. Interestingly, this comment came from a man who had often been praised for bold and courageous decisions. Companies don't fail because they move too swiftly, Hastings had said, but because they move too slowly. That made good sense as long as his swift moves were successful. But when a bold move turned out badly, he pointed to overconfidence.

A few months later, in May 2012, when JPMorgan Chase lost more than $2 billion because its risk-monitoring systems failed to spot the dangers in its derivatives portfolio, chief executive Jamie Dimon pointed the finger at—you guessed it—overconfidence. Overconfidence gave rise to complacency, Dimon explained, which led to the massive error.[15]

Recently I conducted a search for the words *overconfident* and *overconfidence* in the business press. By far the most common use was retrospective, to explain why something had gone wrong. Examples ranged from KFC's initial failure in India ("'They came into the country overconfident,' said a local customer, before biting into a Chicken Tikka Wrap n' Roll"[16]), to Bob Nardelli's bumpy tenure at Home Depot (one investor complained that Nardelli "comes across as arrogant and overconfident"[17]), to why Airbus lost market share when the A380 was delayed ("Airbus managers also quietly concede that they became overconfident after several years in which Boeing gave up market share to a more aggressive Airbus"[18]).

In all of these examples, from politics to natural disasters to sports to business, overconfidence offers a satisfying narrative device. Take any success, and we can find reasons to explain it as the result of healthy confidence. We nod approvingly: *They were confident—that's why they did so well.* Take any failure, and we shake our heads: *They were overconfident—that's why they did poorly. If they hadn't been so sure of themselves, they might have done better.*

There's an appealing syllogism at work:

- Things turned out badly, so someone must have erred.
- Errors are due to overconfidence.
- Therefore, bad outcomes are due to overconfidence.

Unfortunately each of these statements is flawed. First, not everything that turns out badly is due to an error. We live in a world of uncertainty, in which there's an imperfect link between actions and outcomes. Even good decisions sometimes turn out badly, but that doesn't necessarily mean anyone made an error. Second, not every error is the result of overconfidence. There are many kinds of error: errors of calculation, errors of memory, simple motor errors, tactical errors, and so forth. They're not all due to overconfidence.

Those first two flaws lead to the third. It might be convenient to blame bad outcomes on overconfidence, but the logic doesn't add up. Even worse, the effect is to dilute overconfidence to the point where it's all but meaningless. When any failure can be attributed to overconfidence, the term means nothing at all.

In *Decisive: How to Make Better Choices in Life and Work,* Chip Heath and Dan Heath cite the famous comment by a Decca record executive in 1962, who had just listened to an audition by an aspiring quartet called The Beatles, but declined to offer them a contract because he felt guitar groups were a thing of the past.[19] He turned out to be wrong, of course, but is that really evidence of overconfidence? We might just as easily say he was underconfident when it came to guitar groups. (We could even claim he was overconfident in expressing a view of underconfidence, a hair-splitting argument that illustrates the deeper problem—*overconfidence* can be used to mean almost anything.)

There's another danger when we attribute failures to overconfidence, and it's potentially the most serious of all. Accusations of overconfidence carry a moral overtone. When we charge people with overconfidence, we suggest that they contributed to their own demise. We imply that they at least partially deserved their fate. They committed one of the seven deadly sins, sometimes called pride or vainglory. We think: *They were too sure of themselves. They should have known better. They got what they had coming.*

From there, it's a small step to imagine that if *we* can simply avoid the sin of overconfidence, we won't meet the fate that befell others. After all, most people don't think that they suffer from excessive pride or vanity. *Others* might exhibit overconfidence, but we don't imagine the term applies to *us*. And so we comfort ourselves with the notion that we have little to worry about. Did Netflix blunder because Reed Hastings was overconfident? *Too bad for him, but I won't make that mistake, because I'm not overconfident.* Those disasters that befell KFC and Home Depot? *If they were due to overconfidence, I can rest assured they won't happen to me.* We may even experience a bit of *schadenfreude*, taking pleasure at the misfortunes of others.

The irony, of course, is that those people didn't see themselves as overconfident, either. At the time, they believed they were being appropriately confident, and that their actions were bold and decisive but surely not excessive. It's only after things turn out badly that we hear the term. We'll never learn from the errors of others if we attribute them to overconfidence. We end up fooling ourselves.

OVERCONFIDENCE IN THE HERE AND NOW:
NOT ONE THING BUT THREE

Fortunately, overconfidence isn't only inferred after the fact. It can also be studied in the here and now, defined as confidence that exceeds what's objectively warranted. That's the way it has been studied in decision research, and here the evidence seems clear. Decades of research have produced very consistent findings that people really do suffer from a bias of overconfidence.

Some examples have been cited over and over, to the point of folklore. In 1981, Swedish psychologist Ola Svenson found that 93 percent of American drivers rated themselves better than average. Swedish drivers were somewhat less extreme, with only 69 percent claiming to be better than average.[20] Surely this can't be correct. The obvious explanation is that these drivers were overconfident. Another study found that 25 percent of high school seniors believed they were in the top 1 percent in terms of their ability to get along with others,[21] and still another found that 37 percent of engineers rated themselves in the top 5 percent of all professionals.[22] University professors aren't immune either, as a large majority rate themselves above average when it comes to teaching ability.[23] Surely that's incorrect. They must be overconfident.

Other evidence comes from experiments discussed in Chapter One, in which people are presented with questions of general knowledge—the length of the Nile, the year Mozart was born, and so on—and asked to estimate a range that they are 90 percent confident contains the correct answer. The original study, conducted by Marc Alpert and Howard Raiffa in 1969, found that the "90 percent confidence range" contained the correct answer less than 50 percent of the time.[24] Variants of this study have been conducted countless times and produced very consistent results. Time and again, people provide ranges that are far too narrow. The inevitable conclusion: people are overconfident.

Given all of these examples, the evidence seems overwhelming that people suffer from overconfidence. But when we look more closely, however, it's not clear at all. As Don Moore and Paul J. Healy described in a 2008 article, "The Trouble with Overconfidence," the single word—*overconfidence*—has been used to mean three very different things, which they call *overprecision, overestimation*, and *overplacement*. They explain: "Researchers routinely assume, either explicitly or implicitly, that the different types of overconfidence are the same."[25] But they're *not* the same, and when we take them one at a time, the notion that people suffer from a widespread tendency to be overconfident begins to unravel.

Overprecision is the tendency to be too certain that our judgment is correct. Those studies that asked for 90 percent confidence ranges? That's an example of overprecision. In *The Signal and the Noise*, Nate Silver mentions overconfidence as a serious problem when making predictions. He's referring to overprecision: the tendency to believe a prediction is more accurate than it turns out to be.[26]

Overestimation, the second kind of overconfidence, is a belief that we can perform at a level beyond what is objectively warranted. When golfers believe they can sink 90 percent of their six-foot putts, that's overestimation. When we believe we can complete a task in a shorter period of time than we can, that's overestimation. Overestimation is an absolute evaluation; it depends on an assessment of ourselves and no one else.

The evidence for overestimation isn't nearly as strong as the evidence for overprecision. For many ordinary tasks, there's good evidence that people believe they can do better than they really can. As Tali Sharot writes in *The Optimism Bias: A Tour of Our*

Irrationally Positive Brain, most people also believe the future will be better than the present. But there are limits. When it comes to difficult tasks, many people believe they won't do very well and at times even underestimate how well they can do. Overall, it's a stretch to claim that people have a general tendency to overestimate.

Overplacement, the third kind of overconfidence, is a belief that we can perform better than others. It's not an absolute judgment, but a relative one. When 90 percent of American drivers believe they're better than average, that's overplacement. When 80 percent of students believe that they'll finish in the top 20 percent of their class, that's overplacement, too. A well-known example of overplacement is Garrison Keillor's fictional town of Lake Wobegon, where "all the children are above average." Of course it's impossible for a majority to fit in the top half of the distribution, but many studies suggest that we think we do. Sharot writes, "most people perceive themselves as being superior to the average human being." She calls it the superiority bias and says it's a pervasive error.[27]

When it comes to overplacement, much of what we have come to believe isn't just exaggerated but actually incorrect. When I teach executives about decision making, I often ask them to complete a short questionnaire with many questions that call for judgments and choices. First, with a nod to Svenson's study, I ask them to evaluate themselves as drivers, then to compare themselves to their peers. The great majority—71 percent of more than four hundred people I asked over a period of several months—rated themselves above average, a finding that's very consistent with Svenson's results all those years ago.

If I had stopped there, I too might have concluded that people are overconfident. But my questionnaire went on to ask about a very different skill—drawing, as in the ability to draw a good portrait. This time, not only did most people think they were not very good, but they also believed that they were worse than their peers. The great majority—59 percent of the same population—ranked themselves as *below* average. That's *not* what we'd expect if people truly suffered from a pervasive bias of overconfidence.

What should we conclude from these replies? In fact, they're not wrong. They make sense when we consider what people know about themselves and about others. Let's start with driving. What driver do you know best? Yourself, very likely. Unless you have a personal chauffeur, you probably know more about yourself than about any other driver. And what do you know about yourself? Most likely that you're a *very good* driver. You've never been in a major accident, and rarely (if ever) have you been stopped for speeding or any other serious violation. Dozens of times every week, you buckle up, turn on the ignition, put your car in gear, and drive safely to your destination. By any objective measure, you really *are* a very good driver. You might even have a safe driver discount from your insurance company to prove it.

Furthermore, you know there are many bad drivers on the road. Every week you hear about serious traffic accidents and reckless behavior behind the wheel. The US National Traffic Safety Administration reported 32,367 traffic fatalities in 2011, of which 9,878, or 30 percent, were caused by alcohol-impaired drivers. That's an alcohol-related death every fifty-three minutes, and you were (knock on wood) nowhere near any of them.[28] With so much evidence of bad driving, it's entirely reasonable to infer that you're above average. In fact, if you've never been in an accident and have had only a few infractions, you might well conclude that you're among the very best. There's really no obvious reason to believe that anyone is much better! So if you place yourself in the top 20 percent of all drivers, is that an excessive evaluation? Not at all. It's entirely reasonable based on the information you have about yourself and about others.

Now consider drawing. Drawing isn't a routine task that most people come to master. Most of us have never learned to draw very well, and we know it. When we were in school, we found it awkward and even embarrassing to try to draw someone's likeness, and we probably stopped trying long ago. We don't know how well most other people draw, but we do know there are many good artists in the world, and infer that others probably are, on average, somewhat better than we are. And that's exactly what we find. Most people think they're *below* average. Little do they realize that almost everyone else has the same view.[29]

The same holds for other tasks that we find difficult, like juggling.[30] We don't really *know* that others are better, because most of us have never tried to juggle in a group setting, where we could see how frustrating it is for just about everybody. But we're aware there are some very good jugglers out there, and we know that we're not one of them, which makes us think we're worse than average. One study asked US college students to estimate whether they would outperform other students on a quiz about indigenous vegetation in the Amazon basin. Only 6 percent believed they would finish in the top half; the other 94 percent thought they would score below average.[31] That's *not* what we'd expect if people really had a persistent tendency for overplacement. A simpler explanation is that the way we place ourselves depends on the difficulty of the task and the information we have.[32]

Once we break down overconfidence into its different parts and take a close look at each one, we shouldn't conclude that people see themselves as superior to others, period. We're not overconfidence machines at all. Responses depend on the specific skill in question and on the information we have.[33] Rather than claim people are *biased*, it might be more accurate to say they're *myopic*. They see themselves clearly, but have less information about others, and generally make sensible inferences accordingly.

Lumping together three different kinds of overconfidence is convenient, but as Orwell warned us, it can lead to foolish thoughts. As an example, consider a column by David Brooks in the *New York Times* about health-care legislation. Brooks began by making a simple assertion: "Humans are overconfident creatures." For evidence, he mentioned some of the studies we have seen again and again: "Ninety-four percent of college professors believe they are above average teachers, and 90 percent of drivers believe they are above average behind the wheel. Researchers Paul J.H. Schoemaker and J. Edward Russo gave computer executives quizzes on their industry. Afterward, the executives estimated that they had gotten 5 percent of the answers wrong. In fact, they had gotten 80 percent of the answers wrong."[34]

From there, Brooks claimed that the 2008 financial crisis was the result of overconfidence. Then, after declaring that "the bonfire of overconfidence has shifted to Washington," he wrote that the Obama administration's health-care reform was bound to be deeply flawed, because it had been shaped by humans who—as evidence has shown—suffer from overconfidence.

All of this sounds reasonable until we understand that overconfidence is not one thing but several. The studies showing that teachers and drivers rate themselves too highly are examples of *overplacement*, typical for relatively easy tasks, but not for difficult tasks. As for the computer executives who often gave wrong answers, that's *overprecision*. These are very different examples and don't add up to the sweeping claim that "humans are overconfident," nor do they justify the assertion that the 2008 financial crisis was caused by overconfidence, unless of course (as so often happens) we're inclined to blame any failure at all on overconfidence.

As for health-care reform, if the Obama administration had expressed high confidence about the chances of successful reform, that would be *overestimation*. But studies of drivers and teachers who *overplace* and computer executives who are *overprecise* hardly let us conclude that health-care reform is tainted by *overestimation*. In fact, if health-care reform is difficult—and by all indications it may be *very* difficult to carry out successfully—the error may be in the opposite direction. We may actually *underestimate* our ability to bring about this sort of change. Far from undertaking too many difficult projects, we may in fact initiate *too few* complicated and ambitious projects.

WHAT'S THE RIGHT LEVEL OF CONFIDENCE?

So far we have seen that it's not helpful merely to infer overconfidence after the fact, when things have gone wrong. Nor is it correct to use one word for three very different things. There's little reason to suggest that overconfidence is as prevalent as is often claimed.

But we shouldn't stop there. If overconfidence means "greater confidence than circumstances warrant," we need to go another step. We saw previously that positive illusions often help improve performance. Believing we can do something may help us do it well. In that case, is a somewhat exaggerated level of confidence really excessive?

The way forward is to remember the topics of the previous chapters. First, can we exert control and influence outcomes, and second, is performance absolute or relative?

For things we cannot influence—the roll of dice, the weather, or the S&P 500—there's nothing to be gained from overestimation.

Any belief that we can control events is excessive. But when we *can* influence outcomes—whether sinking putts or pedaling a bicycle or carrying out some task—positive illusions can be helpful. A deliberate belief in high performance, maybe even a belief that is somewhat excessive given historical evidence, can boost results.

What's the best level of confidence? An amount that inspires us to do our best, but not so much that we become complacent, or take success for granted, or otherwise neglect what it takes to achieve high performance. In Dr. Thompson's cycling experiment (see Chapter Two), for example, athletes could match the avatar when it was made to go 2 percent faster, but couldn't keep up at 5 percent. That limit surely had to do with oxygen reserves and may have been particular to the task at hand; for other tasks the numbers will vary. Of course knowing that precise balance in advance is difficult, and results will vary among people. Yet the general rule holds. When we can influence outcomes, it can be useful to hold opinions that are somewhat inflated—that is, to overestimate.

When performance is relative, however, the desired level of confidence can only be understood in the context of competition. What's the best level of confidence? It's what we need to do better than our rivals.

That's not to say that a very high level of confidence will *guarantee* success. It won't. The performance of our rivals matters, too. Still, when an ability to influence outcomes is combined with relative performance, only those who push themselves to go beyond what seems reasonable will be in a position to succeed. What might seem like an exaggerated level of confidence isn't just useful, but in the context of competitive rivalry, it is essential.

The problem is, identifying that level of confidence in advance is difficult. There's no formula we can use, which is why we so often resort to ex-post inferences. When things turn out well, we conclude that our level of confidence was appropriate. *We were brimming with healthy confidence.* When things turn out poorly, we conclude it was inappropriate—either too much or too little. *We suffered from overconfidence—or maybe insufficient confidence.* Of course that's really just an easy way out. Ex ante, things are never so clear. Determining the right level of confidence demands more than a simple comparison to past achievements. We need to consider whether we can exert control over outcomes and also the nature of competition. When performance is relative and highly skewed, a very high level of confidence is not excessive but essential.

ARE WE REALLY OVERCONFIDENT?

At the start of this chapter I quoted Mark Twain's remark that all we need in life is ignorance and confidence. That's not a statement to be taken literally, of course. Success is never assured, at least not when it depends on the actions of others, and ignorance isn't generally something we should recommend.

But as was typical of Mark Twain, he had his finger on a larger truth.[35] When confidence can inspire and motivate, what seems excessive by one definition—a level of confidence that exceeds what's objectively justified—may be useful. And when performance is relative and payoffs are skewed, such a level of confidence may be essential. Those who eventually succeed will have exhibited a level of confidence greater than what was, by some definitions, objectively justified: excessive by some definitions, but not by others.

Yes, there are many examples, not only in laboratory experiments but also in real life, of people exhibiting excessive confidence. They're often overprecise, they frequently overestimate, and at times they also overplace. Once we tease them apart, however, we find that overprecision is widespread, but overestimation and overplacement aren't inevitable. In fact, when it comes to difficult tasks, people are more likely to underplace than to overplace. The common image of people as overconfident is justified for routine tasks, but not for many of the greater challenges we face.

Far from people being "overconfidence machines," I suspect a different interpretation is more accurate. As Henry David Thoreau observed, most people lead lives of quiet desperation. Glance at airport bookshelves, and you'd never guess that people suffer from overconfidence. Much more common are books that encourage us to raise our level of confidence. When I recently checked, I found these titles:

- *Self-Confidence: The Remarkable Truth of Why a Small Change Can Make a Big Difference*
- *Brilliant Confidence: What Confident People Know, Say and Do*
- *Confidence: The Power to Take Control and Live the Life You Want*
- *Instant Confidence: The Power to Go for Anything You Want* [36]

These books hardly suggest that the average person is overconfident. Most people seem to want *more* confidence, not less.* Even the most talented among us are at times prone to self-doubt. German violinist Christian Tetzlaff, one of the great musicians of our day

---

* You would be right to question whether a quick check of airport bookstores is the best indicator of how people behave. We can probably find a few books on just about any topic, and the fact that some people want to boost their confidence doesn't mean that most share that concern. We could even argue that only underconfident people buy self-improvement books, because those who are truly overconfident don't feel the need to read!

and acclaimed for his original tone and stunning interpretations, remarked: "Most of the time, we tell ourselves 'I'm confident' or 'I'm doing well.' But then, in a moment alone at home, you feel how close you are to some kind of abyss."[37] We live in a society that is impressed with confidence, and we often try to project confidence because we think others expect it of us. But when we look closely at the evidence, it's questionable whether people are best described as exhibiting overconfidence.

Why has it been reported so consistently that people are overconfident? One problem has to do with the design of experiments. If we ask for ranges that require 90 percent confidence, we shouldn't be surprised to find that most errors are in the direction of too much confidence, not too little. If we ask about routine tasks like driving, we find people tend to overplace. When we run experiments with unbalanced designs, we shouldn't be surprised that the errors are mostly in one direction. The more serious bias isn't with the answers that are given, but with the questions that are asked.

In turn, this raises a deeper question: Why has research not been balanced? I suspect the answer is that for years, economic theory was based on the notion that people are rational actors, capable of making accurate judgments and sound decisions. We find evidence of biases and errors very interesting because it challenged the prevailing orthodoxy. In particular, we report finding overconfidence because that's what is most surprising.

There is another reason, too. Some of the most important research about decision making has been conducted by cognitive psychologists, who have been interested in understanding basic mental processes, but to whom questions about competition among companies are not of central interest. We shouldn't expect psychologists to ask when confidence might be excessive by one definition but useful for competitive purposes. Yet for those of us who are concerned with the world of management, questions of competition are central. We should be careful not to take findings that make sense in one domain and apply them to another—at least not without asking whether the circumstances are the same.

THINKING ABOUT CONFIDENCE . . . AND OVERCONFIDENCE

Early in this chapter, I also quoted psychologist Scott Plous, who wrote more than twenty years ago: "No problem in judgment and decision making is more prevalent and more potentially catastrophic than overconfidence." By now, claims of overconfidence have been repeated so often that they are accepted as fact. Many recent authors have simply repeated the same phrase without taking a critical look.

Now, as I end this chapter, I suggest we turn the phrase on its head: *No concept in judgment and decision making has led to as much erroneous thinking as overconfidence.* Sure, almost all failure can be blamed ex post on overconfidence, but that's not saying much. We know to be skeptical about retrospective attributions. They make good stories, but aren't valid explanations. As for laboratory research, what we often call overconfidence turns out to be three very different errors: overprecision, overestimation, and overplacement. There's very strong evidence of the first, but less of the next two. Evidence of overprecision cannot be used as evidence of overestimation or overplacement. The tendency to rate ourselves better than others—overplacement—is better understood as myopia, with most people sensing their abilities clearly and making reasonable inferences about others. Sweeping claims that people are overconfident do not stand up to close scrutiny.

Overconfidence has been taken to mean so many things, and has been used in so many ways, that the very term has been debased.

My suggestion is that anyone who uses the term should have to specify the point of comparison. If overconfidence means excessively confident, then excessive compared to what? In much of our lives, where we can exert control and influence outcomes, what seems to be an exaggerated level of confidence may be useful; and when we add the need to outperform rivals, such a level of confidence may even be essential.

BASE RATES AND BREAKING BARRIERS

6

ALL PILOTS TAKE CHANCES FROM TIME TO TIME, BUT KNOWING—
NOT GUESSING—WHAT YOU CAN RISK IS OFTEN THE CRITICAL
DIFFERENCE BETWEEN GETTING AWAY WITH IT OR DRILLING A
FIFTY-FOOT HOLE IN MOTHER EARTH.

CHUCK YEAGER, *YEAGER: AN AUTOBIOGRAPHY*, 1985

Overconfidence isn't the only bias that has to be reconsidered when we combine the ability to influence outcomes and the need to outperform rivals. We also need to take a fresh look at the *base rate bias*.

The base rate bias was identified in the early 1970s by psychologists Daniel Kahneman and Amos Tversky. Imagine that at a busy intersection during evening rush hour, a taxicab clips a pedestrian and speeds away. A witness identifies it as one of the Blue Cabs that operate in the city. It happens that 15 percent of taxis are Blue Cabs and the other 85 percent are Green Cabs. The witness has good vision, and tests establish that in evening light she can identify the color of a taxicab correctly 80 percent of the time. If she testifies that the car was blue, what's the probability it really was a Blue Cab?

Most people estimated the probability of it being a Blue Cab to be more than 50 percent, and many said it was close to 80 percent.[1] That may seem reasonable because we were told the witness was correct 80 percent of the time. But what's missing is an appreciation of the overall population, which had more than five times as many Green Cabs as Blue Cabs.

FIGURE 6.1 BLUE CAB OR GREEN CAB?

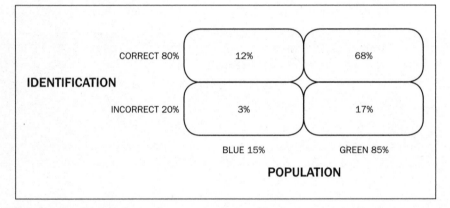

The correct calculation calls for an understanding of *conditional probability*, the probability that the car is blue given that it was identified as blue. It requires using Bayes's theorem, named after Reverend Thomas Bayes, the eighteenth-century English cleric who first laid out the idea of conditional probability, although the formula we use was later elaborated by French mathematician Pierre Simon Laplace.[2]

If our witness is correct 80 percent of the time, then as shown in Figure 6.1, out of eighty-five Green Cabs, she will correctly identify sixty-eight as green but will see seventeen as blue, and out of fifteen Blue Cabs she will correctly identify twelve as blue but incorrectly call three green. Of the twenty-nine cars that she identifies as blue (12 + 17), 41.4 percent (12/29) are indeed Blue Cabs, while 58.6 percent (17/29) are actually Green Cabs.

The answer to the question—If she testifies that the car was blue, what's the probability it really was a Blue Cab?—is therefore only 41.4 percent. Her judgment may be accurate 80 percent of the time, but the question asked about *conditional probabilities*— the chance she was correct given that she identified the car as blue. That calls for a different way of thinking, which doesn't come naturally to most people.

In a related experiment, Kahneman and Tversky described a population composed of 70 percent engineers and 30 percent lawyers. One person, drawn at random, was described as male, with strong quantitative skills, who enjoyed electronics as a hobby. Asked whether this man was an engineer or a lawyer, people overwhelmingly said engineer. That seemed right given the description. Next, with another group the frequencies were reversed—the population was said to be 30 percent engineers and 70 percent lawyers. Even so, most people *still* thought the man with good quantitative skills who enjoyed electronics was an engineer. They gave little weight to the fact that the underlying population comprised mostly lawyers. To their minds, the description sounded more like an engineer, and that's what they guessed.[3]

Both experiments illustrate the same underlying phenomenon: when people make judgments under uncertainty, they tend to focus on the case at hand and overlook the composition of the broader population. They are using what's called the *representativeness heuristic*, which is often helpful but can also lead to error. Kahneman and Tversky noted: "The base-rate frequencies of these categories, which were either known to the subjects from their daily experience or stated explicitly in the question, were largely neglected."[4]

Assessing the color of a taxicab or guessing someone's occupation might not seem very important, but the base rate bias can lead to serious errors. In a 1978 study published in the *New England Journal of Medicine*, researchers gave the following problem to sixty students and staff at Harvard Medical School:

If a test to detect a disease whose prevalence is 1/1000 has a false positive rate of 5 percent, what is the chance that a person found to have a positive result actually has the disease, assuming you know nothing about the person's symptoms or signs?[5]

The most common answer, given by almost half the respondents, was 95 percent. They reasoned that if the false positive rate is 5 percent, there must be a 95 percent chance that a positive test means the disease is present. Once again, they neglected the underlying base rate. If the test is administered to a random sample of the population, where the disease only affects one in a thousand, then only 1.9 percent of positive tests are correct. More than 98 percent of positive results (0.95/49.95) come from *healthy* people, meaning that a positive test is *fifty times more likely* to come from a healthy person than from a person with the disease. Surprisingly, the correct answer was given by just eleven out of sixty respondents at one of the leading medical schools in the country.

Variations of this experiment have been conducted in subsequent years and have produced remarkably consistent findings. Most people, whether ordinary folks or professionals, overlook the population base rates. They don't think in terms of the effect of the probability of one event on the condition of another. (Happily, the story may be changing, at least in the medical profession. While researching this book, I spoke with a professor at UC San Francisco, one of the top medical schools in the United States, who assured me that medical students now receive extensive education about probabilities and statistical analysis.)

By now, the base rate bias is often mentioned as one of the common errors that plague our thinking.[6] It's listed along with overconfidence, the confirmation bias, and others. To avoid the base rate bias, people are counseled to look at the broader population. They shouldn't just focus on the case at hand, but should stand back and consider the larger context. They should develop a basic understanding of conditional probabilities.

That's a step in the right direction, of course. But if the lesson ends there, we have settled for too little. Like Richard Feynman asking about the miracle of Lourdes, we need to probe further and ask another set of questions.

BASE RATES, GIVEN OR FOUND?

In the experiments just described, it was easy to demonstrate the base rate bias because all relevant information was provided. We were *given* the frequency of Blue Cabs and Green Cabs. We were *told* the witness is correct 80 percent of the time. We were *presented* with the split between engineers and lawyers. We were *informed* of the prevalence of disease as well as the rate of false positives and true positives. With all the necessary information before us, all we needed to do was apply the formula and make the correct calculation.

In the real world, however, base rates are rarely just given. They have to be found.[7] They have to be found. As Nassim Nicholas Taleb writes in *The Black Swan*: "The casino is the only venture I know where the probabilities are known. . . . In real life you do not know the odds; you need to discover them, and the sources of uncertainty are not defined.[7]

Discovering base rates is sometimes easy. If you want to know the number of Blue Cabs and Green Cabs, a few well-placed phone calls to the taxi companies might do the trick, or maybe an inquiry to the department of motor vehicles. You'll also want to make sure the information is current; you want this year's registered taxis, not last year's figure.

On second thought, the number of taxis registered in the city might not be the most instructive base rate. If we want to determine whether our witness was right or wrong, even better would be to determine how many Blue and Green Cabs were in service *on that particular evening.* You might learn that all the Blue Cabs but only three-fifths of the Green Cabs were on the road, which would make the relevant base rate very different.[8] Better yet would be to find out how many of each color were in service on that particular evening *and also* were in the general area where the accident took place. With GPS technology, that might be possible. Of course we would need to decide how large an area should be included: a few square blocks, or a somewhat larger area? The more precise our estimate of the time of the accident, the smaller an area we would need; the larger the time window, the larger the area.

If these seem like complications, that's precisely the point. Recognizing the need to consider base rates is only a start. Using Bayes's theorem to make a calculation isn't much good if we don't know which base rate to use.

Similarly, the Harvard Medical School experiment presented all the relevant facts: the prevalence of the disease and the false positive rate. With this information we could calculate that more than 98 percent of positive results actually come from healthy people. But who's to say that the prevalence of disease is one in a thousand?

In the real world, those figures aren't simply given. Finding them is often a very arduous task.

For example, Parkinson's disease is a degenerative disorder of the central nervous system that generally strikes people over fifty years of age. Although the disease has been known for almost two hundred years—it was first described as "shaking palsy" by English doctor James Parkinson in 1817—no accurate laboratory test has been devised, leaving physicians to make diagnoses from (imperfect) neurological examinations. Brain scans can rule out other disorders, but cannot provide definitive evidence of Parkinson's. In fact, sometimes a diagnosis of Parkinson's can only be confirmed when medication, such as levodopa, provides relief for motor impairment. The presence of the disease is only confirmed *after* treatment is effective!

Despite these challenges, it has been estimated that Parkinson's affects 2.1 percent of people sixty-five and over in the United States, 2.2 percent in the Netherlands, and roughly the same in many European countries. Against these fairly consistent figures was a notable outlier: for many years China reported very low rates of Parkinson's, with estimates between 0.1 and 1.0 percent of the elderly population. What could explain such a low rate? Were the Chinese less prone to the disease, perhaps for genetic reasons, or maybe because of diet or lifestyle? Some researchers in Beijing suspected a simpler explanation: lower reported rates of Parkinson's in China reflected inadequate diagnosis. The real problem was that many cases were either not detected or not reported. Over several months a team was trained to conduct initial tests in local clinics, which were then followed up with neurological examinations at three regional centers across the country. Thanks to this approach, many additional cases were identified, and the prevalence of Parkinson's among people sixty-five years of age and older in China was eventually raised to 1.7 percent.[9]

Today it is believed that the prevalence of Parkinson's disease is essentially the same around the world. But that fact wasn't given; it had to be found.

BASE RATES, FIXED OR CHANGING?

The next question is whether base rates are fixed or change over time. At one extreme we have examples like carbon-14, a naturally occurring isotope with a half-life of 5,730 years, meaning that a quantity of carbon-14 will decay by half after that many years, then diminish by half again in another 5,730 years, and so on. That figure wasn't discovered on a tablet but had to be found, yet once found it remains unchanged. The laws of physics that govern the rate of atomic decay are the same today as they were ten thousand years ago or ten million years ago. The same holds for atomic beam magnetic resonance, whose very regular oscillations have given us the most accurate clocks in the world. In 1955, the first atomic clock was developed based on the cesium-133 atom. Its ability to keep time was so accurate that the International System of Units defined one second as the duration of 9,192,631,770 cycles of radiation corresponding to the transition between two energy levels of a cesium-133 atom. That's a *very* precise base rate, and one that doesn't change.

Other base rates have a stochastic element, meaning that the value for any particular sample is subject to random variation. On average, 105 boys are born for every 100 girls, with small variations across some populations.[10] (We'll assume there's no intervention for sex selection, which is common in some countries and produces a different rate of live births, not to mention all sorts of social problems in the next generation.) Today we take that base rate for granted, but it was found through extensive research, much of it conducted by Laplace, who spent decades looking through records of live births in London, Paris, St. Petersburg, Naples, and elsewhere.[11] Although it had to be found, it remains steady over time, although on any given day, and in any town or hospital, the exact proportion of male and female births will vary. If there are forty-one live births in a given hospital during the course of a week, our best guess would be twenty-one boys and twenty girls. In a given week, however, girls may outnumber boys and sometimes by quite a bit, although the larger the number of births the more we expect a ratio that converges toward 105:100.

As another example, cystic fibrosis is related to a gene on chromosome 7. About ten million Americans carry the gene, but because the disease is recessive, only about a thousand children per year are born with cystic fibrosis. That base rate was discovered through research, yet unfortunately not much can be done to change it. The incidence of cystic fibrosis will likely remain steady as long as the underlying gene pool is the same.[12] On the other hand, the mortality rate associated with cystic fibrosis has changed dramatically in the last decades. Thanks to improved treatment and care, children born with the disease survive much longer than they did two generations ago. Two base rates, but shaped by very different forces, and with different implications.

Figure 6.2 shows the incidence and mortality of leukemia in the US population for the last thirty-five years. The rate of incidence—that is, new cases reported—has remained steady, averaging 13.18 per 100,000 for the thirty-five year period, from 12.80 in 1975 and 13.55 in 1976, to 12.95 in 2009 and 13.31 in 2010. Meanwhile, the rate of mortality has edged downward, averaging 7.72 per 100,000 for the period, from 8.09 in 1975 to 7.06 in 2009 and 6.91 in 2010. Do these steady rates mean the incidence and mortality of leukemia are beyond our power to shape? Not at all. The factors that lead to leukemia are still not

FIGURE 6.2 INCIDENCE AND MORTALITY OF LEUKEMIA IN THE US, 1975–2010

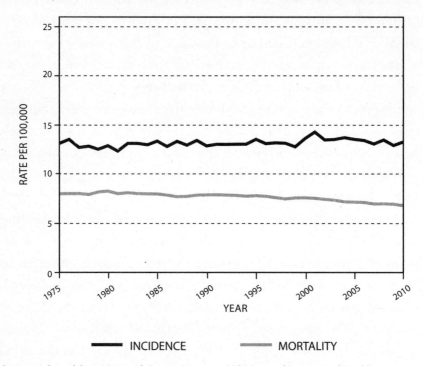

Source: Adapted from National Cancer Institute, US National Institute of Health, Surveillance Epidemiology and End Results, http://www.seer.cancer.gov

entirely known, and efforts to improve treatment are making progress although slowly. That these rates have been relatively steady in the past does not mean they will not change significantly in the future.

For other diseases the rates of incidence and mortality have changed more dramatically. During the same thirty-five years, the incidence of non-Hodgkin lymphoma almost doubled, from 11.07 per 100,000 in 1975 to 20.98 per 100,000 in 2010, as shown in Figure 6.3. There's no steady base rate analogous to Parkinson's disease or cystic fibrosis, or even leukemia. Medical researchers are investigating what forces have led to this rapid increase—perhaps environmental factors, or diet and lifestyle, or maybe the decline of other diseases. The good news, meanwhile, is that the mortality rate has dropped sharply. From

FIGURE 6.3 INCIDENCE AND MORTALITY OF NON-HODGKIN'S LYMPHOMA IN THE US, 1975–2010

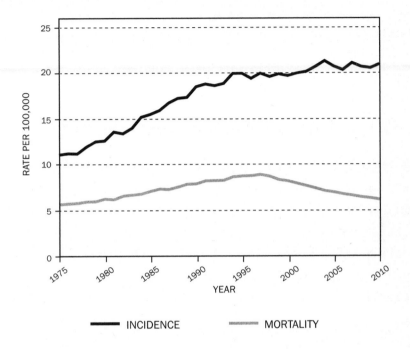

Source: Adapted from National Cancer Institute, US National Institute of Health, Surveillance Epidemiology and End Results, http://www.seer.cancer.gov

1975 to 1997 the mortality rate grew from 5.63 to 8.88 per 100,000, but after 1997 it actually *declined*, all the way to 6.14 in 2010, even though incidence was still on the upswing. Thanks to the efforts of medical researchers, doctors, and other health-care professionals, there has been enormous care in the treatment of non-Hodgkin's lymphoma. For our purposes, the lesson is that when it comes to dreaded diseases, base rates are neither fixed nor entirely beyond our control. We have already affected some, and others may still be within our reach to improve.

In each of these examples, recognizing that people have a tendency to overlook base rates is only a starting point. More important

⁓ is to pose the next set of questions. Are base rates given, or must they be found? Are they fixed, or do they change? And if the latter, what can be done to change them? When it comes to making decisions in the real world, these questions are ultimately more important than identifying the presence of a cognitive bias.

HOW MUCH CAN WE IMPROVE PERFORMANCE?

When we have ability to shape events we confront a different challenge: making accurate estimates of future performance. The danger here is not one of overlooking the base rate of the broader population at a point in time, but neglecting lessons of the past and making a poor prediction of the future. Very often people place great importance on their (exaggerated) level of skills and motivation. The result is to make forecasts on what Kahneman and Tversky call the *inside view*. Unfortunately these projections, which ignore the experiences of others who have attempted similar tasks, often turn out to be wildly optimistic.

The perils of relying on the inside view are described by Daniel Kahneman in a story about the design of a school curriculum.[13] When a committee of educators was appointed to develop the curriculum, most of its members estimated the task would take about two years. That seemed reasonable, until someone suggested that they examine the record of similar initiatives undertaken by other committees. To their astonishment, they found the average time to completion was closer to seven years, and that 40 percent of such efforts never finished at all! Examples like this are actually quite common. A project may begin well—the first steps are often the easiest—leading members to extrapolate what seems like a realistic estimate for the entire project, but which often turns out to be wildly optimistic. They don't see that future steps are likely to be more difficult than early ones, and almost never anticipate the myriad obstacles and complications that arise, as committee members changes jobs, as new assignments take priority, and so forth.

The way to avoid the perils of an overly optimistic inside view is to consider the past history of similar events, known as the *outside view*. We should ask: What have others done in comparable settings? What has been the record of a reference class population? How have others responded to challenges, and what makes us think we will be able to do any better? If we still maintain that we can do better than our predecessors, we should have to justify why we think so.[14]

This is not to say that project leaders should disregard the inside view entirely. Many elements of project management are within our ability to influence, and for that, as we already know, a high level of confidence can be helpful. It may motivate team members and inspire them to achieve greater performance. Managers are therefore advised to seek what Kahneman and Dan Lovallo called "a healthy dose of optimism." They are urged to strike "a balance between optimism and realism—between goals and forecasts."[15]

That sounds good, but it begs an important question: What exactly is a "healthy" dose of optimism? How much is helpful, and at what point might optimism become harmful? If we're not careful, of course, we might just make inferences based on outcomes. When things turn out well, we will conclude that optimism was at a healthy level; and when things turn out badly, we'll infer it was unhealthy, whether excessive or insufficient.

Rather than make ex-post inferences, we need to pose the question in advance. How optimistic should we be? If we commit to do better than historical base rates, by how much can we—must we—improve performance?

To answer those questions, we have to ask whether we can exert control over outcomes and whether performance is absolute or relative. When there is no way to control outcomes, feelings of optimism aren't helpful. There is no point in optimism when we're dealing with a purely random event, like betting on the spin of a roulette wheel. Far better is to have a clear understanding of probabilities and payoffs, and to have a good sense of our risk preference. On the other hand, when we *can* control outcomes, optimism can lead to higher performance. Setting goals that are demanding, but that can inspire our team, may stimulate higher performance. That's the thinking behind "stretch targets."

In addition, we have to consider whether performance is absolute or relative, and if the latter, the distribution of payoffs. Is our goal just to do well, or must we do better than rivals? What's a healthy level of optimism when the objective is to outperform rivals? Enough to help us win.

Think about the example of curriculum redesign. If the goal were simply to carry out a successful design, performance would be absolute. Optimism would be healthy if it stimulated us to do better. If the average time to completion was five years, and by motivating and inspiring our colleagues we could achieve it in four years, that might be a perfectly good result.

But now suppose we're in a competition in which the goal is to design a curriculum faster than other committees that are undertaking a similar project. Maybe the department of education has assigned the same task to six committees in parallel and decreed that the fastest to completion will receive additional grants, or will be able to attract the brightest young teachers, or will benefit in some significant way, while the rest receive nothing at all. Now performance is relative and payoffs are highly skewed—in fact, winner-take-all. Completion in four years might no longer be good enough, because other committees may very likely be setting equally demanding targets for themselves. If our goal is to come out ahead of the others, we may want to make every effort to finish in *three* years, or maybe pull out all the stops and try to finish in *two and a half*. If the payoff is winner-take-all, and there's no silver medal for second place, there's not much to be gained from a cautious approach.

If you think the notion of competition among schools is a bit contrived, think again. Under Arne Duncan, secretary of education in the Obama administration, the US Department of Education initiated a competition called Race to the Top, in which a $4.35 billion fund was earmarked for states that produced the best four-year education reform plans. In two years, forty-six states submitted reform plans, with the twelve best winning grants of between $70 and $700 million. As it happened, merely going through the exercise proved helpful, and even school districts that won no grant money benefited. Jay Altman, responsible for turning around New Orleans schools, commented: "Louisiana ended up not winning Race to the Top, but we got close, and the process stimulated Louisiana and other states to think more broadly about educational reform rather than just approach it piecemeal."[16] For our purposes, however, what is meant by a healthy dose of optimism must take into account both the ability to influence outcomes as well as the nature of performance. Without an appreciation for the need to outperform rivals, we have no way of knowing whether a given level of optimism is healthy or not.

GOING BEYOND BASE RATES

In *Man and Superman*, George Bernard Shaw wrote: "The reasonable man adapts himself to the world; the unreasonable one persists in trying to adapt the world to himself. Therefore all progress depends on the unreasonable man."[17] This is an intriguing statement, and a provocative one. It makes a good story, and it might even seem true, at least in retrospect. We can probably credit an unreasonable person, a visionary who refused to compromise, for any dazzling success. Think of Henry Ford and the Model T, or Steve Jobs and the iPod. We could probably go all the way back to David and Goliath. It seems plausible that stubborn devotion to a vision was the seed of success. (Of course we could probably make the opposite assertion, too: great calamities might be blamed on unreasonable people as well.)

But if we look closer, human progress—in science, business, and elsewhere—does *not* depend on the unreasonable man or on people acting in unreasonable ways. Great outcomes surely involve some risk, but there are often ways to manage risk and reduce it to acceptable levels. It might be more helpful to observe that progress is due to men and women who engage both their capacity for analysis—left brain—as well as moments of daring—right stuff. Indeed, by carefully managing risk they can reduce the potential dangers.

A number of good examples come from aviation. Over the course of human history, few things have had a more prohibitive base rate than human flight. From the tale of Icarus through the drawings of da Vinci, the dream of heavier-than-air flight was persistent yet unattainable. It wasn't just a matter of low probability; the base rate was zero.

Even so, progress was made on several fronts. During the nineteenth century a Yorkshireman, George Cayley, advanced our knowledge of the basic forces affecting aviation, including lift and drag. In the 1880s Otto Lilienthal made more than two thousand flights in the forerunners of today's hang gliders. These experiments led to a greater understanding of stability and control and proved that a glider could support the weight of a human being. Still, the dream of flight remained out of reach.

Wilbur Wright and Orville Wright of Dayton, Ohio, took a different approach. Rather than imagine they were undertaking a single initiative against very long odds, they broke the task into components, each of which became tractable. The Wright brothers identified three separate challenges—wing shape, wing control, and engine thrust and weight—and set about addressing each one.

To learn about wing design, they built a wind tunnel and conducted extensive tests that let them design a more efficient wing with less camber—that is, curve—and a greater ratio of wing length to width. By 1902 the Wright brothers believed they knew more about the movement of air over curved surfaces "a hundred times over, than all our predecessors put together."[18]

As for wing control, they discovered that a crucial element for successful flight was to maintain balance in unstable conditions. When birds encounter turbulence, they maintain control by angling one wing upward and the other down, each one moving independently in response to the forces on that wing. The Wright brothers brought the same capability to their craft with wing-warping, or twisting, to gain lateral control by wire.

Finally, to overcome the problem of thrust, they designed and built their own engine, weighing only 180 pounds and with propellers in which the blade was itself an airfoil, similar to a wing in its aerodynamic design. Their engine was a marvel of efficiency, able to translate 66 percent of its rotational energy into thrust.

Putting these three elements together led to the triumph of December 17, 1903, when the *Wright Flyer* took to the air at Kitty Hawk. The success of the Wright brothers was due in part to their inside view—they weren't short on ambition or self-confidence—but also to the way they thought about the larger problem. They redefined their task from facing a single challenge with a prohibitive base rate, to addressing three component challenges with more feasible probabilities. Once they solved each of the components, the impossible became possible.

BARRIERS OF NATURE OR BARRIERS OF ENGINEERING?

Almost fifty years later, after advances that would have seemed unimaginable in 1903, aviation faced an altogether different challenge, what Chuck Yeager called "the greatest adventure in aviation since the Wright Brothers—the conversion from propeller airplanes to supersonic jets and rocket propelled aircraft."[19]

Now the challenge was to go faster than the speed of sound. Many scientists and engineers feared that shock waves would be so severe that any airplane would break up in flight. Some calculated that the buffeting of air at Mach 1 represented an impenetrable wall—hence the term *sound barrier*.[20] In early 1947 the legendary British test pilot Geoffrey de Havilland Jr. was killed when his aircraft, *The Swallow*, disintegrated at .94 Mach. With that, the British gave up their supersonic experiments.[21] The task seemed too tough. Yeager recalled: "There were a lot of engineer brains who thought that the laws of nature would punch the ticket for anyone caught speeding above Mach 1."

The base rate for supersonic travel? Zero, of course. It had never been done.

But surpassing the speed of sound was hardly a task for unreasonable men. Success would not be a matter of bravado. Rather than accept the prevailing view that the speed of sound could not be surpassed, some believed that the real barrier had more to do with engineering, planning, and precise execution—all of which were things we could control. As pilot Jack Ridley put it, "The only barrier is bad aerodynamics and bad planning."[22]

During 1947 the US Army Air Corps, forerunner to the Air Force, worked with Bell Aircraft to create an experimental aircraft called the X-1, designed for the sole purpose of flying faster than the speed of sound. Their methods were deliberate and systematic. Col. Albert Boyd, in charge of the Army Air Corps' efforts, insisted on a careful approach: "Nobody will know for sure what happens at Mach 1 until somebody gets there. This is an extremely risky mission, and we're not going to take it one step at a time, but one inch at a time."[23]

Of course the effort depended on pilots with very high confidence. As X-1 test engineer Dick Frost put it, "Supreme self-confidence is a big part of a fighter test pilot's baggage, a real cockiness."[24] No test pilot had more confidence in his abilities than Chuck Yeager. Still, Yeager spared no effort to learn as much as he could about the aircraft and agreed to follow strict rules to advance incrementally. As he put it: "You accept risk as part of every new challenge; it comes with the territory. So you learn all you can about the ship and its systems, practice flying it on ground runs and glide flights, plan for any possible contingency, until the odds against you seem more friendly."[25]

Together the team took small steps and evaluated results after every one. For its first flight, the X-1 was dropped from a B-29 and didn't engage its rockets, but merely glided to earth. A next flight engaged one rocket, and a subsequent flight engaged another. Gradually the speeds were increased, rising by increments of just fifteen or twenty miles per hour each time. After seven flights, the X-1 reached .94 Mach.

Then, on the eighth flight, as Yeager pushed the aircraft faster, he pulled back on the control column but got no response. Only when he slowed the X-1 did he regain control of the elevators, the flaps on the horizontal stabilizers of the tail that control the airplane's longitudinal attitude and pitch. Back on the ground, pilots and engineers huddled to locate the problem. They knew that at .88 Mach, a shock wave formed over the thickest part of the wing and the stabilizer; now, at .94 Mach, the shock wave was larger and reached all the way back to the elevator, depriving the pilot of control. A solution was found: if the horizontal stabilizer could be made to pivot up and down with a trim switch, the pilot could retain control without needing to use the elevators.

With that problem solved, the stage was set for the X-1 to go past the speed of sound. Many still harbored doubts, but Yeager had confidence in engineer Jack Ridley's judgment: "If Jackie thinks I can do it, I'll do it. Somebody's got to do it, so I'll do it."[26] On October 14, 1947, the X-1 was dropped from the B-29 and then zoomed upward, past all previous records. At 42,000 feet, Yeager pushed the X-1 forward, past .965 Mach, and then faster than the speed of sound. The needle tipped off the Mach scale and the X-1 carried on, sailing as smoothly, as Yeager put it, "as a baby's bottom." Ridley had been right: the real barrier wasn't outside our control. It was ultimately a matter of engineering and within our power to influence.

An extraordinary feat of skillful flying and courage? Definitely. But Yeager's achievement was hardly a matter of bravado. You don't *take* risks; you *manage* them. You move in small increments, make adjustments and find ways to reduce risk along the way. What seemed like an impossible barrier was broken into small chunks, each one solved through clear-eyed analysis plus a willingness to take a final step beyond what had been done before.

And of course breaking barriers in aviation didn't end with supersonic travel. Today the aim isn't to go still faster, but to push the limits of technology in other ways. The *Solar Impulse*, piloted by Swiss explorer Bertrand Piccard, is a solar-powered airplane. With a single-seat cockpit under a wide wingspan covered by twelve thousand solar panels, it weighs no more than an automobile and has a top speed of just 43 mph. The *Solar Impulse* charges its batteries during daylight flights, reaches a height of 25,000 feet as the sun sets, and then glides gently downward during the night, until the morning sun allows it to recharge its batteries and begin the cycle again.[27]

Like its predecessors, the *Solar Impulse* is advancing in small increments. Its first intercontinental flight took it from Spain to Morocco in June 2012. In May 2013 it left California on the first leg of a ten-day trip across the United States.[28] Piccard's stated goal is to accomplish a round-the-world flight in 2015.

Asked if he was chasing a pipe dream, Piccard explained: "My goal isn't to go beyond physical limits. It's to go beyond the limits we put on ourselves. Human beings prevent themselves from going beyond what they know, from putting themselves in situations where they risk losing control. Those are exactly the situations that interest me, where we venture into the unknown."[29]

Bertrand Piccard, no less than his predecessors in aviation, embodies the right stuff—a willingness to go beyond what has been achieved before—but always governed by careful planning and the intelligent management of risk—elements of the left brain.

THINKING ABOUT BASE RATES

We know from experiments that most people suffer from the base rate bias. They don't naturally think in terms of conditional probabilities. They tend to focus on the event before them, but often overlook important facts about the broader population.

Of course, it's good to be aware of the base rate bias, whether we're trying to interpret the results of a medical test or to make some other judgment under uncertainty. Yet at least as important are a series of second-order questions. Of all the possible base rates we could consider, which is the most relevant for the purpose at hand? Is the base rate fixed, or does it change? If the latter, what causes it to change—and can we take action to change it?

Similarly, it's useful to know the difference between the inside view and the outside view, and to be aware that the view is often inflated by overestimation. It's smart to consider the outside view in order to keep unrealistic the inside view in check. Yet it's also important to consider whether optimism can be useful. To answer that question we not only have to know whether we can influence outcomes, but also need to sense whether performance is absolute or relative.

Finally, although it makes a good story to claim that progress is due to the actions of unreasonable people, the truth is more complex. Going beyond what has been done before isn't the province of the wild and the reckless. It calls for a combination of careful analysis and management of risk—left brain—with the willingness to take a step into the unknown—right stuff.

BETTER DECISIONS OVER TIME 7

THROUGH THE YEARS, I HAVE LEARNED THERE IS NO HARM IN
CHARGING ONESELF UP WITH DELUSIONS BETWEEN MOMENTS OF
VALID INSPIRATION.

STEVE MARTIN, *BORN STANDING UP: A COMIC'S LIFE*, 2007

When the US Army Air Corps set out to fly faster than the speed
of sound, Col. Albert Boyd insisted that they proceed in small increments. They would make one flight of only a few minutes, then
carefully monitor the results, make any adjustments, and push the
envelope the next day by just a bit. Each flight was part of a sequence, in which the lessons from one step would be used to improve the next.

We have seen that great decisions come from understanding
whether we can influence outcomes and whether performance is
absolute or relative. Another important element, epitomized by
Col. Boyd and his aviators, is learning and improving over time. It's
about gaining expertise, which is not the same as simply amassing
experience.

NOAH AND THE ARC

Let's start by looking at an activity that takes just a few seconds: shooting a free throw in basketball. Free throws are a good test of pure shooting skill. The task is the same for everyone: tossing a ball, nine and a half inches in diameter, through a rim eighteen inches wide, placed ten feet off the ground, from a distance of fifteen feet. That's not exactly threading a needle, but it's close. There isn't a lot of margin for error. Furthermore, as when striking a golf ball, performance is entirely up to you. You're not predicting what someone else will do; it's up to you to throw the ball through the hoop.

During the 2011–2012 season, NBA teams attempted an average of 22.5 free throws per game. The Oklahoma City Thunder made 80.6 percent of its free throws, sinking 1,406 of 1,744 attempts. The Orlando Magic had the worst record, making only 66.0 percent, hitting just 995 of 1,508 shots. That's a massive difference between the top team and the bottom, but of course the variance among individual players is even greater. Jamal Crawford of the Portland Trailblazers led the league, sinking 92.7 percent of his free throws, far more than the season's most valuable player, LeBron James, at 77.1 percent, let alone the Magic's Dwight Howard, who made only 49.1 percent from the free throw line.[1] (Howard's dismal performance was the main reason the Magic were the worst team. Without Howard, the rest of the Magic shot 76.3 percent, slightly better than the league average of 75.2 percent.) As good as Crawford shot, he was still shy of the best ever, Mark Price and Steve Nash, who both made 94 percent for their entire careers. That's far better than the average, which has held steady since 1960 at about 74 percent for the NBA and 68 percent for college players.

It makes you wonder: What's the secret to a good free throw?

To find out, a California-based venture capitalist and inventor (as well as former college basketball player and coach) named Alan Marty worked with Jerry Krause, head of research for the National Association of Basketball Coaches, and Tom Edwards, director for aerospace at the NASA Ames Research Center. They were, according to Marty, "the first group to systematically and scientifically confirm what makes great shooters, great."[2]

After months of research, they determined that the best free throw has three features. First, it's straight—neither to the left nor right but dead center. No surprise there. You don't want to throw up a clunker that bounces off to one side or the other. Second, the best shot doesn't aim for the exact center of the basket. The perfect spot is eleven inches past the front rim, about two inches beyond the midpoint. That gives a BRAD shot, the acronym for "Back Rim and Down." Third, and very important, is the arc. The best shots are neither too high nor too flat, but leave the hands at an angle of 45 degrees.

Finding the best arc was the result of three methods. The researchers watched some of the best free throw shooters and mapped their trajectories, which revealed a consistent 45 degree arc. At the same time Edwards, the NASA scientist, modeled the physics of the free throw and determined the best shot had an arc in the mid-40 degrees. Finally, the team built an automated shooting machine and programmed it to throw over and over again in precise and replicable ways. They tried various arcs, from relatively flat shots to high looping shots, and found the best was 45 degrees. Three methods, all of which converged on a single answer.

So far, so good. Of course, it's one thing to calculate the perfect arc, but something else to toss a basketball with exactly that arc, time after time. How do you consistently shoot the ball with a 45 degree arc and a depth of eleven inches past the rim?

The key is immediate feedback, so players can adjust their shots and try again, over and over, until they reach a level of accuracy and consistency. With this in mind, Marty and his team developed a system called Noah (named after the man who built the ark in the Book of Genesis), which links a computer with a camera and an automated voice. When a player releases a shot, the camera records the trajectory and the speaker immediately calls out the angle. Players can take a shot, make an adjustment, and take another, several times a minute. It doesn't take long for the player to get a good feel for a 45 degree arc.

For both individuals and entire teams, Noah has yielded impressive results. One high school coach credited Noah with raising his team's average from 58 to 74 percent. He explained: "This generation wants immediate feedback. They also want visual feedback and this system does both. It's the video-game age now, so having a system available that generates immediate statistics is great."

DELIBERATE PRACTICE AND HIGH PERFORMANCE

The principle behind Noah is *deliberate practice*. Not just lots of time spent practicing, but practice that conforms to a clear process of action, feedback, adjustment, and action again. Not simply experience, but expertise.

The original insights about deliberate practice go back more than two decades, to a study conducted by Benjamin Bloom, president of the American Educational Research Association. At the time, it was widely thought that high performers in many fields were blessed with native talent, sometimes called genius. But as Bloom studied the childhoods of 120 elite performers in fields from music to mathematics, Bloom found otherwise.[3] Success was mostly due to intensive practice, guided by committed teachers and supported by family members.

Since then a great deal of research has tried to uncover the drivers of high performance. Some of the most important work has been conducted by K. Anders Ericsson, professor of psychology at Florida State University. Ericsson is described by Steven Dubner and Steven Levitt, authors of *Freakonomics*, as the leading figure of the expert performance movement, "a loose coalition of scholars trying to answer an important and seemingly primordial question: When someone is very good at a given thing, what is it that actually makes him good?"[4] In one of his first experiments more than thirty years ago, Ericsson asked people to listen to a series of random numbers, then repeat them. At first most people could repeat only a half dozen numbers, but with training they improved significantly. "With the first subject, after about 20 hours of training, his digit span had risen from 7 to 20," Ericsson recalled. "He kept improving, and after about 200 hours of training he had risen to over 80 numbers." Repeated practice led to a remarkable tenfold improvement.

The technique that worked for a seemingly meaningless task turned out to be effective for many useful ones as well. Ericsson studied activities ranging from playing musical instruments to solving puzzles to highly skilled activities like landing airplanes and performing surgery. Very consistently, subjects improved significantly when they received immediate and explicit feedback, then made adjustments before trying again.[5]

You won't be surprised to learn that juggling, mentioned as a difficult task in Chapter Five, lends itself to deliberate practice. Very few people are able to juggle right away, but most of us can learn to juggle three balls with a bit of instruction and a good deal of deliberate practice. Golf, too, lends itself to deliberate practice. Anders Ericsson describes how a novice golfer, with steady practice, can fairly rapidly reach a level of competence, but after a while improvement tapers off. Additional rounds of golf don't lead to further progress, and for a simple reason: in a game setting, every shot is a bit different. A golfer makes one shot and moves on to the next, without the benefit of feedback and with no chance for repetition. However, Ericsson observes: "If you were allowed to take five or ten shots from the exact location of the course, you would get more feedback on your technique and start to adjust your playing style to improve your control."[6] This is exactly what the pros do. In addition to hours on the driving range and the putting green, they play practice rounds in which they take multiple shots from the same location. That way, they can watch the flight of the ball, make adjustments, and try again. The best golfers don't just practice a lot; they practice deliberately.

SHIFTING BACK AND FORTH

Previously we saw that when we can influence outcomes, positive thinking can boost performance. The concept of deliberate practice lets us refine that notion. Positive thinking is effective when it's bracketed by objective feedback and adjustment.

The result is not simply optimism, but what the psychologist Martin Seligman calls *learned optimism*. The key is to replace a static view, which assumes a single mind-set at all times, with a dynamic view, which allows for the ability to shift between mind-sets. Before an activity, it's important to be objective about our abilities and about the task at hand. After the activity, whether we have been successful or not, it's once again important to be objective about our performance and to learn from feedback. Yet in the moment of action, a high degree of optimism even when it may seem excessive is essential. This is the notion expressed by comedian Steve Martin as he looked back on his career: that moments of deluded self-confidence can be useful, provided they are kept in check by valid assessments.

A related idea comes from Peter Gollwitzer, a psychologist at New York University, who distinguishes between a *deliberative mind-set* and an *implemental mind-set*. A deliberative mind-set suggests a detached and impartial attitude. We set aside emotions and focus on the facts. A deliberative mind-set is appropriate when we assess the feasibility of a project, plan a strategic initiative, or decide on an appropriate course of action.* By contrast, an implemental mind-set is about getting results. When we're in an implemental mind-set, we look for ways to be successful. We set aside doubts and focus on achieving the desired performance. Here, positive thinking is essential. The deliberative mind-set is about open-mindedness and deciding what should be done; the implemental mind-set is about closed-mindedness and achieving our aims. Most crucial is the ability to shift between them.[7]

To test the impact of mind-sets, Gollwitzer and his colleague Ronald Kinney conducted an insightful experiment. One group of people was asked to list all the reasons they could think of, pro and con, regarding a particular course of action. The intention was to instill a deliberative mind-set. A second group was asked to list the specific steps they would take to successfully carry out a given course of action. The goal here was to instill an implemental mind-set. Next, all subjects took part in a routine laboratory task. Gollwitzer and Kinney found that subjects with an implemental mind-set showed significantly higher belief in their ability to control the outcome. They

---

* A point on terminology: *Deliberate practice* calls for the shift back and forth between a *deliberative mind-set* and an *implemental mind-set*.

concluded: "After the decision to pursue a certain goal has been made, successful goal attainment requires that one focus on implemental issues. Accordingly, negative thoughts concerning the desirability and attainability of the chosen goal should be avoided, because they would only undermine the level of determination and obligation needed to adhere to goal pursuit."[8] An implemental mind-set, focusing on what it takes to get the job done and banishing doubts, improves the likelihood that you will succeed.

The question we often hear—how much optimism or confidence is good, and how much is too much—turns out to be incomplete. There's no reason to imagine that optimism or confidence must remain steady over time. It's better to ramp it up and down, emphasizing a high level of confidence during moments of implementation, but setting it aside to learn from feedback and find ways to do better.[9]

MIRACLE ON THE HUDSON: SHIFTING MIND-SETS ON THE FLIGHT DECK

An example of shifting between deliberative and implemental mind-sets comes from US Air Flight 1549, which landed safely on the Hudson River in January 2009, sparing the lives of all 155 people aboard.[10]

In the moments after the Airbus 320 took off from La Guardia Airport and struck a flock of geese, causing both engines to fail, Captain Chesley Sullenberger kept a deliberative mind-set. He coolly and systematically considered his options, including a return to La Guardia and an emergency landing at Teterboro Airport in New Jersey. Neither was possible. The aircraft had lost all power and wouldn't be able to reach either airport. At this time, sober deliberation was required.

Once Sullenberger determined that the best course of action was to ditch in the Hudson, his focus shifted to implementation. All that mattered now was a successful landing. For that, he needed to muster a positive mind-set so that this landing—*this* one, right *now*—would be executed to perfection. In an interview with Katie Couric on *60 Minutes*, Sullenberger described his attitude as the plane descended. "The water was coming up fast," he recalled. Kouric asked if during those moments he thought about the passengers on board. Sullenberger replied: "Not specifically. I knew I had to solve this problem to find a way out of this box I found myself in." He knew exactly what was needed: "I had to touch down the wings exactly level. I needed to touch down with the nose slightly up. I needed to touch down at a decent rate, that was survivable. And I needed to touch down at our minimum flying speed but not below it. And I needed to make all these things happen simultaneously."

The time for deliberation had passed; now, success was all about implementation. Sullenberger stayed focused and kept his cool. At all times, he said, "I was sure I could do it." His total focus on implementation helped achieve what was called "the most successful ditching in aviation history." The Guild of Air Pilots and Air Navigators awarded the crew of Flight 1549 the Master's Medal, the citation reading in part: "This emergency ditching and evacuation, with the loss of no lives, is a heroic and unique aviation achievement." It's also a prime example of shifting from one mind-set to another, gaining the benefits of deliberate thinking, but then shifting completely to implementation.

THE RIGHT STUFF AT AMEN CORNER

The need to shift mind-sets is clearly seen in golf—and not just once, as in landing a plane, but over and over. We have seen how golf is a game of confidence. As golfer Mark O'Meara said, you have to *know* the ball is going in. That's true enough when you're standing over the putt. But before a shot, a golfer needs to assess matters objectively and impartially. *What's the distance to the pin, the strength of the wind, and the length of the grass? Given all these factors, what shot should I play? Which club should I pick, the five-iron for greater distance or the six-iron for higher loft?* These questions call for a deliberative mind-set, unaffected by wishful thinking.

Once the club is chosen and the golfer settles into his or her stance, the focus shifts. Now it's all about executing this shot—*this one shot*—to perfection. An implemental mind-set is needed.

Next, once the golfer strikes the ball and watches its flight, the need for impartial observation returns. *Am I playing long today, or are my shots falling short of their usual distance? Do I have my best game, or do I need to compensate in some way?* The emphasis is on seeing things as they are, free from illusions or distortions. Moments later, when standing over the ball with club in hand, the implemental mind-set returns. Again the golfer must believe that *this* swing, *this* shot, will be perfect. I can—*I will*—make this shot exactly as I wish.[11]

And so it goes, back and forth between deliberation and implementation, perhaps seventy-two times—for a par golfer—in a few hours. No wonder the mental game is paramount. According to Bob Rotella, one of today's most respected coaches: "To play golf as well as he can, a golfer has to focus his mind tightly on the shot he is playing now, in the present. A player can't think about the shot he just hit, or the shot he played with the tournament on the line a week ago. That's thinking about the past. He can't think about how great it would be to win the tournament, or how terrible it would feel to blow it. That's thinking about the future."[12]

One of Rotella's students is the Irish champion Padraig Harrington, a fine player but with the reputation of analyzing too much. At the Doral Open in March 2013, Rotella had Harrington wear a cap with electrodes to measure which areas of Harrington's brain were most active as he played, the more analytical left brain or the more instinctive right side. Rotella said: "We want Padraig in the right brain. During a round, you shift back and forth but when he's trying to swing, you definitely want him in that right side."[13] Another of Harrington's coaches, Dave Alred, added: "One side of your brain lets you get on with stuff and the other side of your brain clutters what you are trying to do. That's it in a nutshell. Golfers have to oscillate between the two sides, which is where it gets complicated."[14]

Nowhere was the ability to shift between mind-sets illustrated as clearly as at the 2010 Masters. Coming into the final day of the tournament, Lee Westwood held a slim lead over Phil Mickelson, followed closely by Tiger Woods and K. J. Choi. Any of them was in position to win, with a few good shots and accurate putts. Performance was relative and payoffs were highly skewed, with the winner getting a payday of $1,350,000, compared to $810,000 for second place and $510,000 for third. A single stroke could be worth half a million dollars—as well as the fabled Green Jacket.

By the 8th hole, Mickelson and Westwood were tied at 12 under par. Then Mickelson nosed into the lead, taking a one-stroke advantage on the 9th hole, and held onto that barest of margins for the next three holes. Coming to the 13th hole, Mickelson had a two-stroke lead with only six holes left to play. Called Azalea, the 13th is one of the most difficult on the course, a 510-yard, par-five hole at the end of a demanding series of holes known as Amen Corner.

Clutching a driver, Mickelson came to the tee and powered the ball far and deep, but it veered off course and came to rest in the rough, lying in a patch of pine straw behind some trees. Still two hundred yards from the green, Mickelson faced a very difficult approach shot. Making matters worse, a tributary of Rae's Creek fronted the green. Disaster loomed.

Most observers expected Mickelson to lay up—that is, to hit onto the fairway, and from there to make a safe approach shot over the creek and onto the green. He would very likely lose a stroke, and if Westwood birdied the 13th the Masters would be tied. But at least Mickelson would avoid a very risky shot through the trees, which could go badly wrong and cost several strokes, with little chance to recover.

Even his caddy advised him to take the safe route. But Phil Mickelson thought differently. Judging the line through the trees, he figured that a well-hit shot could split the trees and maybe even find the green.

Determining the best shot was a matter of deliberation: understanding his capabilities, assessing the competitive setting, and bearing in mind the holes yet to play. Then, having committed himself to attempt the risky shot, Mickelson's mind shifted to implementation. As he later said: "I had to shut out everything around me. The fact that most people, most spectators, family friends, and even my caddy, wanted me to lay up. I had to focus on making a good golf swing because I knew if I executed that swing, the ball would fit between the trees, and end up on the green."[15]

As the gallery watched in silence, Mickelson made a clean shot that threaded the ball between the pines, cleared the creek, bounced twice, and ended up just a few feet from the hole. It was a stunning shot, the stuff of legend. From there, his lead secure, Mickelson went on to win the 2010 Masters.[16]

An example of the right stuff? Absolutely. Once Mickelson made up his mind to go for the shot, he blocked out all distractions and summoned utter confidence. As he later put it, "I just felt like at that time, I needed to trust my swing and hit a shot. And it came off perfect."[17]

Of course not all risky shots turn out so well. It's easy to pick a memorable shot and infer, after the fact, that it was brilliant. (When asked the difference between a great shot and a smart shot, Mickelson gave a candid reply: "A great shot is when you pull it off. A smart shot is when you don't have the guts to try it."[18]) As are many instances of brilliance, it was shaped by careful analysis. In addition to a keen sense of the shot itself, Mickelson also understood the competitive situation. He wouldn't have attempted such a shot on the first day of the Masters, or even on the second day. During the early rounds the main idea is to play well, to look for chances to make a birdie, but above all to avoid major errors. As the saying goes, you can't win the tournament on Thursday, but you can lose it. Better to make a Type II error of omission than a Type I error of commission.

The final found, on Sunday, is a different matter. With just a few holes to play and victory within reach, a different calculus takes over. Phil Mickelson showed talent and guts, as well as a clear understanding of strategy.

THE LIMITS OF DELIBERATE PRACTICE

With so many examples of improved performance through deliberate practice, it's tempting to conclude, as Ericsson puts it, that "outstanding performance is the product of years of deliberate practice and coaching, not of any innate talent or skill."[19] Others have made much the same argument. In recent years deliberate practice has been invoked as the key to high performance in books ranging from *Talent Is Overrated*, by Geoffrey Colvin, to *Outliers*, by Malcolm Gladwell.[20] It's mentioned prominently in *Moonwalking with Einstein*, in which science reporter Joshua Foer sought out Anders Ericsson for guidance in his (highly successful) quest to improve his memory.[21] How can we increase our ability to recall information, whether the items on a shopping list, names of people we have met, or the exact sequence of fifty-two cards? The key is to practice deliberately. Set a specific goal, obtain rapid and accurate feedback, make adjustments, and then try again. And again.

No question, the message of deliberate practice is very encouraging. It appeals to our can-do spirit. We like to think that genius isn't born. We like to believe that even Mozart had to practice long hours, and that Einstein's success was the result of good teachers and hard work. It makes us feel good to imagine that Bobby Fischer wasn't a creature from a different world, but got an early start and persisted. It makes us think there may be hope for us, too. If Joshua Foer went from a novice to national champion in one year, why not me?[22]

Yet we should be careful. Deliberate practice is hardly the cure-all that some would like to suggest.

First, there's a growing body of evidence that talent matters—and a great deal. Researchers at Vanderbilt University found that children who performed very well on intelligence tests at a young age had a significant edge over others in later accomplishment. Very high intellectual ability really *does* confer an enormous real-world advantage for many demanding activities.[23] Second, if we're not careful, we can always pick examples after the fact, then look back and claim that extensive practice led to success. Among Gladwell's examples in *Outliers* were The Beatles and Bill Gates, both chosen to illustrate the value of long hours of practice, whether playing music late into the night at clubs in Hamburg and

Liverpool, or programming computers for hours on end while growing up in Seattle. Missing, however, are the legions of people who also practiced diligently but *didn't* find the same success. (Psychologist Steven Pinker found Malcolm Gladwell's approach particularly maddening: "The reasoning in *Outliers*, which consists of cherry-picked anecdotes, post-hoc sophistry and false dichotomies, had me gnawing on my Kindle.")[23]

More important, deliberate practice is very well suited to some activities but much less to others. Look again at the examples we have seen: shooting a basket, memorizing a deck of cards, hitting a golf ball. Each action has a short duration, sometimes taking just a few seconds or maybe a few minutes. Each one produces immediate and tangible feedback. We can see right away whether the basketball went through the hoop, we got all fifty-two cards right, or the shot landed on the green. We can make modifications and then try again. Furthermore, each action was a matter of absolute performance. Even if a golf shot was made with an eye toward the competition, the shot itself—swinging a club to drive a ball onto the green and then into the hole—was a matter of absolute performance. Executing the task didn't depend on anyone else.

These sorts of tasks are described in the left column of Table 7.1. Duration is short, feedback is immediate and clear, the order is sequential, and performance is absolute. When these conditions

TABLE 7.1 WHEN IS DELIBERATE PRACTICE USEFUL?

	USEFUL	LESS USEFUL
DURATION	SHORT	LONG
FEEDBACK	IMMEDIATE	SLOW
ORDER	SEQUENTIAL	CONCURRENT
PERFORMANCE	ABSOLUTE	RELATIVE

hold, deliberate practice can be hugely powerful. As we relax each of them, the picture changes. Other tasks are long in duration, have feedback that is slow or incomplete, must be undertaken concurrently, and involve performance that is relative. None of this is meant to suggest their deliberate practice isn't a valuable technique. But we have to know when it's useful and when it's not.

To see how these differences can matter, consider the job of a sales representative. Imagine you're a cosmetics salesperson, going door to door in your neighborhood. This sort of task is in the left column. The entire transaction is quick, taking maybe a few minutes. Feedback is immediate; you know right away if you made a sale or not. You finish one visit before going on to the next. Performance is absolute in the sense that you're not directly competing with another offer. The logic of deliberate practice applies nicely. How you describe the products, how you present the options, the words you use and jokes you tell, and the way you try to close the sale—all of these can be practiced and refined, with feedback from one encounter applied to the next. The best salespeople approach each encounter as a new opportunity and do their best to project confidence and self-assurance. They can't afford to be discouraged by the last rejection or worried about rejections to come. They have to believe that *this* customer, *this* call, *this* time can be successful—and muster positive thinking to help make it so. After each call, they can stand back and reflect. *What did I do well, and what can I improve for next time?* They shift rapidly from deliberation to implementation and back again.

For other kinds of sales representatives, the story is entirely different. Consider the sale of, say, a complex enterprise software system. The sales process—it's a sales *process*, not a sales *call*—demands a deep understanding of the client's needs and takes place over weeks and months. During that time, feedback is either uncertain or nonexistent. You might not know for several months if your efforts will bear fruit. Furthermore, because you're working on many potential sales in parallel, you can't easily incorporate the lessons from one client and apply them to the next. Your efforts are concurrent, not consecutive. And finally, for something like an enterprise software system, performance is better thought of as relative, not absolute, because the client is very likely talking with multiple vendors but will buy from only one. If nothing comes of your efforts, you may never know if it was because your sales presentation was poor, a rival's products and services were better, or another sales rep was more effective. In this sort of setting, rapid and immediate feedback that can be applied right away is simply not possible.

DELIBERATE PRACTICE IN THE BUSINESS WORLD

In the business world, some decisions lend themselves nicely to deliberate practice, but others do not. Rapidly occurring and routine activities, including not only operations but many customer-facing encounters conform very well to the rigor of deliberate practice. That's the essence of Kaizen, the system of continuous improvement at the heart of so many manufacturing techniques. There's a disciplined sequence—plan, do, act, check. The cycle time is short and repeated over and over. Feedback is rapid and specific and can be applied to a next effort. Performance, whether gauged in quality or defects or some other operational measure, is absolute. It depends on you and no one else.

For other activities, the benefits of deliberate practice are less obvious. Examples go well beyond software sales. Consider the introduction of a new product. The entire process may take months or even years. By the time results are known, additional products will have been introduced. Furthermore, performance is at least partly relative. If a new product was unsuccessful, is that because we did a poor job, or did a rival introduce a better one?

Or consider setting up a foreign subsidiary. Years may elapse before we can assess whether we have been successful. Many factors are out of our control, including the actions of competitors as well as global economic forces. Was entry to a new market successful because of superior insights about customer needs, or mainly because of favorable economic conditions? Managerial decisions like these rarely afford us the luxury of trying once, receiving feedback, refining our technique, and trying again.

In *Talent Is Overrated*, Geoff Colvin offers an explanation of why two young men, Steve Ballmer and Jeff Immelt, office mates at Procter & Gamble in the late 1970s, became successful.[25] Although they had graduated from excellent business schools, Stanford and Harvard, respectively, neither seemed much different from hundreds of other new hires at P&G. Twenty-five years later, however, they were hugely successful, Ballmer as the chief executive of Microsoft, taking over from Bill Gates, and Immelt as the chief executive of General Electric, where he succeeded Jack Welch. Colvin claims that Ballmer and Immelt owe their success to deliberate practice, and at first glance that seems plausible. If deliberate practice helps people improve at everything from hitting golf balls to landing airplanes, perhaps it's an important element for executive success, too.

Certainly the message is very encouraging. It's comforting and even inspiring to imagine that with diligence and deliberate practice, you too can become the chief executive of a major company. But Colvin's claim is doubtful. To conclude that Steve Ballmer and Jeff Immelt were better at deliberate practice than their contemporaries, we would have to know who was in the next office and whether *those* people engaged in deliberate practice. Which of course we don't. Even if we *could* compare them with their peers, the most important factors in career success are rarely the sorts of things that lend themselves to rapid and explicit feedback, followed by adjustment and a new effort. Much of Immelt's success at GE had to do with the business division he ran, medical instruments, and decisions he made about product strategy and market development. As for Steve Ballmer, some of the most important factors in Microsoft's success had to do with devising a propriety standard, MS-DOS, that was not controlled by IBM and could be sold to makers of PCs—so-called IBM clones. A shrewd move by Gates and Ballmer, no doubt, and one that showed enormous vision about the evolution of hardware and software, as well as a keen understanding about crucial points of leverage in a rapidly changing industry. But it's not the sort of decision that lends itself to deliberate practice. You don't have the opportunity to try, monitor the feedback, and try again.

Executive decisions aren't like shooting baskets. In fact, as a general rule the more important the decision, the less opportunity there is for deliberate practice. We may wish it were otherwise, but there's little evidence that in business, deliberate practice is "what really separates world-class performers from everybody else."

Even Anders Ericsson misses this crucial distinction. In a 2007 article for *Harvard Business Review*, he writes: "[D]eliberate practice can be adapted to developing business and leadership expertise. The classic example is the case method taught by many business schools, which presents students with real-life situations that require action. Because the eventual outcomes of those situations are known, the students can immediately judge the merits of their proposed solutions. In this way, they can practice making decisions ten to twenty times a week."[26] This assertion is questionable. In business, eventual outcomes are rarely known with either the speed or clarity of, say, landing an airplane or striking a ball. Nor do students learning by the case method have the chance to make a decision and see how their actions would have played out. At best, they learn what another person did and get a sense of what followed (at least as described by the case writer, who very likely gathered facts and constructed a narrative with the eventual result in mind). The case method can be a very effective means of learning, and well-constructed cases can give rise to thoughtful discussions with powerful insights. But let's not exaggerate. Most strategic decisions are very far removed from the logic of deliberate practice, in which rapid and precise feedback can be used to improve subsequent decisions. When we fail to make this distinction, we mislead our students and maybe even fool ourselves.

Ericsson recommends that managers and other professionals set aside some time each day to reflect on their actions and draw lessons. "While this may seem like a relatively small investment," he notes, "it is two hours a day more than most executives and managers devote to building their skills, since the majority of their time is consumed by meetings and by day-to-day concerns. The difference adds up to some 700 or more hours more a year, or 7,000 hours more a decade. Think about what you could accomplish if you devoted two hours a day to deliberate practice."[27] I'm all for reflection and evaluation. Stepping back to ponder one's actions and trying to draw lessons from experience is a good idea. But when feedback is slow and imprecise, and when performance is relative rather than absolute, we're in a different domain. Although deliberate practice is ideal for some activities, it is much less appropriate for others.

THINKING ABOUT DECISIONS OVER TIME

Winning decisions call for more than identifying biases and finding ways to avoid them. As we have seen, we first need to know whether we're making a decision about something we can or cannot directly control. We also need to understand whether performance is absolute or relative.

In this chapter we have added the temporal dimension. We need to ask: Are we making one decision in a sequence, where the outcome of one can help us make adjustments and improve the next? If so, the logic of deliberate practice works well. We can oscillate between deliberative and implemental mind-sets. For many activities, especially those that offer rapid and concrete feedback, and for which performance is absolute, the benefits of deliberate practice can be immense.

Yet many decisions do not lend themselves to deliberate practice, and it's crucial to know the difference. The opening example of Skanska USA Building and its bid for the UDC is a case in point. The bidding process alone took months, and the actual construction would take years to complete. Precise lessons would be hard to distill and difficult to apply to a next project, which would be different from the UDC in many respects. Plus, bidding against four other companies added a competitive dimension, so that performance was relative. As much as Bill Flemming would have loved to derive the benefits of deliberate practice, and whereas he surely used his accumulated experience to help make a smart bid, a large and complex decision like the UDC bid demanded a different approach.

Wise decision makers know that for sequential decisions that provide clear feedback, we can err on the side of taking action, monitoring results, and then make adjustments and try again.

When circumstances are different—when decisions are large, complex, and difficult to reverse—a different logic applies. Now the premium is on getting *this* decision right. Rather than err on the side of taking action that may be wrong but that can be rapidly corrected, we may prefer to err on the side of caution and avoid a mistake with potentially devastating long-term consequences.

DECISIONS OF A LEADER

8

IF A COMMANDING OFFICER LACKS CONFIDENCE, WHAT CAN HE EXPECT OF HIS MEN?

STANLEY KUBRICK, *PATHS OF GLORY*, 1957

Up to this point, we have looked at decisions made by individuals, such as golfers or cyclists or pilots. That's consistent with the vast majority of decision research which has studied the way individuals make choices and judgments that suit them best. That's a fine way to learn about everything from consumer choices to financial investments.

But other decisions are made by people who have responsibilities in an organizational setting. They're made by the chief executive of a company, the manager of a team, or the leader of a group. These decisions are different in a fundamental way. They introduce a social dimension. To understand winning decisions, we have to appreciate what's distinctive about the role of a leader.

We got a glimpse of leadership decisions in the story of Bill Flemming and the Utah Data Center. As president of Skanska USA

Building, Flemming had to think about more than what bid would be low enough to win but still high enough to be profitable. He was concerned with how his decision would be perceived by his staff. He wanted to be seen as aggressive but not reckless. He was also concerned with the way rival companies would evaluate his actions. The amount Bill Flemming bid was inextricably linked to his understanding of the role of a leader.

A BIT ABOUT LEADERSHIP

At its core, leadership isn't a very complicated idea. It's about mobilizing people to achieve a purpose.[1] Jack Welch, General Electric's legendary chief executive, put it this way: "As a leader, your job is to steer and inspire."[2] That pretty much sums it up. To steer is to set a direction, and to inspire is to mobilize others to get there.[3]

Of course, *how* to determine the best direction, and *how* to mobilize and inspire followers, is no small matter. Some have conceived of leadership as primarily *transactional*: the person in charge uses rewards and punishments to appeal to the self-interest of followers. Another view, currently in vogue, sees leadership as *transformational*: the aim is to induce followers to transcend their narrow self-interest and pursue a set of higher purposes—perhaps achieving a mission or serving a cause. For transformational leadership, the ability to communicate effectively and to persuade others is essential. If a leader isn't perceived to be authentic, genuine, and trustworthy, others won't follow.[4]

Now we run into a complication. We know that a high level of confidence can be useful for success. We saw in Chapter Five that an exaggerated level of confidence may even be essential—in which case we need to rethink what is meant by overconfidence. That's fine if you're an individual, like Phil Mickelson on the 13th hole at Augusta. The only person you're trying to inspire is yourself.

But what if you're the leader of a group or the chief executive of a company? You're not acting on your own, but through other people. You need to inspire them to achieve great things, maybe even to do something that's risky or unprecedented. You may need to instill in them a level of confidence that exceeds what can be justified by past experience or present capabilities. How should we think about our responsibilities now? How do we reconcile the need to inspire others with leadership traits we admire, such as honesty, transparency, and authenticity?

These issues don't arise when we study individual decisions, but they are central when it comes to the decisions of leaders. They raise some of the most excruciating questions of all. When we're leading others, where does transparency end and deception begin? What is the boundary between authenticity and manipulation? Questions like these don't figure in most laboratory experiments, but they're the stuff of real-world decisions.

LEADING AGAINST THE ODDS

To see how leaders can inspire people to achieve more than seems possible, let's look at an example from the manned space program of the 1960s and 1970s, the setting that gave us the notion of the right stuff.

In 1962, President John F. Kennedy declared that we chose to go to the moon not because it was easy, but because it was hard.[5] If anything, that was an understatement. An extraordinary number of elements—man and machine—had to work together perfectly. The base rate for space travel? Zero, of course. It had never been done before. The Americans and Soviets were blazing a new trail.

The dominant culture at the National Aeronautics and Space Administration (NASA) was one of thorough preparation and extensive practice. While astronauts like Alan Shepard and John Glenn were promoted as heroes in the eyes of the public, Mission Control was firmly in charge of the space program. From the very first days, detailed procedures were developed for every step of each mission. The top minds at NASA—men like Walt Williams, Bob Gilruth, and Chris Kraft—established a policy known as "three nines," or Three Sigma. All critical systems were designed for 99.9 percent reliability, allowing no more than one chance of failure in a thousand. There was a premium on a deliberative mind-set. There was no fudging or guessing, just careful analysis. In this setting, there was no room for positive illusions.[6]

The foundations of Mission Control were codified in six points: discipline, competence, confidence, responsibility, toughness, and teamwork. The definition of competence read: "There being no substitute for total preparation and complete dedication, for space will not tolerate the careless or the indifferent." Confidence was essential, too: "Believing in ourselves as well as others, knowing that we must master fear and hesitation before we can succeed."

The program progressed smoothly, from Project Mercury's suborbital and orbital flights with a single astronaut, to Project Gemini's increasingly long flights with two men aboard. By 1965, NASA's first flight director, Chris Kraft, commented: "There was a confidence that I'd never seen before flowing between engineers at the Cape, the astronauts, the worldwide network, and the flight control teams. The only word I could find to describe it was *professional*. We were good before. Now the Gemini V mission took us to a new level of professionalism that I didn't know existed."[7] They had a high level of confidence, born out of clear-eyed competence.

Gemini flew five manned missions in 1965 and five more in 1966, all of them successful.

Yet risks were always present, and in January 1967 a launchpad fire killed three astronauts during a routine test for the first Apollo mission. NASA halted missions and conducted a thorough investigation. A review board concluded that the fire was the result of three factors: a spark from faulty wiring, the all-oxygen environment, and a sealed hatch that prevented escape. Together they proved fatal.[8] Now there was an even greater emphasis on safety. More than 120 separate items in the command module alone were redesigned, from the escape hatch to flame retardants to nonflammable cooling liquids. At every turn NASA insisted on even greater reliability. Astronaut training became even more thorough, with lengthy hours spent in simulators followed by extensive debriefings, known as "wakes"—precisely the stuff of deliberate practice. More than ever, NASA was obsessed with thorough preparation and complete professionalism.

Manned space flights resumed in October 1968, and two months later Apollo 8 successfully circled the moon. The following summer, Apollo 11 landed on the moon, a triumph watched live by millions around the world, and Apollo 12 followed with another success in the autumn of 1969.

The third lunar mission, Apollo 13, lifted off on April 11, 1970, with the crew of Jim Lovell, Fred Haise, and Jack Swigert. Fifty-five hours into the mission, Apollo 13 was 200,000 miles from the earth and entering the moon's gravitational field.[9] At Mission Control in Houston, Flight Director Gene Kranz's team was nearing the end of its shift. One last duty remained: the crew had to stir the oxygen tanks, a routine procedure to make sure the slushy contents didn't stratify. Suddenly a jolt rocked the capsule. Lovell radioed: "Houston, we've had a problem."[10]

The first symptoms were electrical: a main bus fault, a malfunc-
tioning antenna, and broken computer switches. As Kranz later put
it: "Initially when the crew called down I thought it was an electrical glitch. We'd solve it quickly and be back on track." Very soon,
however, the data monitors at Mission Control showed "multiple
simultaneous failures." Critical fuel cells weren't working. Oxygen
levels were falling rapidly. The spacecraft lurched and veered out of
control. This combination of problems was not just unprecedented,
but almost unimaginable.

Moments later Jim Lovell's voice crackled over the radio: "Hey,
Houston, I see something venting." Through the capsule window
he could see gas spewing into space. Now the magnitude of the
problem was clear. An explosion in the service module had ripped
out the cryogenics and fuel cells, and blown a hole in the oxygen
tanks. The force was the equivalent of seven pounds of TNT, powerful enough to level a three-thousand square foot house.[11] At Mission Control, Kranz looked over at Kraft: "Chris, we're in deep
shit." In an instant the mission's objective was transformed. A
moon landing was out of the question. Kranz recalled: "The only
thought on my mind was survival, how to buy the seconds and
minutes to give the crew a chance to return to Earth."[12]

As flight director, Kranz's responsibilities were partly analytical,
figuring out what had happened and what to do next. After considering the alternatives, he instructed the men in the crippled spacecraft to follow a free return trajectory, continuing around the moon
and using its gravity to propel the ship back toward Earth. But
Kranz's role was about more than selecting the right option. As
team leader, his job was to influence outcomes. He wasn't trying to
predict a safe end to the story; he had to guide his team to achieve a
safe return. The necessary mind-set was not just deliberative but
implemental.

Kranz had no illusions about the severity of the situation: "We were in a survival exercise from now on and it was going to be tough, maybe impossible to get the crew home."[13] That may have been what Kranz was thinking, but it was *not* what he said. Gathering his team around him, he spoke bluntly:

> Okay, team, we've had a hell of a problem. There has been some type of explosion on board the spacecraft. We still don't know what happened. We are on the long return around the Moon and it is our job to figure out how to get them home. The odds are damned long, but we're damned good.
>
> When you leave this room, you must leave believing that *this crew is coming home.* I don't give a damn about the odds and I don't give a damn that we've never done anything like this before. Flight control will *never* lose an American in space. You've got to believe, your people have got to believe, that this crew is coming home. Now let's get going.[14]

Kranz's job was to instill in his team the absolute conviction that they could—*they would*—prevail. He exclaimed: "We've never lost an American in space, and it's not going to happen on my watch. *Failure is not an option!*"[15] Their task was to bring the astronauts back, no question.

Over the next hours, Apollo 13 faced a series of challenges: the loss of oxygen in the spacecraft, a buildup of harmful carbon dioxide, a shortage of power, and an untested burn that was required to gain speed, all compounded by the astronauts' growing exhaustion. It was a seemingly endless set of problems, several of them potentially catastrophic, but each one resolved as Mission Control and the astronauts worked together closely.[16] The odds of a safe return may have seemed insurmountable, but the problem was broken into components, each of which could be—and had to be—solved. Three harrowing days later, Lovell, Haise and Swigert splashed down safely in the Pacific.[17]

THE LEADER MUST NEVER WAVER

The story of Apollo 13 is dramatic and inspirational, but for students of decision making it offers something more. It's a brilliant example of leading others to be successful in a moment of extreme difficulty.

To learn more, I contacted Gene Kranz. How, I wanted to understand, did he get others to achieve their very best in the face of such a challenge? Kranz explained that as flight director, he knew that all eyes were on him. It was imperative that he project complete confidence in the face of long odds. As he put it: "The leader must set the expectations and no matter what the difficulty must never waver." Kranz compared his role to that of a heart surgeon with a patient: "I've got his chest open and I'm ready to make a first incision down there and he looks into my eyes. Do you want to see any doubt?"[18]

In his memoirs, Chris Kraft echoed that view: "The control teams and backroom support technicians were on top of their game. Not once did I hear the words 'If we get them back . . . '. It was 'When we get them back . . . ' and 'Here's what we have to do.' . . . It was never a question of if. The only question was how. That confidence affected us all. I was worried, all right. But I didn't doubt."[19]

In the 1995 movie *Apollo 13*, there's a scene in which a call comes from the White House, asking for an estimate of the probability of a safe return. Kranz (played by Ed Harris) waves the question away, refusing to offer any odds. Eventually his colleagues, feeling obligated to answer President Nixon, place the odds at between 3 to 1 and 5 to 1 *against* a safe return. I asked Kranz if such an exchange had ever taken place. He replied that probabilities were explicitly considered in the planning and preparation stages, but not afterward:

> Prior to liftoff we address performance in mission design, trajectory, resources, etc., targeting in most cases for a 3 Sigma probability of accomplishment. Once we lift off, when it comes to crews and missions, we no longer address probability. . . .
>
> As a Flight Director, I never considered failure to return the crew of Apollo 13. I believe that the White House staff requested probabilities. I never provided them. Always I said "The Crew is coming home."[20]

I didn't ask Gene Kranz whether he had been *overconfident* during the crisis aboard Apollo 13. Given how the word is typically used—inferred after the fact to explain something that went wrong—the question would have seemed out of place. It might even have seemed offensive. The values of Mission Control, which Kranz himself had helped draft, emphasized competence and confidence—surely not the sort of reckless behavior that we commonly associate with overconfidence.[21]

But as we know, overconfidence has more than one meaning. By insisting that the men were coming home, by refusing to countenance the possibility of failure, Kranz clearly *did* communicate a level of confidence that exceeded what was objectively warranted. Because there *was* a chance of failure, and indeed a very great one. Yet when a very high level of confidence is essential to inspire people to succeed, it's really not excessive at all. It's *necessary*. And getting people to believe they can perform at that level is a supreme act of leadership.

During the crisis aboard Apollo 13, Gene Kranz demonstrated a blend of leadership skills. He displayed courage and strength, of course. But he was also wise, recognizing that his team could exert control and influence outcomes, and that his responsibility as a leader was precisely to get them to do so. He knew there was nothing to be gained from dwelling on the possibility of a grim outcome. There was nothing to be gained from an error of omission, or failing to do everything possible to succeed. Of course the odds were long, but by managing risk there was a way to improve the chances of success—and by simultaneously holding a deliberate mind-set as well as emphasizing implementation, Kranz led his team to a successful outcome.

AUTHENTICITY, RECONSIDERED

Few leaders face a challenge quite as extreme as the one that Gene Kranz faced, but many instances of leadership have some of the same elements. Leadership is about influencing outcomes, and when only the very highest levels of performance are acceptable, leaders need to convey high levels of confidence. Jack Welch used words very similar to Kranz's: "Business leaders gain nothing by showing uncertainty and indecision. . . . [They] undermine success by talking about the risk of failure. . . . Your team won't give its all if it senses you're prepared to say, 'Well I told you it might not work out.' They know you can't win unless the leader believes you can."[22]

For another example, consider Steve Jobs, who repeatedly convinced his coworkers that they could do the impossible. During his first stint at Apple, in the early 1980s, Jobs created the Macintosh, a breakthrough personal computer with graphical user interface, which allowed control with a mouse. Two decades later, back at Apple's headquarters in Cupertino for his second time at the helm, he revolutionized consumer electronics with a pocket-sized music player, the iPod, which could hold more than a thousand songs, something that was at the time utterly unimaginable. Jobs possessed what those around him called a "reality distortion field."[23] It came, biographer Walter Isaacson asserts, from "willfully defying reality, not only to others but to himself." Jobs challenged, prodded, encouraged, berated, cajoled, and demanded that his employees do things that had never been done. He talked about creating products that were "insanely great." A bit of hyperbole, perhaps, but it's a short step to imagine that great products come from minds that are, if not insane, at least not limited by conventional thinking. Inspiring people to accomplish the impossible is part of the role of the leader—particularly in an industry where competition is intense and constant innovation is required.

These examples force us to take a fresh look at the notion of *authenticity*. The best leaders, we're often told, share a common feature: they're authentic. They are genuine and true to themselves.[24] In recent years, the term has been used by everyone from Oprah Winfrey, who spoke about discovering your "authentic self," to Pope Benedict XVI, who issued a papal statement titled "Truth, Proclamation and Authenticity of Life in the Digital Age." In business, too, authenticity has become a popular phrase. Former Medtronic executive Bill George wrote a book, *Authentic Leadership*, which emphasizes above all the need for executives to be, well, *authentic*.[25]

No question, authenticity is an attractive word. (Who can be against it, when the opposite is to be, what, *inauthentic*?) It's also wonderfully affirming to suggest that anyone can be an effective leader if only he or she is authentic. It's a bit like the promise of deliberate practice: *As long as you're authentic, you can achieve anything.*

If we look closer, however, things become more complicated. First, we can always find evidence of authenticity when someone is successful. Take any high performing organization, and we can make a case that the leader is true to himself or herself. (It's analagous to the way we commonly use *overconfidence*.) But it's too easy to make inferences based on outcomes. If we can find evidence of authenticity for any successful leader, we have said nothing at all. The term loses all validity.

Assuming we *can* define authenticity in an objective way and not merely infer it from outcomes, we run into a different problem. If a leader instills in others a level of confidence that exceeds what is objectively warranted, is that authenticity or is that deception? When does one give way to the other?

Our instinctive answer is to assert that Kranz, Welch, and Jobs are paragons of authenticity. After all, they were all highly successful. Surely their followers were right to believe them, because the results were favorable. But if that's nothing more than an inference based on outcomes, it's hardly a satisfying answer.

To break this impasse, it's useful to make the distinction between *authenticity* and *sincerity*. Authenticity generally means acting in accordance with our inner selves. We're authentic when we express what we truly feel. Sincerity is about behaving in accordance with the demands of our role. We're sincere when we meet our obligations and fulfill our responsibilities.[26]

In the Western world, for centuries the more admired virtue was sincerity. We were taught to do our duty and to meet our responsibilities—whether to country, family, or religion—even if that involved hardship and sacrifice. Being steadfast and faithful trumped the desire to express one's inner feelings. General Douglas MacArthur captured this ethos in just three words in his address to the Corps of Cadets at West Point in 1962: *Duty, Honor, Country*.[27]

In recent decades, the pendulum has swung toward authenticity. Popular culture now holds that the greater virtue is to act in accordance with our innermost feelings. Leaders, we are told, should strive to be authentic.

To Harvard sociologist Orlando Patterson, this change has not been for the better: "Authenticity now dominates our way of viewing ourselves and our relationships, with baleful consequences. Within sensitive individuals it breeds doubt; between people it promotes distrust; within groups it enhances group-think in the endless quest to be one with the group's true soul; and between groups it is the inner source of identity politics."[28]

Why should authenticity breed doubt? Because we spend time worrying about which of our many and sometimes conflicting feelings are the authentic ones, rather than concentrating on doing our duty.[29] As for distrust, Patterson is less concerned with what people feel than with how they behave. An African American of Jamaican birth, Patterson explains: "I couldn't care less whether my neighbors and co-workers are authentically sexist, racist or ageist. What matters is that they behave with civility and tolerance, obey the rules of social interaction and are sincere about it. The criteria of sincerity are unambiguous: Will they keep their promises? Will they honor the meanings and understandings we tacitly negotiate? Are their gestures of cordiality offered in conscious good faith?"[30]

Although we love words like *transparency* and *honesty* and *authenticity*, let us recall that the ultimate responsibility of a leader is to mobilize others to achieve a purpose. And when they must guide others to reach high levels of performance, leaders may at times need to communicate less than the full truth. They may withhold information that could be disheartening or lead to defeatism. They may need, a bit like the experiment of cycling we saw previously, to deceive others into thinking they can achieve more than they have done in the past. Effective leadership calls for much more than remaining true to one's inner beliefs, or being open and honest at all times. It means being sincere to a higher purpose and may call for something less than complete transparency. That's not a view we have come to associate with exemplary leadership, not in our age of authenticity. Nor do such questions of communication and disclosure in organizational settings appear in most decision research, which has tended to focus on the way individuals make judgments and choices. But when we think of decisions by leaders, these sorts of complications are always present.

THE LOOK OF A LEADER

The decision facing Gene Kranz was unusual in another important way. Once the explosion occurred and the lunar landing was no longer possible, the mission changed to one of survival. The outcome would be known in a few days at the most, and there were only two possible outcomes: the astronauts would return safely or they would perish. There was an immediacy and a clarity to the problem at hand. To paraphrase Samuel Johnson, when we know the crew might die in a matter of days, it concentrates the mind wonderfully.[31]

In many leadership situations, neither of these conditions holds. Decisions take longer to reach an outcome, and those outcomes are more difficult to assess. That makes it harder to evaluate a leader, which in turn changes the way leaders make decisions.

Consider a recent example. Carly Fiorina was chief executive of Hewlett-Packard from 1999 to 2005. Revenues rose during her tenure, in part because of the merger with Compaq in 2001. Was she a successful leader? Not according to Carol Loomis, who wrote a withering critique in *Fortune*, calculating that under the terms of the deal HP gave away 37 percent of its highly profitable printing and imaging business to Compaq, with little to show in return.[32] After Fiorina's ouster in 2005, the company went on to record several years of profitable growth, improving the efficiency of operations and boosting the bottom line. Was that due to the new chief executive, Mark Hurd, and his widely praised talent for execution? So said the press, and it made for a good story. Or was HP's improved performance the result of strategic choices made by Fiorina while she was in charge—decisions that simply took a long time to bear fruit? That was the narrative that Fiorina offered in her book, *Hard Choices*. Which story is correct? It's not entirely clear, for the reasons we explored in the previous chapter. Executive decisions play out over months and years, sometimes long after a term of office has ended. And indeed, when Hurd was forced out for personal improprieties a few years later, many were highly critical of his tenure at the helm, claiming that apparent improvements had come at the expense of building for the future.

It's a paradox: as we go higher in an organization, decisions become more complex and take longer to produce results, making it more difficult to evaluate the leader. For the very highest positions of all, at which decisions often are the most consequential, evaluating those decisions can be the most difficult of all.

When Rakesh Khurana of Harvard Business School undertook a study of CEO selection, he expected to find rigorous and objective appraisals, with the highest salaries offered to executives who were demonstrably the most effective.[33] Instead, he discovered that the market for CEOs was fraught with imperfections and largely based on highly subjective perceptions. Khurana described the process of executive search as "the irrational search for a charismatic leader," best understood as a ritual in which boards of directors make choices that *appear* to be reasonable and can be defended no matter how things eventually turn out. Because leaders cannot easily be assessed on what should matter most—the quality of their decisions—they are often evaluated on whether they conform to our image of a good leader. Above all, it helps to have the look of a leader.

As for those people selected to be chief executives, they know their decisions will take years to play out and will be confounded by so many other factors that a definitive evaluation will be close to impossible. As a consequence, they often act with an eye toward how they will be perceived. They try to conform to what we associate with effective behavior, chief among which is to appear decisive. As James March and Zur Shapira explain: "Managers are expected to make things happen. Managerial ideology pictures managers as making changes, thus leading to a tendency for managers to be biased in the direction of making organizational changes and for others to be biased in expecting them to do so."[34]

There's that word again: *bias*. March and Shapira aren't referring to a cognitive bias, or an unconscious error of judgment, but to a strong tendency or inclination. We saw that previously with *bias for action*: a deliberate preference to act rather than to wait. Here it means that leaders are expected to take decisive action. They'll be perceived as performing well as long as they seem to be inclined toward taking action and acting with self-assurance.

As well, leaders want to be seen as persistent. They're expected to have a clear sense of direction and to be steadfast in the pursuit of associated goals. In a remarkable experiment, Barry Staw and Jerry Ross asked four groups to read a description of a leader's actions in a business setting. Each group was given a different reading. One was about a leader who stuck to a policy despite repeated failure and was never successful (persist/fail—persist/fail—persist/fail). The second persisted and eventually succeeded (persist/fail—persist/fail—persist/succeed). The third kept changing the policy but never succeeded (change/fail—change/fail—change/fail), and the fourth kept changing and ultimately succeeded (change/fail—change/fail—change/succeed). After reading, participants were asked to evaluate the leader's actions. The leader who received the highest evaluation was the one who followed a consistent policy and ultimately succeeded (persist/fail—persist/fail—persist/succeed). He was credited for eventual success and also lauded for his steadfast behavior, for persevering even in the face of initial failure. As for the leader who changed policies and eventually succeeded? He was rated *lower* for clarity of vision and strength of character. In fact, because he changed course, eventual success was sometimes ascribed to chance. Far from praising his adaptability and flexibility, he was questioned for a lack of consistency. The implication for leaders is profound: being perceived as consistent and steadfast was as important as the eventual outcome—and sometimes more so.[35]

Staw and Ross ran their experiment three times: with practicing managers, business school students, and undergraduate psychology students. Who do you think placed the greatest importance on consistency? Practicing managers, followed by business school students, with the least importance placed on consistency by psychology undergraduates. It appears that leaders come to appreciate the importance of perception through their own (sometimes painful) experience. They have learned—often the hard way—that results only count for so much. At least as important is to look strong and constant, and avoid the appearance of being wishy-washy or indecisive. As Staw summed up in an article titled "Leadership and Persistence": "Few actions are so visible, consequential, or accountable as those of leadership. . . . Most leaders try to avoid the appearance of vacillation so that their constituents can have faith in a program or philosophy of management and can understand the direction that the organization is going. As we've seen, strong leaders are perceived to be consistent."[36]

‑The desire to be seen as persistent helps explains why decision makers are prone to escalate their commitment to a losing course of action.[37] Escalation of commitment attracted attention in the 1970s as a way to explain US policy during the Vietnam War. Ground forces were introduced in 1965, but progress was slow and more were added, until by 1969 the United States had more than 500,000 soldiers in Vietnam and was taking heavy casualties. How had it arrived at this position? Each step in the process had seemed like only a small additional investment, but one that held out the hope of changing the outcome of the war. When viewed on the margin, each decision to escalate seemed sensible, at least until a point was reached at which it became clear that a decision to desist should have been made long before. In retrospect, the folly of escalation was clear; at the time, discerning the moment when one more step forward should *not* be taken was all but impossible. As Barry Staw explained, "Individuals may persist in a course of action simply because they believe consistency in action is an appropriate form of behavior, thereby modeling their own behavior on those they see as successful within organizations or society in general."[38] What seems to the leader like a reasonable decision—to take just one more step, perhaps a small one, and to remain persistent, disciplined, and steadfast—can lead to a disastrous outcome.

THINKING ABOUT LEADERSHIP DECISIONS

Much of what we know about decision making is based on laboratory experiments with individuals, acting on their own. That's a fine way to isolate cognitive mechanisms of judgment and choice.

That's also a good way to shed light on many real-world decisions.

Generalizing the results of those studies to leadership decisions, however, is problematic. Leaders mobilize others to achieve a purpose, which means that they do their work through the actions of other people. Leadership means shaping outcomes, which involves exercising control, of which we often have more—not less—than we imagine. Furthermore, leaders often make decisions that are, almost by definition, more complex and consequential than routine decisions made by individuals. For these reasons, as well, they often do not lend themselves to deliberate practice.

For leaders, there are several implications for making winning decisions. First is to recognize that they may need to instill in others a level of confidence that might seem exaggerated, but is necessary for high performance. Terms that are currently in vogue, such as transparency and authenticity, don't do justice to the challenges facing leaders. More appropriate may be the concept of sincerity. Ultimately, the duty of a leader is to inspire others, and for that, the ability to personify confidence is essential. As General Rousseau, a character in *Paths of Glory*, asked rhetorically, *If a commanding officer lacks confidence, what can he expect of his men?*

Second is that unlike the decisions that offer rapid feedback, so that we can make adjustments and improve for the next one, leaders often make decisions that take a long time to bear fruit. Deliberate practice is impossible; leaders often get only one chance to make truly strategic decisions. For this reason it is especially important to deliberate wisely, considering the implications of Type I and Type II errors.

Third, because it is difficult to evaluate complex and long-term decisions with precision, leaders often act with an eye to how they are expected to behave. Put another way, they decide how to decide. When in doubt as to the best course of action, leaders will tend to do what allows them to be seen as persistent, as courageous, and as steadfast.

This final point introduces important questions of governance and oversight. In *The Powers to Lead*, Joseph Nye writes: "History tends to be kind to the lucky and unkind to the unlucky, but we can still judge them in terms of the means they use and the causes of their luck."[39] Certainly we should *try* to judge them in that way. In practice, however, it's difficult to separate luck and skill, especially for the most far-reaching and long-term decisions. It is not always easy to evaluate outcomes, much less to appraise objectively the means used to achieve them. It's so much simpler and offers a more satisfying story to make attributions based on results. When they're good, we naturally infer the process was sound and the actions authentic.

For individuals making routine decisions, we know a lot about common biases and errors of judgment. At its core, however, leadership is not a series of discrete decisions, but calls for working through other people over long stretches of time. It is not transactional but transformational. Making great decisions calls, above all, for us to recognize that the most important and consequential decisions leaders face are fundamentally different from what has been studied at length in laboratory settings. The controls that have been so useful to isolate cognitive mechanisms, like a strobe light capturing a single frame at a time, distract us from appreciating what truly defines the decisions of a leader.

WHERE MODELS
FEAR TO TREAD

I WAS SO ENAMORED OF THE POWER AND ELEGANCE OF THE MORE
MATHEMATICAL ASPECTS OF THIS EMERGING FIELD THAT I IGNORED
THE NON-MATHEMATICAL UNDERPINNINGS: HOW TO IDENTIFY A
PROBLEM OR OPPORTUNITY TO BE ANALYZED, HOW TO SPECIFY
THE OBJECTIVES OF CONCERN, HOW TO GENERATE THE ALTERNA-
TIVES TO BE ANALYZED.

HOWARD RAIFFA, "DECISION ANALYSIS: A PERSONAL ACCOUNT OF HOW
IT ALL GOT STARTED AND EVOLVED," *OPERATIONS RESEARCH*, 2002

In the preceding chapters we considered a number of elements of
making great decisions. We made the distinction between outcomes we can influence and those we cannot, between performance that is absolute and relative, between decisions that lend
themselves to rapid feedback and those that do not, and between
decisions made by individuals acting alone and those made
by leaders.

In coming chapters I'll bring these elements together and look at
a few comprehensive examples. But first let's take a closer look at a
topic of current interest: decision models.

MODELS, MODELS, EVERYWHERE

The insight that even simple models can lead to surprisingly accurate decisions has been around for some time. In 1954, Paul Meehl, a psychologist at the University of Minnesota, compared expert forecasts with the predictions of simple statistical models. Although the models used only a fraction of the data available to the experts, they were almost always more accurate. A number of similar studies have reached the same conclusion. Even seemingly crude models often do very well.

Models are accurate in part because they avoid common errors that plague humans. People suffer from the *recency bias*, placing too much weight on recent information while downplaying earlier data. They pay too much attention to information that is readily available. They're also unreliable: give someone the same information on two different occasions, and he or she may reach two rather different decisions. Models have none of these problems. They can also crunch copious amounts of data accurately and reliably.

For decades decision models have made important contributions to a wide variety of fields. Colleges rely on models to evaluate applications for admission. By using formulas that assign weights to variables—high school grade point average, test scores, recommendations, and extracurricular activities—colleges can make better predictions of academic success than by relying on a one-at-a-time review of each candidate. Admissions officers can't apply a consistent standard across a large pool of applicants, but models can. Banks use models to grant loans. In bygone times, bankers relied on the three Cs: credit, capacity, and character. They asked: *Does the applicant have a strong credit record? Does his monthly income leave enough money, after other expenses, to make the payments? Does she seem trustworthy?* Those aren't bad rules of thumb, but bankers, like everyone else, are prone to error. Models do a better job of predicting whether a loan will be repaid, and by updating them continually with the latest information, we can make them even more accurate over time.

In recent years the use of decision models has surged. The combination of vast amounts of data—stored in places like the NSA's Utah Data Center—and increasingly sophisticated algorithms has led to advances in many fields. Some applications are deadly serious. Palantir, based in Palo Alto, California, analyzes masses of financial transactions on an ongoing basis to detect money laundering and fraudulent credit card usage. It also serves the US military by examining photographic images on a real-time basis to spot suspicious objects that might be roadside bombs—so-called improvised explosive devices or IEDs. San Francisco-based Climate Corp. gathers years of data about temperature and rainfall across the country to run weather simulations and help farmers decide what to plant and when. Better risk management and improved crop yields are the result.[1]

Other applications border on the humorous. Garth Sundem and John Tierney devised a model to shed light on what they described, tongue firmly in cheek, as one of the world's great unsolved mysteries: How long will a celebrity marriage last? By gathering all sorts of facts and feeding them into a computer, they came up with the Sundem/Tierney Unified Celebrity Theory, which predicted the length of a marriage based on the couple's age (older was better), whether either had tied the knot before (failed marriages were not a good sign), and how long they had dated (the longer the better), as well as fame (measured by hits on a Google search) and sex appeal (the share of those Google hits that revealed scantily clad images). With only a handful of variables, the model did a very good job of predicting the fate of celebrity marriages over the next few years.[2]

Models have shown remarkable power in fields that are usually considered the domain of experts. Two political scientists, Andrew Martin and Kevin Quinn, developed a model to explain recent Supreme Court decisions—whether the nine justices would uphold or overturn a lower court ruling—based on just six variables.[3] For all the lengthy arguments, with detailed discussions of precedent and arcane points of law, most decisions came down to a few key factors. Of course, hindsight is one thing. To see whether the model could actually *predict* decisions, University of Pennsylvania law professor Ted Ruger applied it to the upcoming Supreme Court term. Separately, he asked a panel of eighty-three legal experts for their predictions about the same cases. At the end of the year he compared the two sets of predictions and found that the model was correct 75 percent of the time, compared to 59 percent for the experts. It wasn't even close.[4]

Models can even work well for seemingly subjective tasks. Which would you think does a better job of predicting the quality of wine, a connoisseur with a discerning palate and years of experience or a statistical model that can neither taste nor smell? Most of us would put our faith in the connoisseur. We picture an elegant man or woman holding up a glass of a dark red liquid and swirling it slowly, breathing in the bouquet and savoring the subtle undertones— blackberry here, cinnamon there. We believe that personal experience, gained over many years in the vineyards of Burgundy and Napa, should lead to a finely calibrated ability to judge the quality of a vintage. The facts tell a different story. Using data from France's premier wine-producing region, Bordeaux, Princeton economist Orley Ashenfelter devised a model that predicted the quality of a vintage based on just three variables: winter rainfall, harvest rainfall, and average growing season temperature.[5] To the surprise of many and embarrassment of a few, the model outperformed the experts—and by a good margin.[6]

These last two examples were described by Yale law professor Ian Ayres in *Super Crunchers: Why Thinking-by-Numbers Is the New Way to Be Smart*. Ayres explained that models do so well because they avoid common biases. Not surprisingly, he mentioned overconfidence, noting that people are "damnably overconfident about our predictions and slow to change them in the face of new evidence."[7] (As evidence, Ayres mentioned the study we have seen several times: when people make estimates with 90 percent confidence for questions of general knowledge, they consistently provide ranges that are far too narrow. He's right—people *are* overprecise, but we know that overprecision is not evidence of overestimation or overplacement.) Decision models, of course, don't suffer from such biases. They weigh all data objectively and evenly. No wonder they do better than humans.

So are decision models really "the new way to be smart"? Absolutely. At least for some kinds of decisions.

But look back over our examples. In every case the goal was to make a prediction about something that could not be directly influenced. A model can estimate whether a loan will be repaid, but can't change the likelihood that a given loan will be repaid on time. It won't give the borrower any greater capacity to pay or make sure he doesn't squander his money the week before payment is due. A model can predict the rainfall and days of sunshine on a given farm in central Iowa, but can't change the weather. It can estimate how long a celebrity marriage might last, but won't help one last longer or cause another to end sooner. A model can estimate the quality of a wine vintage, but won't make the wine any better. It can't reduce the acidity, improve the balance, or add a hint of vanilla or a note of cassis.

For these sorts of situations, in which our aim is to make an accurate estimate of something we cannot influence, models can be enormously powerful. But when we *can* influence outcomes, the story changes. Let's return to the example about cycling, in Chapter Two, in which Dr. Kevin Thompson used a deceiving avatar to spur cyclists to go faster. If Thompson ran many trials of the same experiment and accumulated a large data set, he could surely devise a model that could predict the relationship between "surreptitiously augmented feedback" and cyclist performance. He might be able to show, for example, that most athletes can match the avatar when it speeds up by 2 percent, and that a few can keep up at 3 percent, even fewer at 4 percent, and almost none can match the avatar when it goes 5 percent faster. That's fine for the researcher, wearing a lab coat and holding a clipboard or adjusting the dials on the controls. He's using the data to predict an outcome he does not directly influence. But for the cyclist, the reality is very different. For the person pushing the pedals, positive thinking is vital. Believing you can achieve high performance—even holding a belief that goes beyond what you have done before—can lead to better performance.

The same goes for Dr. Witt and her study of putting accuracy. With enough subjects, and by varying the size of the circles and the distance, she could surely build a model to predict the effect of the Ebbinghaus illusion. She might show that the small surround leads to a certain average improvement with a given variance. But for a subject in the experiment, holding the putter in hand and taking aim at the hole, predictions about average improvements are beside the point. The golfer has to draw back the club and bring it forward to strike the ball with just the right force to propel the ball toward the hole. The model doesn't strike the ball; the golfer holding the club does. This distinction is simple, but it's crucial and often overlooked.

MODELS AND *MONEYBALL*

The failure to distinguish between what we can control and what we cannot has led to quite a bit of confusion, and nowhere more so than in the application of statistics to baseball. For decades, baseball managers made tactical decisions according to an unwritten set of rules, known as *going by the book*. Beginning in the 1970s a group of statistically minded fans—practitioners of *sabermetrics*, a term coined for the Society for American Baseball Research—began to apply the power of data analysis to test some of baseball's cherished notions, often with surprising results. Take a common tactic, the sacrifice bunt. With a runner on first base and fewer than two outs, should the batter bunt the ball to advance the runner? Conventional wisdom often said yes. As Bill James, a pioneer of sabermetrics, put it: "The experts all knew that when there was a runner on first and no one out, the percentage move was to bunt."[8]

Until recently there was no way to conduct a decent empirical analysis of the sacrifice bunt, but now there is. A simple test compares the runs that result from two situations: a runner at first base with no outs, and a runner at second base with one out. Analyzing an entire season of major league games revealed that a runner on first base with no outs led to an average of 0.93 runs, whereas a runner on second base with one out led to 0.71 runs.[9] All else being equal, making an out to advance a runner from first base to second base led to 0.22 *fewer* runs, or a drop of almost 24 percent (22/93 = .237). What if there is already one out? Now a sacrifice bunt is even less effective, as the runs scored drop from 0.55 to 0.34. That's a smaller absolute decrease of 0.21 runs, but an even steeper drop in percentage terms (21/55 = .382). In either case, making an out to advance the runner is a bad move. These findings came as a surprise to many, but they confirmed the hunch of Baltimore Orioles manager Earl Weaver, who had long doubted the effectiveness of sacrifice bunts. In Weaver's day the data and computing power didn't exist to test the hypothesis, and he was maligned for rejecting conventional thinking. Now we know he was right. The sacrifice bunt is just one example of conventional wisdom in baseball being wrong. As Bill James concluded, "A very, very large percentage of the things that the experts all knew to be true turned out, on examination, not to be true at all."[10]

The use of data analysis in baseball was the key insight of Michael Lewis's 2003 best seller, *Moneyball: The Art of Winning an Unfair Game*. Lewis described how the Oakland Athletics, a low budget team in a small market, posted several consecutive years of excellent results. Rather than relying on traditional scouting reports, Athletics general manager Billy Beane used statistical analysis to calculate what really led to offensive productivity. He focused on key metrics that were highly correlated with scoring runs, like on-base percentage, which includes not just base hits but also the ability to coax bases on balls. Based on these insights, Beane assembled a team of very good players at bargain prices. In decision-speak, he was trying to *optimize runs scored per dollar spent*. Oakland's strong record for several consecutive years, achieved in spite of a low payroll, was very likely the result of the team's use of decision analytics. Beane explained that he was merely doing in baseball what was already happening elsewhere: "In the Eighties, on Wall Street, there was still a group of 'gut feel' traders and there was this collision with these people who were using complex mathematics. In sports it was exactly the same thing."[11] Quants had already revolutionized finance and were now making their mark in baseball.

With the publication of Moneyball, the use of statistical analysis in baseball became widely accepted. Statistically minded general managers, several of them disciples of Billy Beane, spread throughout major league baseball. Since then legions of young men and women have come out of college or left Wall Street, searching for a job in baseball in which they can exercise their statistical chops, building proprietary databases and creating ever-more-sophisticated formulas to predict performance. By 2013 a host of new statistics had been devised to measure increasingly esoteric aspects of play. PITCHf/x tracks the location and velocity of every single pitch, and allows ever-finer analysis of pitcher performance.[12] Park Adjusted Defensive Efficiency (PADE) records every ball in play and extends statistical analysis to fielding, the aspect of play that has been least amenable to quantification.[13] Based on these insights, teams are now able to shift the position of their fielders for each batter. Still other algorithms are kept secret, the equivalent of a carefully guarded formula.

The San Francisco Giants, winners of the World Series in 2010 and 2012, are one of many teams that use statistical analysis to gain an edge. They work with more than ten companies, including Inside Edge and Sportvision, to acquire not only statistics but extensive video of on-field performance. The Giants were the first team to use FieldF/X, which records fielding data. Coaches and players now have a trove of information to help them understand the performance of pitchers and hitters—both their opponents' and their own. Not only do the Giants use statistics to understand what happens on the field, they're also at the forefront of using decision models for marketing and customer relations.[14] Today, America's pastime has fully embraced the digital age, bringing together Cooperstown and Cupertino.

As for the Oakland Athletics? A baseball team's performance is relative, not absolute.* If Oakland was the only major league team to rely on statistics to evaluate players, it would enjoy—all else being equal—a clear advantage over the other twenty-nine teams. What would happen if a second team took the same approach? Very likely both teams might be able to find undervalued players, and both would have an edge over the other twenty-eight. But now suppose that six teams played "Moneyball," or maybe twelve, or eventually twenty. The market price for undervalued players would go up, and what Michael Lewis described as an *unfair game* would become a *fair market*. At some point, when almost all teams played "Moneyball," there would no longer be any relative advantage at all. True, any teams that still rejected the power of data analysis would perform worse than the rest, but the use of statistics wouldn't be enough to ensure high performance. It would become necessary, but insufficient to win.

And that pretty much describes what happened to the Oakland Athletics, whose performance tapered off as they posted a losing record for five straight years, before returning to their winnings in 2012 and 2013. In a 2009 interview—"No More Talk about Moneyball, Please"—Billy Beane expressed mild irritation at the continued attention paid to his earlier triumphs. He commented: "Listen, you can't get stagnant in this business and we certainly haven't. There are teams that are probably far beyond what we can imagine in this office based on their intelligence and their resourcefulness. . . . You can't do the same things, in this case, seven years later. There are too many changes in the game and it's more and more competitive."[15]

---

* I'm referring here to its win-loss performance; if we mean financial performance, the story changes. There are ways to earn a solid profit without bringing home championships—witness the Chicago Cubs.

Statistical analysis is a powerful tool, and by now it's indispensable for baseball teams. But in baseball, as in so many other competitive arenas, absolute improvements don't ensure relative success. The bar keeps rising.

WHY BILLY BEANE AND JOE MORGAN ARE BOTH RIGHT

Given how widespread the use of statistics in baseball has become, it's easy to forget the passions that were unleashed when Michael Lewis's *Moneyball* was published. At that time, the notion that players could be evaluated by statistical models touched off something of a holy war. Players, managers, and scouts were incensed. They insisted that player performance couldn't be reduced to figures. Statistics don't capture the intangibles of the game, they argued; numbers don't grasp the subtle human qualities that make players great.

Lewis, whose background was in finance, concluded that baseball was little more than a glorified social club, a bunch of good ol' boys with shared values forged by long hours of batting practice, bullpen chatter, and chewing tobacco. It was a tight-knit fraternity that jealously guarded its traditions. As Lewis observed, the growing emphasis on statistics "drove baseball's clubby traditionalists crazy. . . . Members of the Club flipped out. Over and over during the 2003 season I found myself facing one reaction from the reading public and another from the Club."[16]

At one level, skepticism about statistical analysis reflected an unwillingness to accept new ideas. Scouts and coaches no doubt felt threatened by the growing use of statistics. (It turned out they had good reason to worry: by 2011, more than one hundred scouts had lost their jobs, their opinions and hunches no longer needed.[17]) But there was a deeper issue, one that touches on the difference between making predictions and influencing outcomes.

Of all Billy Beane's critics, none was more outspoken than Joe Morgan, a star player from the 1960s to the 1980s and one of the best second basemen of all time.[18] Morgan was also, according to Michael Lewis, the de facto social chairman for the club, a guardian of baseball tradition and a self-appointed arbiter of what was acceptable. And to Joe Morgan, the growing use of decision models was definitely *not* acceptable. When Morgan talked about *Moneyball*, Lewis wrote in a 2004 article for *Sports Illustrated*, "the tone of the discourse, already unhinged, came untethered from reality." Something about the use of statistics was deeply upsetting. "I don't think that statistics are what the game is about," Morgan insisted. "I played the Game. I know what happens out there. . . . *Players* win games. Not theories." The incomprehension was mutual. To adherents of statistical analysis, Joe Morgan seemed hopelessly naïve. Reporters dismissed him as a head-in-the-sand Luddite, a simpleton who was unable to absorb new ideas or accept the truth. Tommy Craggs of *SF Weekly* mused: "Alas, I realize, Morgan will never get it. The only comfort is that this sort of argument will be a relic within a matter of years. Morgan is in the middle of a paradigm shift and doesn't even know it."[19]

But Joe Morgan wasn't entirely wrong. He understood that players don't *predict* performance; they have to *achieve* it. As Brian Wilson said: *You make what's going to happen.* For that, all the statistical analysis in the world is insufficient. For the man in the arena—whether Joe Morgan at bat or Phil Mickelson on the 13th hole at Augusta—positive thinking is vital.[20]

It's not surprising that of all people, Morgan should feel so strongly on this point. His entire career was testimony to the power of self-confidence. Standing just five foot seven, he had to overcome doubters his whole life. As a high school ballplayer, Morgan recalled, "No scouts were interested in me. Whenever someone had something kind to say, there was nearly always a double edge to it: I was known as a good little player—with emphasis on the second of the two adjectives."[21] Through hard work and diligent effort, he signed a professional contract. At just twenty-one, Morgan was promoted to the major leagues and broke into the starting lineup for the Houston Astros, where thanks to relentless practice and brimming self-confidence he became a fine player. After six years in Houston he joined the Cincinnati Reds, where he blossomed into a superstar—in part by working with Reds' hitting instructor Ted Kluszewski, a pioneer in the use of video to make small adjustments and an early practitioner of deliberate practice. Morgan was named the National League's most valuable player in 1975 and 1976, thanks to a combination of outstanding hitting, superb base running, and deft fielding. He continued playing until 1985, and in 1990 he received baseball's ultimate honor, induction into the Hall of Fame. No wonder Joe Morgan resisted the growing emphasis on statistical analysis. His life story was an example of achievement over adversity, of defying expectations through positive thinking and self-confidence.[22]

When we stand back from the claims and counterclaims, Billy Beane and Joe Morgan are both right, just about different things. We come back to one of the central questions of great decision making: Am I predicting something I cannot influence, or can I exert control? The job of a general manager is to assemble a team that will perform well on the field. When he evaluates players, when he decides whom to sign and how much to pay, whom to promote and whom to trade, he does best by relying on dispassionate analysis. There's nothing to be gained from wishful thinking or biased judgments. Billy Beane was known to work out in the clubhouse gym during games rather than watch the action on the diamond. Why? Because as general manager, he doesn't throw a ball or swing a bat. He can exercise control over the composition of the team and makes an impact by putting together the best team possible, but once the game begins, he's powerless.

The job of a player is entirely different. If you're a batter, walking to the plate with no outs and a runner at first, your team isn't somehow entitled to an average of 0.93 runs. Your job is to hit the ball and drive in the runs. If you strike out, the expected number of runs goes down—or if you hit into a double play, even worse. If you hit the ball over the fence, you score two runs. At that moment, an implemental mind-set with high self-confidence is vital.

Between at bats, it's important to shift to a deliberative mind. *What happened during my last time at bat? Are my mechanics sound? What is the pitcher likely to do? What adjustment should I make for the next time?* Then, when next standing in at the plate, deliberation gives way to implementation. Now, thinking that you can succeed is vital: believing that you can and will succeed *now*, against *this* pitcher.

The field manager, in the dugout, has duties that are a blend of both. For some decisions, such as whether to order a sacrifice bunt, which relief pitcher to summon from the bullpen, or how to position the defense, statistical analysis can be very useful. Yet he can also shape outcomes, at least indirectly, through the tone he sets and the encouragement or criticism he offers. When the Moneyball controversy was at its height, St. Louis Cardinals manager Tony LaRussa wisely observed that no single approach was best: "The 'Moneyball' kind of stuff has its place, but so does the human. Really, the combination is the answer."[23]

Pitting baseball traditionalists against proponents of statistical analysis makes for a spirited debate, but it's a false dichotomy. It's not conducive to a better understanding. Both approaches have merit, but for different things.

POLITICAL JUDGMENT . . . AND JUDGMENT ABOUT POLITICS

The need to distinguish between making predictions and influencing outcomes is seen in fields other than sports. Over a span of more than twenty years, from the 1980s to the 2000s, psychologist Philip Tetlock asked a wide range of people, from experts to college students to ordinary citizens, to make predictions about a variety of political events. These included the possible breakup of the Soviet Union, the prospect that Quebec would separate from Canada, the end of apartheid in South Africa, the outbreak of nuclear war, and more. The results of his study, published in his acclaimed book *Expert Political Judgment*, were sobering. So-called experts were generally no better than ordinary citizens at predicting political events, and both were less accurate than simple linear models that made projections based on a handful of variables. Tetlock's study was a tour de force in the field of the psychology of prediction, its findings providing further evidence of the power of models.[24]

Yet for all its strengths, Tetlock's study examined only one kind of political judgment, that of estimating events that could not be directly influenced. After all, none of his subjects were in a position to affect the events they were asked to predict. They could not influence the future of the Soviet Union or of Quebec, or end apartheid in South Africa, or deploy nuclear weapons. For these sorts of judgments, in which the premium is on objective and accurate evaluations, Tetlock demonstrated persuasively that decision models do better than most people and much better than pundits. The standard lesson of decision research—that we should beware of common biases and find ways to avoid them—makes good sense.

But predicting events is *not* the only kind of political judgment, nor necessarily even the most important. *Political judgment* is not the same thing as *judgment about politics*. The mark of a skilled politician isn't the ability to forecast events but to shape them. That calls for leadership, which means influencing people to bring about desired results. Political leaders—whether John F. Kennedy during the Cuban missile crisis, Lyndon Johnson passing civil rights legislation, Richard Nixon opening diplomatic relations with China, Jimmy Carter engineering the Camp David Accords, or Ronald Reagan facing down the air traffic controllers—don't just predict what will happen. They have to get things done. The presidency is called the bully pulpit because it's a forum for influence. Good political judgment means using power and persuasion and levers of influence to shape the course of events. As Nixon once remarked, "The mark of a leader is whether he gives history a nudge."[25]

INFLUENCE, DIRECT AND INDIRECT

Decision models can be very accurate at predicting things we cannot influence, like Supreme Court decisions and wine vintages. For the person who actually has to get things done, models are far from sufficient. There's also a third category between direct influence and no influence: *indirect influence*. If a model's prediction is communicated in a way that changes someone's behavior, we may still be able to shape outcomes. Indirect influence can take two forms. If it increases the chance of an event occurring, that's a self-fulfilling prediction. If it lowers the chance of an event occurring, that's a self-negating prediction.

Suppose you work at a bank that uses a model to review loan applications. You have no direct influence on the borrower's behavior; you don't control her spending habits, and you can't make sure she saves enough money each month to pay the loan. But suppose that instead of simply turning down the application, you meet the aspiring borrower and explain the reasons for your concern. Your intervention could cause her to alter her behavior, perhaps devising a monthly budget or even asking her employer for an automatic deduction from her earnings so as to avoid the possibility of missing a payment. In that case the model, although aimed at predicting an event it cannot directly influence, will have exerted an indirect influence: a self-negating one. (Do this many times, and you may have enough data about the interventions to build a model that predicts their effectiveness.)

Or consider the model that predicted Supreme Court decisions. If the political scientists kept their predictions in a sealed envelope until the Court issued its rulings, the model would have no influence on the outcomes. But suppose the findings were publicized and got quite a bit of attention in the press *before* the Court deliberated. It's possible—although one would hope unlikely—that the Court's decision could be altered. If the justices became more inclined to decide as the model predicted, we'd have a self-fulfilling prediction. If the justices felt offended that a model had the temerity to predict their decisions, and were prompted to rule in a contrary fashion, we'd have a self-negating prediction. And of course, if it was known that the Court had a tendency to rule contrary to predictions, some clever people might announce that their model made one prediction in order to steer the justices in the *other* direction—a bit of reverse psychology.

The Supreme Court might not pay much attention to the pronouncement of a decision model, but efforts to sway the Court through public statements happen all the time. In March 2012, following oral arguments about the constitutionality of the Obama administration's Affordable Care Act, several prominent Democrats offered their views. Speaking on a Sunday news program, Vice President Joe Biden "predicted" that the Court would uphold the legislation.[26] House Minority Leader Nancy Pelosi went further, saying that she expected the Court to rule overwhelmingly that the law was constitutional: "Me, I'm predicting 6–3 in favor."[27]

These weren't predictions in the strict sense, of course. They weren't dispassionate judgments that sought to estimate the outcome with accuracy, but thinly disguised efforts to put a finger on the scale and influence the outcome. The paradox, of course, is that efforts at persuasion will be most effective when they are able to disguise their true intentions—that is, when they appear to be purely objective and impartial.

NOT JUST A ONE-TERM WONDER

The need to distinguish among different kinds of influence—none, direct, or indirect—was keenly apparent during the 2012 presidential campaign. Four years earlier Nate Silver—at that time a little-known thirty-year-old with a background in baseball statistics and poker— surprised the pundits by correctly predicting the results of the Obama-McCain presidential race in forty-nine out of fifty states. He missed only Indiana, a traditionally Republican state that went for Obama by a very small margin. It was a remarkable achieve-ment, which Silver parlayed into a blog called *FiveThirtyEight* (the number of electors in the Electoral College) for the *New York Times*, in which he brought the power of data analytics to politics.

In the spring of 2012, Silver's models showed that President Obama enjoyed a small edge in the popular vote over the likely Republican nominee, Mitt Romney, but held a clear advantage in the Electoral College. Various scenarios involving key battleground states, like Ohio, Colorado, Virginia, and Wisconsin, pointed to the likelihood of an Obama victory. There were simply more com-binations of events that favored Obama. For Romney to win, he would have to take almost all of the close states, which was unlikely.

Silver was candid about his methodology, describing the algorithm he used and explaining that he was simply trying to make the most accurate prediction the data would allow. Yes, he had voted for Obama in 2008 and intended to do so again, but Silver claimed that his personal views had nothing to do with the forecasts. He was doing the best job he could as an impartial pollster—the political equivalent of an umpire calling balls and strikes the way he saw them.

Of course supporters of Mitt Romney were having none of it. They understood that a pollster has no *direct* influence on the outcome—Nate Silver is allowed to cast one vote for president, the same as you and I are—but that communicating polling data, especially by someone who had established his credibility so powerfully in 2008, can have a powerful *indirect* effect. If undecided voters believed that Obama was likely to win, they might jump on the presidential bandwagon, whereas Romney supporters might lose enthusiasm or turn their attention to races that their preferred candidates had a better chance of winning. Either way, it would be a classic self-fulfilling prophecy. Announcing that Obama had a clear lead would raise the likelihood of his victory. Ironically, the more Silver took pains to describe the scientific nature of his methods, the more credible his polls became, and the more vigorously Romney supporters tried to impugn his motives.

As it happened, President Obama maintained his edge in the polls through the national conventions in August and well into September. Then the race tightened considerably in October, when Obama fared poorly in the first of three televised debates. Support for Romney surged. Several polls showed the race to be too close to call, and the Gallup Poll, the oldest and most revered name in American political polling, put Romney in the lead. Conservative Web sites began to prominently feature polls that showed a Romney victory was likely. They wanted to create momentum, encourage donors, embolden supporters, and thereby affect the outcome of the race.

Alas for Romney, by late October his surge had faded. As the election approached, *FiveThirtyEight* reported with increasing levels of confidence that Barack Obama would win, putting the probability between 75 and 85 percent. Meanwhile, Romney supporters became ever more shrill in denouncing Silver. Dylan Byers of *Politico.com* speculated that Nate Silver would turn out to be a "one-term celebrity." On the eve of election day, when Silver put the chances of an Obama win at 85 percent, *The Drudge Report*, a conservative Web site, featured stories that predicted a Romney victory from three prominent pundits: Peggy Noonan, Michael Barone, and Dick Morris, who said it would be a Romney landslide.

When the votes were counted, Nate Silver got all fifty states right. As for those who had predicted a Romney win? The Gallup Poll acknowledged that its sampling methods had been flawed and promised to improve in the future. Some Republican pundits, on the other hand, admitted that their so-called predictions had been little more than attempts to influence the vote. Two days after he called a Romney landslide, Dick Morris admitted that he had mainly wanted to keep Romney supporters from becoming discouraged: "I did the best I could—and I also worked very hard for Romney. . . . I think there was a period of time when the Romney campaign was falling apart, people were not optimistic, nobody thought there was a chance of victory. And I felt that it was my duty at that point to go out and say what I said."[28] Morris confirmed one of the less savory principles of punditry: it's better to be outrageously wrong and get lots of attention than to be correct but blend into the crowd.[29] He underscored another truth as well: not all predictions are created equal.

BAYESIAN MODELS, USED WISELY

Understanding the uses and limits of decision models brings us back to the topic of base rates, discussed in Chapter Six. We saw from the examples of the taxicabs and medical tests that people don't naturally think in terms of conditional probabilities. They don't often pay attention to the overall population when making judgments about specific events.

In those examples, of course, all the relevant facts were provided to us, so that calculating conditional probabilities was just a matter of applying the formula and crunching the numbers. But as we know, very often data are not simply given but have to be found, and are not fixed but can change. In such cases, we can incorporate new information into our models through a process of Bayesian updating.

Consider weather forecasting. By taking measurements every day, we can update our models so that over time they become better and better. The steady improvement in predicting temperatures—from an average error in the maximum temperature of 6 degrees in the early 1970s, to 5 degrees in the 1990s, to just 4 degrees by 2010—is testimony to the power of updating models.[30] In this instance, not only are data abundant, but they deal with something we cannot directly influence (at least within the time frame of the prediction—the climate *can* be changed over time, as we are learning). The same goes for models that predict the performance of a basketball team. Our aim is to predict something we don't influence directly (we neither dribble nor shoot) or even indirectly (the Knicks and Lakers don't know what our model is predicting). With several games played per week, we can continually refine our models to become more and more accurate. Thinking of our models as works in progress, continually updated to become more accurate over time, makes good sense.

But let's be careful. What works so well for taking daily readings of the temperature, or predicting the performance of a basketball team, may not be especially useful for other kinds of events. The time frame is different, and our efforts to update the model may affect the event of interest.

In *The Signal and the Noise*, Nate Silver uses an interesting example to suggest how conditional probabilities and Bayesian updating can be useful. Suppose you live with a partner and return from a business trip to discover a strange pair of underwear in the dresser drawer. Let's say you're female, your partner is male, and this is a distinctly female item. You wonder: Given that you've found this strange item, what's the chance that your partner is having an affair?[30]

Silver explains that Bayes's theorem can provide a good initial estimate if we furnish three base rates: the prior probability in absence of evidence, the true positive rate, and the false positive rate.[31] First, we need an estimate of the probability your partner is having an affair setting aside the current evidence, for which—in the absence of other information—we might as well use the overall population base rate of infidelity, which Silver puts at .04. Second, we need to estimate the probability of underwear appearing conditional on his cheating, which Silver sets at 50 percent, or .5.[32] Third is the probability of underwear appearing if he is not cheating, which is estimated at 5 percent, or .05. We don't know for sure that those rates are exactly right, but they're a decent starting point to estimate what we want to know: the probability that our partner is having an affair given that we discovered the mystery underwear. The idea behind Bayesian updating is that if we make this initial calculation, then gather more data over time, much like weather forecasting we can revise our model to make estimates that are more and more accurate.

So far, so good. If we apply Bayes's theorem, as we did in the taxicab and medical test examples, we'll get the figures on Table 9.1. There are two possibilities of finding the underwear: If your partner is not having an affair (five percent of 96 percent, or 4.8 percent) or if your partner is having an affair (fifty percent of four percent, or two percent). Thus, the chance that your partner is having an affair given that you discovered mystery underwear is calculated by 0.02 / (0.02 + 0.048) = .294, or 29.4 percent.

FIGURE 9.1 HAVING AN AFFAIR?

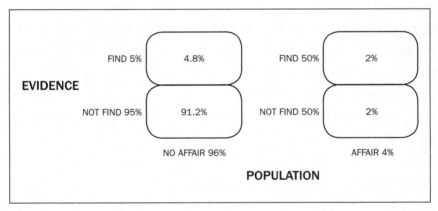

That might seem like less than you would imagine, given the apparently incriminating evidence, but that's what the numbers show. As for the other 70.6 percent of the time? Relax. There's no hanky-panky going on, just a mistake in the laundry, or something left over from the visit of a relative, or a similarly innocent explanation.

This is an intriguing example—bringing Reverend Bayes into the bedroom, so to speak—but I submit it's not a good way to show how models can become more and more accurate through continual updating. It neither considers the importance of rapid updating, nor does it recognize how the very act of taking measurements can affect the likelihood of future events.

To see what I mean, suppose that based on these assumptions you calculate the chance your partner is having an affair at 29.4 percent. If we were predicting tomorrow's weather, we'd know what to do next. We'd record tomorrow's correct temperature, compare it to our prediction, and then tweak our model to make a better prediction next time. We would do the same thing if we wanted to predict how many points the Knicks were likely to score: see what really happened and refine our model to make a better prediction for the next game. The process works when we get new data quickly and accurately, and—crucially—when gathering that information doesn't alter the probabilities of a future occurrence. After all, the weather doesn't know what you predicted, nor do the Knicks know what your model estimated. There's no question of influencing outcomes, whether directly or indirectly.

Things change, however, when it comes to finding mystery underwear. How exactly do you determine whether your partner is really having an affair, and then adjust the model to make a more accurate prediction, without altering the probability of a future event?

If you ask a question—not even as direct as "So, are you having an affair?" but a milder variant such as "Gee, I wonder whose underwear this is?"—you'll change the likelihood of a future occurrence. If nothing was going on your inquiry may not make an affair more likely, but if your partner really was having an affair he or she might do a better job of hiding evidence in the future, which would lower the probability of underwear in your dresser. Or your partner might quietly bring the affair to an end, which again would lower the likelihood of a recurrence. Either way, the very effort to learn the truth introduces a feedback loop that makes this example entirely different from predicting the weather or a basketball score.

Maybe you decide not to say or do anything. You act as if nothing is unusual and wait to see what happens next. That raises a different problem: waiting for the appearance of more underwear could take a long time, especially if you go on business trips only once a month. You won't gather data rapidly enough to update the model to any meaningful extent, certainly not fast enough to shed light on such a burning questions. Bayesian updating can be very powerful, but we should recognize its practical limits, as well.

THINKING ABOUT DECISION MODELS

Decision models can be immensely useful, often making very accurate predictions with relatively little data, and they can help us avoid some of the common biases that undermine our judgments. In the past decade their use has expanded enormously, thanks to growing access to large databases. Models are becoming more important all the time.

In our embrace of decision models, however, we have sometimes overlooked the need to use them well. Especially for things we cannot directly influence, there's no benefit to anything other than accurate judgment. When we have direct influence, the challenge is different. Our task isn't to predict what will happen, but to make it happen. Here, positive thinking can make the difference between success and failure.

We need also to acknowledge a third category: indirect influence. Even if we have no direct influence on a given outcome, we may communicate our model's predictions in such a way that we can alter behaviors and ultimately shape events. Publicizing the results of a political opinion poll is but one example. In baseball, too, the results of statistical analysis can be used to encourage or motivate, indirectly affecting what happens on the diamond, but never in a way that replaces the need to swing the bat and throw the ball. Statistics don't play the game; ballplayers do.

Decision models are often a way to be smart, but even more important is to be wise, which means understanding what models can and cannot do. To quote one blogger, the growing popularity of "technically-sophisticated, computationally-intensive statistical approaches" has an unfortunate side effect: to think less about what the numbers actually mean. There's a "shut up and calculate the numbers" ethos, rather than one that promotes critical thinking.[33] When we use models without a clear understanding of when they are appropriate, we're not going to make great decisions—no matter how big the data set or how sophisticated the model appears to be.

WHEN ARE WINNERS CURSED? 10

THE *ONLY* WAY TO MAKE PROGRESS IN BUSINESS IS THROUGH CHANGE. AND CHANGE, BY DEFINITION, HAS A CERTAIN AMOUNT OF RISK ATTACHED TO IT. BUT IF YOU PICK YOUR SHOTS, USE YOUR HEAD, AND APPLY GOOD MANAGEMENT, THOSE ROLLS OF THE DICE CAN TURN OUT PRETTY GOOD.

ED WHITACRE, *AMERICAN TURNAROUND: REINVENTING AT&T AND GM AND THE WAY WE DO BUSINESS IN AMERICA,* 2013

Experiments offer a powerful way to isolate a single phenomenon while holding other things constant. Many real-world decisions, however, don't oblige our wish to deal with one element at a time. They confront us with many elements, interlinked and interdependent. They often combine an ability to control outcomes with a need to outperform rivals, they often unfold over months and years, and they involve leaders in an organizational setting.

In these next two chapters I'll look at two very different kinds of leadership decisions: making a high-stakes competitive bid and starting a new venture. In both instances, we'll see how a careful analysis and deliberation—left brain—is essential, but that winning decisions also call for moments of calculated risk—right stuff.

A GOOD PLACE TO LOSE YOUR SHIRT

Competitive bids have been a frequent topic of study in decision research, with much attention paid to the winner's curse. The winner's curse appeared briefly in Chapter One, when Skanska USA Building was trying to determine how much to bid for the Utah Data Center. An aggressive bid was surely needed, but a danger loomed: if Skanska made a very low bid in order to win, it would very likely end up losing money. As we will see, the standard lessons about the winner's curse make sense for some kinds of competitive bids, but aren't appropriate for others.

The story of the winner's curse goes back to the 1960s, when managers at the Atlantic Refining Company noticed a worrying trend. Some years earlier, Atlantic (later known as Atlantic Richfield and then ARCO) had won several auctions to drill for oil in the Gulf of Mexico. Later, as the company reviewed the performance of those leases, it found that it was losing huge sums of money. Oil had been discovered, yes, but revenues weren't enough to make the leases profitable. Winning bids had turned into losing investments.

A few members of Atlantic's R&D department decided to take a closer look. Ed Capen, a research geophysicist, found that Atlantic wasn't alone. Virtually every company that acquired oil fields in the Gulf of Mexico through public auctions ended up losing money. Since 1950, investing in Gulf of Mexico oil fields had "paid off at something less than the local credit union."[1] Competitive bidding, Capen concluded, "is a good place to lose your shirt."[2]

To get at the root of the problem, Capen looked at the auction process itself. He discovered an insidious dynamic: when a large number of bidders place secret bids, it's almost inevitable that the winning bid will be too high. Capen called this the winner's curse.

From there the story gets even more interesting. Once Atlantic understood the danger of overbidding, it took precautionary steps. Each department was instructed to become more conservative. Geophysicists were told to be more cautious when estimating the size of oil deposits. Geologists were directed to assume a lower rate of drilling success. Accountants were instructed to raise the discount rate, which lowered the net present value of future revenue streams and made fewer projects appear attractive. Every one of these measures seemed reasonable, but together they had an unanticipated effect. Ed Capen recalled, "By the time everyone was through subtracting value, our bids were so low we didn't buy anything."[3] Now Atlantic had a different problem: it had found a way to avoid losses from overbidding, but also precluded the possibility of any wins.*

Working with two colleagues, Bob Clapp and Bill Campbell, Ed Capen designed a Monte Carlo model to simulate bidding among many parties. Eventually they devised a method aimed at limiting losses while providing a reasonable chance of success over the long run. Capen and his colleagues set out three rules: The larger the number of bidders, the lower you should bid. The less information you have relative to the information possessed by rival bidders, the lower you should bid. And the less certain you are about your information, the lower you should bid. When more than one condition

---

* If the words "Atlantic" and "auction" have a familiar ring, you might remember the Marx Brothers movie *The Cocoanuts*. Groucho says, "I'll show you how you can make some real money. I'm gonna hold an auction in a little while at Cocoanut Manor. You know what an auction is, eh?" Chico answers, "Sure. I come from Italy, on the Atlantic Auction!"

is present, it's even more important to reduce your bid; when all three are present, be extra careful. In those cases, Atlantic's rule of thumb was to make its best estimate of the value of the lease, then bid only 30 percent of that amount. Granted, this approach would lead to fewer wins, but any purchase would be at a price that would give the company a good chance of earning a profit. It was a practical way to mitigate the dangers of competitive bidding.

Capen and his colleagues were modest about their method. The complexities of competitive bidding remained daunting: "So what is the best bid strategy? We cannot tell you and will not even try. The only thing we can do is show you one approach to the mathematical modeling of competitive sales. . . . The bidding model gives us a bid that we can make with confidence, and be happy with when we win. Yes, we may have overestimated value. But we have bid lower than our value estimate—hedging against expected error. In a probability sense, we 'guarantee' that we obtain the rate of return we want."[4] In 1971, Capen, Clapp, and Campbell published their findings in a seminal article, "Competitive Bidding in High-Risk Situations," in the *Journal of Petroleum Technology*. It remains a classic to this day.[5]

COUNTING NICKELS IN A JAR

In the following years, the winner's curse was studied in a variety of experiments. In one, Max Bazerman and William Samuelson filled a large glass jar with nickels, then asked a group of students to come close and take a good look, so they could inspect the jar from various angles. Unbeknownst to the students, the jar contained 160 nickels, worth $8. Each student then made a sealed bid, stating how much he or she was willing to pay for the contents of the jar, with the highest bid winning the nickels.

Some students' estimates were high, many were low, and a few were very accurate. Overall the average of their bids was $5.01, a good deal lower than the true value of the nickels. Most students were cautious and tended to underbid, which isn't surprising because people are often risk averse, and in this experiment there was nothing to be gained by erring on the high side. But in every auction, some people bid well above the correct figure. Over the course of several auctions, those high bids had a mean of $10.01, which meant that on average the winner paid 25 percent more than the contents were worth.

This simple demonstration had all the virtues of laboratory experiments. It was easy to do: just assemble the students and show them the jar, invite them to place their bids, and calculate the result. The entire process took just a few minutes. Other versions used a variety of different items, including things like paper clips, but the results were the same. The larger the number of bidders, the greater the chance that at least one bid would be wildly high, and the less likely it was that an accurate bid could hope to win. Bazerman and Samuelson published their findings in an article with a title that made the point nicely: "I Won the Auction but I Don't Want the Prize."[6]

Today, *winner's curse* has entered the general lexicon. It's often mentioned when questions are raised about an ambitious bid. It's not a cognitive bias, because it doesn't arise from an error of cognition. Rather, it stems from the bidding process itself. Bring together enough people—even people who are somewhat conservative in their bids—and it's very likely that at least one will bid too much. Richard Thaler described the winner's curse as "a prototype for the kind of problem that is amenable to investigation using behavioral economics, a combination of cognitive psychology and microeconomics."[7] So well did the term capture the essence of behavioral economics that Thaler used it for the title of a 1992 book, *The Winner's Curse: Paradoxes and Anomalies of Economic Life.*

AUCTIONS, PUBLIC AND PRIVATE VALUE

Of course it's good to be aware of the winner's curse. Anyone thinking of taking part in an auction should understand the basic paradox that the apparent winner often ends up a loser. You don't want to be drawn into a bidding war for some item on eBay when you can find it somewhere else and perhaps more cheaply. The winner's curse is particularly important in the world of finance, where it poses a serious danger for investors in publicly traded assets. Because market analysts and investors have access to roughly the same information, anyone willing to pay more than the market price is very likely paying too much. The implication is sobering. Imagine you spot what seems like a bargain—a stock that you think can be bought on the cheap, for example. Rather than believe you know something that others don't, it's wiser to conclude that you're wrong.[8] Much more likely is that your generous valuation is in error. Seminars on behavioral finance teach investors to watch out for the winner's curse and to avoid its ill effects.[9]

But let's stand back for a moment. What do a nickel auction and buying a stock have in common? By now, I hope you have spotted the answer. In both cases, there's no way to exert control over the value of the asset.

Both are examples of a *common value auction*, meaning that the item on offer has the same value for all bidders.[10] The jar contains the same number of nickels for everyone; not even the most eagle-eyed buyer can find an extra nickel hiding somewhere in the contours of the jar. Further, a nickel has the same value to everyone. You cannot, through skill or persistence or positive thinking, go into a store and buy more with a nickel than I can. The same goes for a financial asset, like a share of Apple or General Electric. It's worth the same for you and for me. You can decide to buy a share, or you can decide not to buy and spend your money elsewhere, but you won't have any effect on its value.

In common value auctions, our bids reflect our estimates of the asset's value. If you think the jar contains more nickels than I think it does, you'll bid more than I will, simple as that. The same goes for a share of stock. For these sorts of assets, there's nothing to be gained from anything other than careful and dispassionate assessment.

There's another reason you don't want to overpay. If you need nickels you can always go to a bank and buy a roll of 40 for $2. There's no reason to pay more. You wouldn't worry about losing a nickel auction—or making a Type II error. Rather, you should worry about making a Type I error—winning the bid and realizing you have overpaid. The same is true for a share of Apple or GE. There's a ready market with plenty of liquidity, and unless you're planning to mount a takeover bid and want to accumulate a large block of shares, you can buy as many as you want without moving the market. Paying more than the market price makes no sense.

Other auctions are very different. They're known as *private value auctions*, in which the value for you and for me is not the same. Differences might be due to entirely subjective reasons, as with a collectible. What would you be willing to pay for John Lennon's handwritten lyrics to "A Day in the Life"? They were sold at Sotheby's in New York for $1.2 million after a vigorous bidding war among three parties, each of whom placed a high personal value on a small piece of paper.[11] In other cases the difference in value is for commercial reasons, such as different abilities to generate revenues or profits from the asset. Here again, what bidders are willing to pay may differ sharply. Offering more than others isn't necessarily wrong, but should reflect a sound understanding of the value of that asset today—and what it can earn tomorrow. Paying more than other bidders might make good sense, provided you can explain your rationale.

DRILLING FOR DOLLARS

Let's return to bidding for oil tracts. It's not a common value auction, and it doesn't take place in a few minutes, but rather unfolds over years. Determining the amount to bid is much more complicated than at a nickel auction.

If you saw the 2007 movie *There Will Be Blood*, you might think that drilling for oil is a bit like drinking a milkshake—you sink a straw and drain it dry. A few wells might be something like that. The famous 1901 Spindletop gusher near Beaumont, Texas, comes to mind; the oil was so close to the surface that even before the well was tapped, fumes were wafting up through the soil. Today, of course, oil exploration takes place in much more demanding settings. Drilling was already complex when Atlantic was drilling in the Gulf of Mexico back in the 1950s, and it's much more challenging now. Some of the complexities became apparent to the general public in a dramatic fashion in 2010, with the explosion and spill at BP's Deepwater Horizon platform.

The cost of developing new oil fields continues to rise because of the challenges of working in more and more remote locations, but if we hold constant the level of difficulty, the cost of producing oil has *declined* on a per-barrel basis. That's because there have been major improvements at every step of the process. Let's start with exploration. Oil companies now have much better seismic imaging technology and more powerful software to interpret the data they gather. In the 1970s two-dimensional imaging was the state of the art. By the 1980s more oil could be located thanks to three-dimensional imaging along with better algorithms to analyze data. Then came four-dimensional imaging, with the fourth dimension of time. By comparing images taken at regular intervals, exploration companies could monitor how extraction causes the remaining oil to shift, allowing them to position subsequent wells with even greater precision. Companies are also more efficient at drilling. Drill bits are made of increasingly durable materials that are less likely to break, and wells no longer have to be vertical but can be drilled at any angle, including horizontal. Oil companies are also better at extraction, using techniques known as enhanced oil recovery. In addition to advanced drilling muds, some companies inject natural gas and carbon dioxide to push the oil up to the surface.[12]

The combined impact of these improvements has been huge.[13] If exploration, drilling, and extraction each improved by 1 percent per year—a conservative assumption—and if each had the same weight, we would see a total improvement of 3 percent, compounded annually. That's not exactly Moore's Law, which famously stated that the power of semiconductors would double every eighteen to twenty-four months, but it's still very significant. Get better by 3 percent each year, and you will increase productivity by 23 percent in seven years and by 55 percent in fifteen years. What used to be produced for $3 now costs less than $2. These improvements have made it possible to develop oil fields more fully and to extend their useful lives for many more years. BP's oil field at Prudhoe Bay, Alaska, which opened in the early 1970s, was expected to shut after 40 percent of the oil was extracted. Now, with greater efficiency and lower costs, it may well continue operation until 60 percent has been extracted, half again as much as originally anticipated.[14]

All of these factors are crucial when deciding how much to bid for an oil tract. The oil in the ground may be the same for all bidders, but how much we bid differs according to the technology we use, the equipment we employ, and the skills of our engineers and drilling crews. And that's just at a point in time. The vital question isn't how good we are today, but how much better we are likely to become at exploration, drilling, and extracting over the life of the field.

To see what this means, I designed another Monte Carlo simulation. This one assumed that the oil field has a useful life of fifteen years, during which three capabilities—exploration, drilling, and extraction—each improve at an average of 1 percent per year.[15] The result shows a median improvement over fifteen years of 49.2 percent (see Figure 10.1). In other words, the same quantity of oil should cost about half as much to bring to the surface. The amount a company should be willing to pay reflects the present value of the

FIGURE 10.1 15 YEAR IMPROVEMENT OF OIL EXPLORATION, DRILLING, AND EXTRACTION

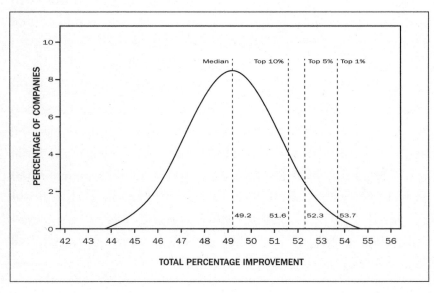

stream of cash flow over the life in the field, with each year's volume extracted more and more efficiently.

Is making a bid based on anticipated improvements an example of overconfidence? By one definition, yes. It smacks of overestimation. It exceeds our current level of ability. But by another definition, betting on an annual improvement of 3 percent isn't excessive at all. It's in line with the historical rate of improvement. The problem is, your rivals are also likely to improve at a similar rate, meaning that betting on a 3 percent rate of improvement probably won't be enough to win. It will only bring you to the midpoint of expected improvements.

To have a good chance of winning, you might want to make a bid that puts you in the top 10 percent, which means betting on an improvement of 51.6 percent over fifteen years. To stand a better chance, you might want to go still further—toward the high end of what could be justified by historical rates. An improvement of 52.3 percent could be expected to occur one in twenty times. Such a bet would seem to be an example of overestimation, but even then you wouldn't win the auction if a rival was willing to be even more ambitious. To have a *very* good chance of winning the auction, you might want to be in the top 1 percent, which means betting on an improvement of 53.7 percent.

We're not far from what happened when we combined an ability to improve performance with the need to do better than rivals—much like in the Tour de France, but without any illicit doping. Anyone hoping to win a competitive battle, in which the winner takes it all, will have to bid more than seems warranted and then exert control to achieve those gains. Put another way, anyone *not* willing to go out on a limb won't stand much of a chance of winning.

Of course it's wise to beware of the winner's curse. The analysis conducted by Atlantic Refining Company, all those years ago, helped identify an insidious problem. The rules suggested by Ed Capen to moderate bids are a step in the right direction. But it's a mistake to take a simple classroom experiment using a common value auction and apply its findings to private value auctions, where capabilities can improve over many years. When we can exert influence and improve outcomes, and in particular when we have many years in which to do so, a very different logic applies. Seeking to avoid losses and steer clear of dangers may seem prudent, but it will not lead to success. In addition to a clear understanding of base rates and a careful analysis of possible improvements, we also need to take calculated risks.

FROM BUYING SHARES TO BUYING COMPANIES

Beyond nickel auctions and shares of stock, the winner's curse has also been used to explain the high prices paid for corporate acquisitions. Consider this question from a leading text in the field, *Judgment in Managerial Decision Making*:

> Your conglomerate is considering a new acquisition. Many other firms are also "bidding" for this firm. The target firm has suggested that they will gladly be acquired by the highest bidder. The actual value of the target firm is highly uncertain—the target firm does not even know what they are "worth." With at least half a dozen firms pursuing the target, your bid is the highest, your offer is accepted, and you obtain the acquisition. Have you been successful?[16]

According to the author—Max Bazerman, who conducted the nickel auction—it's likely your firm has *not* been successful. If you paid more than other bidders, you probably paid too much. The reason, of course, is the winner's curse, coupled with common biases we have already discussed, notably overconfidence. Managers are therefore cautioned to temper their optimism and recognize that the acquired company is likely worth much less than they imagine. They should bid less than they would otherwise offer, or perhaps refrain from making a bid at all.

There's another syllogism at work:

- Most acquisitions fail to deliver value.
- Bidders are prone to the winner's curse.
- Therefore, acquisitions fail to deliver value because of the winner's curse.

From there, it's a short step to suggesting that excessive bids stem from overconfidence.[17] We point the finger at excessive optimism, perhaps due to the runaway ego of chief executives. That makes for a satisfying explanation, of course. We love to see the mighty fall. We're pleased to see the rich and arrogant get their comeuppance. But as we know, it's too easy to make these sorts of judgments after the fact. As long as executives are successful, they're likely to be described as bold and confident; it's only when things go badly that we talk of overconfidence or hubris or arrogance. (The only exception I know of is the chairman of French conglomerate Vivendi, Jean-Marie Messier, who was seen as a personification of arrogance even before his company foundered. His nickname, J4M, stood for Jean-Marie Messier, *Maître du Monde*.)

What's a better way to explain the poor track record of acquisitions? Very likely there's a combination of forces at work. One is overestimation. Even if it's not as pervasive as often suggested, some managers surely *do* overestimate their ability to drive revenue growth and cost savings. Chief executives who are the most optimistic about the benefits they expect to achieve will be willing to pay much more than others. Second is the paradox that successful managers may be the worst offenders, having grown accustomed to past success and therefore imagining they will succeed in the future, even when attempting something much more difficult. They focus on their own personal rate of success—the inside view—and neglect the rate of success in the population—the outside view. Third is the problem of asymmetrical incentives. Chief executives may be willing to take a dubious chance if they know they will benefit handsomely for getting good results but will suffer little if things go poorly—or even walk away with a large severance payment if the deal goes badly. *Heads I win, tails I win even more.*

Given the generally poor record of acquisitions, it's easy to conclude that any time we are tempted to bid more than other buyers, we're committing an error. But this is too simple a view. Morally laden terms like hubris aren't helpful, either, because most people don't think that concepts like hubris and arrogance apply to them—at least not until they have the same wrenching experience, at which point they ruefully admit that they suffer from the same flaws.

To blame the poor performance of so many acquisitions on overconfidence and the winner's curse diverts us from making important distinctions. Acquisitions are typically matters of private value, not common value. A company may be justified in paying more than another if it can identify potential gains that are unique to it. Furthermore, value isn't captured at the point of acquisition, but is created over time, sometimes several years. For that, companies can influence outcomes.

Rather than conclude that acquisitions are bound to fail, we should ask a series of second-order questions. If most acquisitions fail, do some kinds have a greater chance of success than others?

What can be done to influence outcomes and raise the chances of success? Are there circumstances in which it might be reasonable to undertake even a very risky acquisition?

Let's take these questions in order. Extensive empirical research has concluded that most acquisitions fail to create value.[18] The evidence goes beyond the handful of high-profile disasters, like the TimeWarner merger with AOL at the height of the Internet bubble. Mark Sirower of New York University studied more than one thousand deals between 1995 and 2001, all worth more than $500 million, and found that almost two out of three—64 percent—lost money. On average, the acquiring firm overpaid by close to 10 percent.[19]

But do some kinds of acquisitions have a greater chance of success than others? A significant number—the other 36 percent—were profitable, and they turned out to have a few things in common. The buyer could identify clear and immediate gains, rather than pursuing vague or distant benefits. Also, the gains they expected came from cost savings rather than revenue growth. That's a crucial distinction, because costs are largely within our control, whereas revenues depend on customer behavior, which is typically beyond our direct control.

For an example of successful acquisitions that sought gains from cost savings, consider the string of deals carried out by Sandy Weill in the 1980s and 1990s, when he merged Commercial Credit with Primerica and then with Travelers. Each deal was aimed at finding cost synergies, usually by combining back office functions and consolidating operations, and each was successful. Later, when Weill engineered the 1999 merger of Travelers with Citibank, the outcome was different. This time the logic of acquisition depended on revenue gains through cross-selling of banking and insurance products; sadly for Citigroup, those gains never materialized. What had been intended as the crowning achievement of Sandy Weill's career turned out to be a deal too far.

As for circumstances in which it might make sense to attempt a risky acquisition, we need to consider the competitive context. We need to look at questions of relative performance and the intensity of rivalry. The amount a firm is willing to pay should reflect not only the direct costs and expected benefits, but broader considerations of competitive position. In 1988 the Swiss food giant, Nestlé, was willing to pay a high price to acquire English confectionary company Rowntree, maker of Kit-Kat and Smarties, not only because it saw a potential to create value, but also to make sure that Rowntree was *not* acquired by a rival Swiss chocolate company, Jacobs Suchard. Nestlé's offer of $4.5 billion reflected a calculation of gains achieved—revenue growth and cost savings—as well as strategic considerations, the latter of which could only be calculated in the most general terms. It preferred running the risk of making a Type I error—trying but failing—rather than a Type II—not trying at all.

To understand the dynamics of decision making in an acquisition, we need to do more than look at the overall (often poor) record of acquisition success, then cite the results of laboratory experiments like the nickel auction, and suggest one is due to the other. We also have to think about some of the elements we have discussed in previous chapters: control, relative performance, time, and leadership.

For that, let's take a close look at a real acquisition. Let's go back a few years and recall the bidding war for AT&T Wireless.

THE TEXAS SIZE SHOOT-OUT FOR AT&T WIRELESS

This story began in the autumn of 2003, when the US wireless industry was moving from a phase of rapid growth to one of price competition and consolidation. After years of generous profits, cell phone carriers were feeling the strain of declining profit margins. AT&T Wireless, spun off from AT&T Corporation in 2000, was among the worst hit, beset by technical problems and losing subscribers. Its share price had slipped all the way down to $7, barely half the level of one year earlier. Rivals were gaining ground.

The largest US carrier, Verizon Wireless, had 37.5 million customers from coast to coast. The number two carrier, Cingular, was a joint venture owned 60 percent by San Antonio–based SBC and 40 percent by Atlanta-based BellSouth. Cingular had 24 million customers and a strong regional position, but was seeking a national position.

The chief executive of SBC was Ed Whitacre, a six foot four Texan known as "Big Ed" who had climbed the ranks at Southwestern Bell, a regional carrier in the old Bell system. In 1996, when the Telecommunications Act opened local markets to competition, Whitacre was fast out of the gate, buying one rival after another. In 1997 Whitacre's company, now known as SBC, acquired Pacific Telesis for $16.5 billion, and the next year it added Southern New England Telecommunications Corp. for $4.4 billion. Whitacre's goal was to build the country's largest telecommunications company, offering both fixed and wireless services.[20] In 1999 SBC paid $62 billion for Ameritech Corp., the leading phone carrier in the Midwest.[21] In 2000 it teamed up with BellSouth to create Cingular, which soon became the number two wireless carrier behind Verizon Wireless.

In late 2003, as AT&T Wireless was struggling, Cingular sensed an opening. On January 17, 2004, it offered to buy AT&T Wireless for $11.25 a share. It was a nonbinding offer, little more than an opening gambit, but when the word got out shares of AT&T Wireless rose sharply. If Cingular was willing to pay $11.25, an eventual sale might go for more—maybe much more. Three days later the AT&T Wireless board formally decided to entertain offers from buyers. The auction would be handled by its banker, Merrill Lynch. Its law firm, Wachtell Lipton, was a specialist in mergers and acquisitions and had invented the "poison pill" defense. No one bought its clients on the cheap.[22]

For Cingular, the attraction was obvious. Adding AT&T Wireless's 22 million customers would give it a national position and vault it into first place. The cost savings could be massive. By combining operations and back office functions, Cingular might lower costs by $2 billion a year, maybe more.[23] An SBC executive commented, "This is the most strategic acquisition for Cingular with compelling synergies, and we are determined to be successful." Whitacre later explained: "There are only so many national licenses in existence, and they rarely become available for purchase. So when the 'For Sale' sign went up, *everybody* in the wireless world sat up and took notice. . . . For SBC to become a major player over the long term we needed a national footprint—a regional presence wasn't going to carry us. With the assets of AT&T Wireless in our back pocket, we'd instantly gain national standing and recognition. Without it, we'd always be a second-string player."[24]

But Cingular wouldn't be alone. The world's largest network operator, Vodafone, based in the United Kingdom, was also interested in buying AT&T Wireless, and if anything Vodafone had an even more audacious record of acquisitions. In 1999 it doubled in size by scooping up California-based AirTouch, gaining in the process a 45 percent minority share in Verizon Wireless. A year later it doubled again with the takeover of Mannesmann, the first hostile takeover in German industrial history, for a staggering €112 billion. Yet Vodafone was dissatisfied with its minority share in Verizon Wireless and was looking to build its own position in the United

States. The acquisition of AT&T Wireless would give Vodafone what it desperately wanted, and chief executive Arun Sarin indicated he was ready to bid. The *Wall Street Journal* described the looming contest between the two titans as "a Texas-size shootout."[25]

AT&T Wireless's banker, Merrill Lynch, used a number of ways to estimate its client's value and converged on a range between $9.00 and $12.50 per share.[26] In parallel, Cingular and Vodafone made their own calculations. Meeting privately, Vodafone's board approved a ceiling of $14, but hoped it could make the deal for much less. One industry analyst described the contest: "It is scale—Cingular, versus scope—Vodafone. Cingular is betting on cost synergies, particularly the opportunity to work on redundant infrastructure overhead, while Vodafone is betting on economies of scope, trying to apply the same aggressive recipe they have used in Europe to the US."[27] But of course anything can happen when executives get caught up in a bidding contest. The initial bids would be sealed, but after that the bidding would go back and forth, so that AT&T Wireless could secure the highest price possible.

Bids were due at 5:00 PM on Friday, February 13, 2004. They came in just after hours. Vodafone offered $13 a share, which valued AT&T Wireless at $35.45 billion. Moments later Cingular's bid arrived, offering just a bit less: $12.50 a share, for a value of $33.75 billion. Both parties proposed all-cash bids—no stock swaps, just cash. All of this was good news for AT&T Wireless on two counts. Both bids were above the range that Merrill Lynch had calculated, meaning that AT&T Wireless shareholders would receive a solid premium. Even better was that the bids were close to one another. With just fifty cents separating the bids, the process would go on, as one of the bankers explained to me, "until the seller is satisfied that the bidders have exhausted their ammunition."

On Saturday morning the AT&T Wireless board directed its bankers to seek "improvements in prices and terms," a polite way of saying it wanted more money. Merrill Lynch sent word to Cingular and Vodafone that a second round of bids was due the following day, at 11:00 AM on Sunday.[28] Now a protracted battle was shaping up among parties spread across Manhattan. The AT&T Wireless team, led by its president, John Zeglis, settled in at Wachtell Lipton's offices on 52nd Street. The Cingular team, led by Stan Sigman, set up a war room at the offices of SBC's lawyers in lower Manhattan. The Vodafone team dug in with its lawyers at 425 Lexington Avenue across from Grand Central Station, where it stayed in close contact with company headquarters in England.[29]

The next bids arrived on Sunday morning. Vodafone didn't know how much Cingular had bid, but had been told only that its offer of $13 wasn't enough. One of Vodafone's bankers explained to me: "The psychology was, we had to move up. If we didn't move up, the seller would get the sense we were maxed out. We were each eyeing the other, wanting to keep it moving." After some deliberation, Vodafone submitted a bid of $13.50, still under the board limit of $14. Meanwhile, Cingular executives decided it was time for a major push and upped their bid all the way to $14, for an astonishing sum of $38.2 billion.[30] Now Cingular was in the lead.

On Monday morning, the President's Day holiday, Merrill Lynch contacted Vodafone and said that Cingular had pulled ahead. Vodafone now raised its bid once again, to $14.[31] Although the bids were even, a tie worked in Vodafone's favor. A takeover by Cingular would likely raise antitrust concerns, which could delay the deal or block it altogether. Another reason was the impact on AT&T Wireless. Combining with Cingular could lead to significant layoffs, with AT&T Wireless employees likely to bear the brunt. Vodafone, on the other hand, would probably expand the business and add jobs. If the bids were tied, AT&T Wireless would go with Vodafone. The only question now was whether Cingular would raise its bid once again.

After lunch on Monday, AT&T Wireless board member Ralph Larsen called Cingular and Vodafone and read the same script: Best and Final Offers were due at 4:00 PM. Larsen wouldn't say who was in the lead. Cingular's Sigman later recalled: "They said, 'Just because you may have been in the lead before doesn't mean you are anymore.'"[32]

When the deadline came, Vodafone reaffirmed its bid of $14 but went no higher. It had reached its limit and wouldn't be drawn into a bidding war. Cingular didn't raise its bid, either, but added a provision aimed at one of AT&T Wireless's concerns: in the event the deal was held up by regulators, it would pay a 4 percent interest fee every month after ten months. A good attempt, but not enough to make a difference. Vodafone still held the advantage. A final decision was imminent.

At 7:00 PM AT&T Wireless chief executive John Zeglis reached Vodafone's Arun Sarin by telephone. It was midnight in London. Vodafone's bid was accepted, Zeglis said. All that was needed was approval of Vodafone's board, scheduled to meet the next morning.

As he monitored events from San Antonio, Ed Whitacre saw the deal was slipping away. He recalled, "In my mind, that was not acceptable. Wireless was the way of the future. Millions of new wireless customers were piling on by the quarter, with no signs of slowing. The mobile web was also showing a lot of promise. We simply could not afford to permanently relegate ourselves to second-tier status."[33]

Although AT&T Wireless had given a verbal acceptance to Vodafone's offer, the deal wasn't done until the Vodafone board gave its formal approval. Whitacre figured there was still a chance that AT&T Wireless could change its mind, provided it received a higher offer. At 9:00 PM he contacted Duane Ackerman, his counterpart at BellSouth. By now, all the numbers had been analyzed. There was no new information to consider. The only remaining question was this: How much of a risk were they willing to take? Was it worth taking an even bigger risk? Whitacre recalled the conversation as direct and blunt: "'There's only one of these things,' I told Duane. 'This is beachfront property, and once it's gone, it's gone.'"[34] They agreed to raise their bid to $15 a share, a full $1 more than what Vodafone had offered. A Cingular executive later recalled, "We thought we had a decent chance of winning at 4 o'clock, and when we didn't win, we wanted to end it. So we ended it. Winning was the only option."

Moments before midnight, Sigman called Zeglis at Wachtell Lipton offices and made the offer: Would AT&T Wireless accept $15 a share? That worked out to $41 billion, the largest cash deal in US history. One person recalled that the air seemed to go out of the room: "Everybody was like, 'Whoa.'"[35] Zeglis tried to keep a calm voice. Sure, we'll accept $15, he said, as long as the offer is signed and delivered by three in the morning. That would be 8:00 AM in London, when Vodafone's board planned to meet. Everything had to be settled by then.

With that, SBC and BellSouth called snap board meetings. Some directors were tracked down by cell phone and others were rousted out of bed. Polled by telephone, both boards approved the bid. Within minutes a detachment of bankers and lawyers, offer in hand, headed uptown to the offices of Wachtell Lipton on 52nd Street. At 2:00 AM, Zeglis recalled, "We had just finished our third pizza when Stan and his team brought over their piece of paper."[36] Zeglis checked the figures and signed on the line. The deal was done. Moments later he performed one last duty. Reaching Arun Sarin at Vodafone headquarters, Zeglis recalled, "I told him we went another way." Vodafone's celebratory announcement was quickly scrubbed.

HOW MUCH IS ENOUGH, HOW MUCH IS TOO MUCH?

The bidding war for AT&T Wireless had all the ingredients of great drama: a head-to-head duel between large companies, a record sum of money, and a surprise late-night ending. The press found the story irresistible. The headline in the *Financial Times* was typical: "Cingular grabs AT&T from sleeping Vodafone."[37] Cingular was seen as the winner, capturing the prize with a gutsy midnight move. Vodafone was portrayed as the loser, its failure to close the deal described as a "significant setback."[38]

Others saw it differently. The enormous sum of money smacked of the winner's curse. Surely Cingular had paid too much. The market was skeptical, too, sending shares of SBC and BellSouth lower, while shares of Vodafone rose.[39] That's normal. Investors have come to assume that winning bidders pay too much and routinely punish the shares of the buyer, while bidding upward the shares of a would-be buyer, relieved that they dodged a bullet.

But on closer inspection, both sets of executives made reasonable bets. Vodafone set a limit of $14 a share before the bidding began and stayed with that limit.[40] Far from getting caught up in the bidding war, it calculated the maximum it would pay and didn't get swept up by ego or emotion. Neither Arun Sarin nor his top team gave in to the psychology of the moment to try to get the Vodafone board to raise its limit.

As for Cingular, the last-minute decision to raise the stakes raised the specter of the winner's curse. Phrases like "winning was the only option" sound like bravado. As Whitacre later put it, he and Ackerman made a desperate effort to throw a touchdown pass and win the game. No question, alarm bells should sound when an executive justifies spending a record amount of money by reasoning that the opportunity is unique. Even beachfront property can be overvalued.[41]

We might conclude that Cingular fell victim to the winner's curse if this were a common value auction, but a corporate acquisition is different. It's a private value auction in which gains aren't captured at the time of the deal, but created over time. Furthermore, much of the value to Cingular would come from cost savings, a more predictable source of gain than revenues. There were also competitive considerations. Whitacre recalled: "There was only one AT&T Wireless, and we had exactly one shot to get it right."[42] That's not to say *any* price, no matter how high, would have been justified. Cingular was surely at the upper limits of what it could pay. The fact that Whitacre and Ackerman were trying to salvage a deal that had almost slipped away suggests they had already reached the limit they set for themselves. But if the choice was between spending $1 per share more to clinch the deal or letting AT&T Wireless get away, deciding to push ahead was not obviously wrong. The cost of a Type I error—at $15 a share, paying too much—was less onerous than the cost of a Type II error—failing to grasp the nettle and losing the bid. Whitacre saw it in precisely those terms: "The financial implications for SBC and BellSouth were not insignificant. But the downside to not winning AT&T Wireless could be devastating over the long term."[43] Long-term strategic considerations trumped short-term financial calculations.

There was, finally, the question of leadership. Whitacre had a reputation for bold moves. He was not known for shrinking from big deals, but for rallying his team to greater heights. Making a strong push to win this deal would reinforce his reputation as a leader. As Whitacre saw it, it was crucial to press ahead: "That, ultimately, is what builds enthusiasm and momentum within a company—the feeling that *By God, we're actually doing something here; this company is on the move; I can be proud of where I work.*"[44]

How did the acquisition of AT&T Wireless work out? Once the deal went through, Cingular moved quickly to capture combination benefits. Through concerted efforts at cost reduction, it more than achieved expected synergies. By 2006 those savings had reached $18 billion, 20 percent more than had been estimated at the time of the deal. There were strong revenue gains, too.[45] Overall, the acquisition of AT&T Wireless turned out to be profitable for Cingular. One of the bankers involved in the deal later told me, "At $15 [per share] the deal worked out fine for Cingular. They were the right buyer, and they created value."

And the story doesn't end there. The following year, in January 2005, Whitacre announced plans to acquire the rest of AT&T Corporation, the parent of AT&T Wireless. He was still determined to create a global leader, with powerful positions in both wireless and fixed line communications. In a surprising move, Whitacre took the name of the company he bought, calling the combined entity AT&T Inc., commenting, "While SBC was a great brand, AT&T was the right choice to position us as a premier global brand." The new AT&T became a market leader in wireless communication, with strong positions in DSL broadband lines, local access, and long distance lines.[46]

Even then, Whitacre wasn't finished. He next acquired Bell-South, his partner in the Cingular joint venture, bringing the entire network under his control. In January 2007 Cingular was rebranded as AT&T Wireless. Just three years after AT&T Wireless put itself up for sale, the AT&T brand was reborn, this time as the US market leader. As for Ed Whitacre, he was in charge of what

Fortune magazine in 2006 named "America's Most Admired Tele-communications Company." The record bid for AT&T Wireless in February 2004 had been an essential element of a winning strategy.[47] Looking back in 2013, Whitacre observed: "That deal cemented our place in the US wireless industry. It also changed the landscape of the industry for all time. I knew that going in, which was why I pushed so hard. And man, I want to tell you, we pushed that one about as far as you could push."[48]

By one definition, paying $15 per share for AT&T Wireless was an excessive bid. It surpassed what could be justified based on current calculations of costs and revenues. If the deal had failed to deliver value, Whitacre would surely have been castigated for hubris. Critics would have blamed the winner's curse. But $15 per share was *not* excessive given that AT&T Wireless offered benefits that were unique in the landscape of telecommunications, and once lost might be gone forever. Ed Whitacre understood that in a competitive arena, where managers can shape outcomes, the only way to succeed is to take calculated risks—not just risks that lend themselves to precise analysis, taken out to several decimal points, but risks that are understood in broad brush strokes. Only those willing to take large and even outsize risks will be in a position to win.

THINKING ABOUT COMPETITIVE BIDS

Many complex decisions involve competitive bids, whether tendering a low bid to win a contract or making a high bid to acquire a property or a company. For anyone engaged in competitive bidding, familiarity with the winner's curse is vital. You don't want to pay more than $2 for a roll of 40 nickels—certainly not when you have ready alternatives. You don't want to pay more than market value for a share of stock, thinking that you know something others don't.

Yet once again, we sometimes generalize the lessons from one situation without understanding important differences. Classroom demonstrations about the winner's curse are a good way to illustrate the perils of common value auctions, but we need to be careful when we apply them to private value auctions, let alone to situations in which we can influence value and performance is relative. Very different circumstances call for a different mind-set.[49]

So when are winners cursed? In simple experiments, the bidder who wins the prize is almost always cursed. The real winners are those who keep their wallets shut and refuse to be drawn into a bidding war. But in many real-world situations, the truth is more complex. When we can influence outcomes and drive gains, especially when the time horizon is long, we can and should bid beyond what is currently justified. And where competitive dynamics are crucial, it may be essential to do so. We must consider not only the dangers of paying too much—a Type I error—but also to the consequences of failing to push aggressively—a Type II error.

The real curse is to apply lessons blindly, without understanding how decisions differ. When we can exert control, when we must outperform rivals, when there are vital strategic considerations, the greater real danger is to fail to make a bold move. Acquisitions always involve uncertainty, and risks are often considerable. There's no formula to avoid the chance of losses. Wisdom calls for combining clear and detached thinking—properties of the left brain—with the willingness to take bold action—the hallmark of the right stuff.

STARTING UP, STEPPING OUT

THE WORLD THINKS OF STARTUP FOUNDERS AS HAVING SOME KIND OF SUPERHUMAN CONFIDENCE, BUT A LOT OF THEM WERE UNCERTAIN AT FIRST ABOUT STARTING A COMPANY. WHAT THEY WEREN'T UNCERTAIN ABOUT WAS MAKING SOMETHING GOOD—OR TRYING TO FIX SOMETHING BROKEN.

JESSICA LIVINGSTON, *FOUNDERS AT WORK: STORIES OF STARTUPS' EARLY DAYS*, 2008

The acquisition of AT&T Wireless stands at one extreme: buying an established company for a massive amount of money in the face of a firm deadline. At the other extreme is a very different kind of decision: starting a new business, often with very little money and with no particular deadline. Both, however, capture some of the complexities of making winning decisions in the real world.

From the perspective of decision making, new venture creation poses a puzzle. Many studies show that the great majority of new businesses fail. According to the US Small Business Administration, only 69 percent of businesses founded in 2000 survived for at least two years; the rest did not. After five years only 51 percent survived; almost half were out of business.[1] By seven years, only 20 percent were still in business; fully 80 percent were gone. This wasn't just a bad patch linked to the dot.com bubble, either. The survival rate for businesses founded ten years earlier, in 1990, was about the same.[2]

All of this poses the inevitable question: If most new ventures fail, why do people keep starting them? Economic theory offers a couple of explanations. Maybe enough new businesses succeed, and a few succeed so spectacularly, that starting one is still a good bet. In the language of economics, there's a *positive expected value*. But unfortunately most studies don't claim that a few large successes outweigh the many failures. The reason people keep starting new businesses must lie elsewhere.

A second explanation looks to something called *subjective expected utility*. The idea is that people don't make decisions based on financial returns alone. Entrepreneurs enjoy the thrill of starting a new business. They take satisfaction from running their own company and love to be their own boss. These nonfinancial benefits might be large enough to offset financial losses. In fact, according to this logic they *must* be, for otherwise rational individuals wouldn't keep founding businesses.[3] But this argument isn't very persuasive, either. The thrill of starting a business won't last long as the red ink piles up. Being your own boss wears thin when you're losing money. (It also smacks of a rationalization; anything at all can be explained as somehow maximizing subjective expected utility.)[4]

Decision research offers a different explanation. Why do people continue to start new ventures despite a low chance of success? Because of errors in judgment. Two biases stand out, and by now we know them well: overconfidence and the base rate bias. People often overestimate their abilities, thinking they're better than they really are, and they also overplace, believing themselves to be superior to others. They also disregard base rates and assume that the experience of others doesn't apply to them. They emphasize the optimistic inside view and dismiss the more realistic outside view. Take these two biases together, and it's no wonder that entrepreneurs launch new businesses despite the low chance of success.[5]

There's another appealing syllogism at work:

- Most new ventures fail.
- People suffer from cognitive biases.
- Therefore, new ventures fail due to cognitive biases.

Supporting this view is evidence from laboratory experiments. Colin Camerer and Dan Lovallo designed an experiment in which people could pay an entry fee to play a competitive game, with payoffs clearly posted. Although each subject could see how many others had already entered the game and could calculate at what point it made little sense to enter, many of them *still* paid the entry fee to play the game. They seemed to be saying, "I expect the average entrant to lose money, but not me!"[6] Each acted as if he could do better than the others, who also believed *they* could outperform the rest. Camerer and Lovallo concluded that people tend to be overly optimistic about their chances of success, displaying reference group neglect. This bias, they suggest, explains why people continue to start new businesses that so often fail.[7]

If biases are to blame for so many failed businesses, presumably aspiring entrepreneurs should be advised to guard against these errors and refrain from starting so many new businesses. No doubt some aspiring entrepreneurs do suffer from delusions of success, and some harebrained schemes that stand little chance of success should be discouraged. But curiously, for all the fuss made about new business failure, it's seldom suggested that the US economy suffers from an excess of new ventures, or that entrepreneurial activity is somehow destroying economic value. Indeed, other countries strive to emulate our record for new business creation. Of all the ills in American society—education, health care, crime, and so forth—the high rate of new venture creation is rarely mentioned. If anything, the vibrant climate for starting new companies is thought to be an asset of the US economy.

THE ROMANCE OF THE RECKLESS ENTREPRENEUR

How should we reconcile concerns about the high rate of entrepreneurial failure with a sense that overall it's good to have lots of start-ups? One way to square the circle is to suggest that even if most new businesses go bust, there's a spillover benefit for the economy at large. By this thinking, entrepreneurs are "optimistic martyrs" who sacrifice themselves for the greater good.[8] Overconfidence may be harmful at the individual level, but it serves as an engine of capitalism and benefits the economy as a whole.[9]

This notion is reflected in the widespread view that entrepreneurs are—in fact must be—a bit nutty. The title of a recent book sums it up: *You Need to Be a Little Crazy: The Truth About Starting and Growing Your Business.*[10] It's a variation of George Bernard Shaw's comment that all progress is due to unreasonable men. If entrepreneurs didn't suffer from delusions, they wouldn't attempt the innovations that are so important for the economy as a whole. There are many proponents of this view, including Michael Lewis, author of *Moneyball*:

> The job of an entrepreneur isn't to act prudently, to err on the side of caution. It's to err on the side of reckless ambition. It is to take the

risk that the market allows him to take. What distinguishes a robust market economy like ours from a less robust one like, say, France's, is that it encourages energetic, ambitious people to take a flier—and that they respond to that encouragement. It encourages nerve, and that is a beautiful thing."[11]

Note the words: entrepreneurship isn't about taking smart risks, but *reckless ambition*. Moreover, the resulting energy and ambition are a *beautiful thing*. Lewis goes on to suggest that if Jeff Bezos hadn't been willing to take outsize risks against all odds, Amazon.com wouldn't exist. We need more of this kind of beauty, not less.

Similarly, Martha Lane Fox, cofounder of Internet start-up lastminute.com, recalls that she had believed so passionately in the success of her venture that she used the words of her doubters—those who pointed out that success was highly unlikely—as a source of motivation:

> When you start a business, you have to have a blind faith that you can prove the critics wrong. If we had listened to the people who said it was rubbish, bankrupt, we'd have failed to get out of bed in the morning. So whether blindly, arrogantly, or whatever, we always thought we could make it work. . . . Anybody who starts their own business, you are going to constantly be told no, by people all along the whole journey, right from the word go. The first people we showed the business plan to, our parents, both said no one's going to give you money for this idea, you're crazy. You have to have that passion to carry you through it.[12]

Comments like these reflect the widely-held view that inordinate levels of confidence are necessary for success. Rather than warn would-be entrepreneurs about the dangers of overconfidence, we should celebrate people with the audacity to pursue their ambitions in the face of overwhelming odds. Sure, many will fail, but that's part of a healthy process of innovation and value creation. We're all better off because of their willingness to push beyond what's reasonable; society at large benefits from their *reckless ambition* and *arrogance*.

This is an appealing view, but it's not entirely accurate. In fact, it contains several errors.

We have already questioned the common view that overconfidence is a pervasive bias. We know it's not one thing but several. Some entrepreneurs probably *are* far too confident—perhaps wildly overestimating their chances of success—and would be well advised not to chase an impossible dream. Discouraging the least likely to succeed is a good thing. At the same time, a high degree of confidence is good for many entrepreneurs much of the time, especially when they can improve outcomes. Blaming failures on overconfidence is far too simple.[13]

So what explains the high rate of new business failure? On closer inspection, it's not even clear that most new businesses fail. The very premise is questionable to begin with. True, a majority shut their doors in less than five years, but let's be careful. If success means selling shares through an initial public offering, then less than 1 percent of all new ventures would be considered successful. Surely that cannot be the only yardstick. If, however, success means that a business closes with no debt, the rate of success after five years is much higher, estimated by some studies to be as high as 92 percent! If that seems surprising, bear in mind that small businesses cease operation for all sorts of reasons: family circumstances change, better opportunities arise, and so forth. Many companies close down but are able to pay their debts and even have something left over—perhaps even enough to start another business. One study found that one in four companies that closes down actually made a profit. The fact that many businesses don't last very long shouldn't be taken as proof that most new businesses fail.[14] Furthermore, many companies that end up in the red have losses that are quite modest, such that entrepreneurs state they would do it all again, which is not something we normally associate with failure. That's not just a rationalization either. Losses are often modest and don't pose a barrier to trying again.

It makes a good story to begin with the premise that most businesses fail, observe the presence of cognitive biases, and then claim that one is the result of the other. But this syllogism doesn't stand up to scrutiny. Even worse, by perpetuating the myth that cognitive biases are a major cause of failure, we divert our attention from understanding how entrepreneurs successfully manage risk, finding ways to take advantage of opportunities while limiting their losses.

STEPPING INTO THE CLOUD

For a good example of the launch of a new business, let's consider VMware. Today VMware is one of the leaders in the booming field of cloud computing. It has grown rapidly and earned healthy profits, but we shouldn't infer that everything it did was brilliant. Let's not make the mistake of selecting a winner and working backward. To the extent we can, we should try to set aside its eventual success and look at the decisions made during its early days.

The story of VMware began in the 1970s, when the computer landscape was dominated by powerful but expensive IBM mainframes. To offer its clients greater cost efficiency, IBM pioneered the practice of time sharing, which was eventually superseded by a software breakthrough called *virtualization*. Now a mainframe could be partitioned into multiple environments, each running a different operating system and application software. Multiple users shared a single computer, each one sensing that it had the use of the entire machine.[15]

By the 1990s improvements in microprocessor technology led to a shift away from IBM mainframes, toward networks of PCs and servers, most of which ran on a family of Intel chips known as x86. Unfortunately Intel had not designed those chips to accommodate virtualization. The reason was simple: no one imagined there would be such a need. At the time, PCs were small and inexpensive, and if a client wanted multiple computers it could easily afford them. However, as the power of PCs grew and companies began to rely on server networks, the same problems of underutilization and inefficiency that had plagued mainframes now extended to the x86.

At Stanford University, computer science professor Mendel Rosenblum and a team of graduate students had been studying virtualization by looking at the architecture of a machine built at Stanford called MIPS CPU. They wondered if they could also virtualize the x86 architecture. At first their interest was mainly theoretical. Rosenblum recalled: "We viewed it as a project. It was a challenge to do what people thought was impossible, to virtualize the x86. We had confidence that virtualization of the x86 could be useful. We didn't have a vision of exactly *how* it could be useful. One of the things we liked was that it was sufficiently different from what other people were doing that we had the space to ourselves."[16]

The prospect of virtualizing the x86 chips was exciting enough that Rosenblum took leave from his academic duties and began to work with two of his students, Ed Bugnion and Scott Devine. Rosenblum's wife, Diane Greene, was an experienced Silicon Valley entrepreneur and helped on the business end. She recommended they hire a fifth person, Ed Wang, a doctoral student they knew from Berkeley with industry experience. "When we were starting out, it was truly a research experiment," Rosenblum recalled. "We didn't know if we could pull it off. We thought we could get something that would run, but we feared it would be unacceptably slow, so it wouldn't be interesting. The question was whether we could get it to run fast enough to be interesting. That's what we set out to do."

The nascent venture incorporated in 1998 and faced many uncertainties. It wasn't clear their idea was technically feasible, and even if it was, no one knew if any new products would be commercially viable. Since they didn't know what a product would look like or what it would cost, they couldn't be sure if the potential market was large or small. Then there was the question of competition. In the event they could develop a successful product, there would surely be a strong response from established players, some of them rich and powerful, which could quickly sink their new business.

Given all the risks, many outside their control, they set up shop with a minimum of resources. They began with no outside funding, relying on their own funds and some contributions from friends. The operative phrase during this early phase was *fail fast*. If the new product wasn't going to work, they wanted to know quickly so they could call a halt and not waste lots of time and money. Accordingly, they stayed small, with just five employees, and kept costs to a minimum. Their first offices were in a modest suite above a cheese shop at the edge of a shopping plaza, hardly a hotbed of computer innovation.

Despite the many uncertainties, the founders were excited to undertake the challenge. One of them, Ed Bugnion, later explained to me:

> We were taking a leap into an area not imagined before. Even Intel people didn't think it was possible. The common knowl-

edge at Intel was that their architecture was not virtualizable. We took a contrarian point of view.

Our confidence was grounded in the fact that virtualization had been a dominating way of working in mainframes. So it was not a crazy new idea. It just seemed crazy to apply it to the x86.

There's no point doing something slightly different. You need to be extremely disruptive, need to be extremely "outside the box." As we started VMware, we started with a clean sheet of paper, a lot of confidence, not a lot of knowledge of the issues ahead of us, but we knew where the mountain was and what peaks were ahead of us.[17]

Mendel Rosenblum and Diane Greene instilled a belief that the team was on the cusp of an important breakthrough, and they were exactly the right people, with the right abilities and drive to pull it off. They might have been making a leap into the unknown, but they had confidence they could succeed. Bugnion commented: "Even in a small organization, you need to be able to rally people and give people confidence that we know what we're doing, we have a path, even though the details are murky."[18]

In the early days the VMware team ran into one technical problem after another. Days on end were spent at the screen, working out possible solutions. "It was very, very hard," Rosenblum recalled, then quickly added, "It was a fun time."[19] The most immediate hurdle was technical feasibility. They had to break their task into chunks and solve each one. A first goal was to virtualize the x86 for Windows 95. For weeks they worked long hours, with little progress. Eventually they succeeded in getting Windows 95 to boot using their new program, a process that took eight hours. That was far too slow to be commercially viable, but it was a start. They had shown that a solution was technically possible. Rosenblum recalled: "We knew how to do it, now we just had to go back and solve it to make it faster."[20]

From there, improvements were measured in faster speed, getting their program to run at 1/100 the speed of Windows 95, then at 1/30, and eventually at 1/10. It would only be commercially viable when it ran at the same speed. Getting there took many more weeks and months.

In time, they reached their goal thanks to two breakthroughs. First they devised a way to let a virtual machine monitor run on top of a host operating system. Next they created a way to virtualize x86 chips by combining an existing approach, called trap and emulate, with a new one they called dynamic binary translation. This innovation was "the spike in the punchbowl," the special ingredient that made it all work. For both, VMware owned the fundamental patents.

Within months they developed their first product, called VMware Workstation, designed to have a low barrier to deployment. It was expected to be a loss leader that would pave the way for a larger and eventually profitable enterprise product. To keep costs down, VMware relied on a "Web-only" route to market, avoiding the need for a sales force or channels of distribution. A sales force would be added only when revenues could justify the expense.

VMware Workstation was unveiled in February 1999 at the Demo 99 conference, where it drew rave reviews from technology writers. Customer demand was strong, and revenues surpassed expectations. Far from being a modest first product, VMware Workstation turned out to be a cash cow that funded VMware's activities for the next two years. During that time VMware continued to develop its product line. Soon it was able to hire additional employees, attracting engineers from other companies and new graduates from top schools. In 2003, with an expanded product line and rapidly growing revenues and profits, VMware was acquired by EMC for $635 million. Since then VMware has gone from strength to strength, and by 2012 it could claim that 97 percent of the *Fortune* Global 500 used its products for virtualization and cloud infrastructure.

It's easy to imagine in view of VMware's later growth that its success was inevitable. It's tempting to think that VMware did well because its founders were brilliant, or maybe a bit crazy. Those sorts of phrases make a satisfying story, but they really don't capture what happened at VMware. The truth is simpler but no less impressive. First, VMware's founders were smart to identify a problem that was difficult enough to discourage all but the best computer scientists, yet was not impossible to solve. They also picked one that had the potential to be commercially successful, although the size of the market was unclear. But they were hardly reckless or imbued with blind faith. They kept an eye on what was within their control: solving a technological problem while risking as little as possible in terms of funds. Had they been unable to solve the technical challenge—a very distinct possibility—they would have closed their doors. They would have been listed among the many small businesses that fail, but really would not have been a failure at all. They would have risked only what was affordable. The gamble they made had a large upside, but they made sure to keep the downside small. They were smart and they were fortunate, but above all they were wise.

MANAGING RISKS, SEEKING REWARDS

The approach taken by VMware is fairly typical of many new ventures. Starting a company isn't a one-time decision. Entrepreneurs don't just make a bet and hope they can defy the odds. Their job is to manage risk, which means controlling what they can and finding ways to grasp the gains while guarding against losses.

To learn more about the crucial decisions facing entrepreneurs, I met with Brad Mattson, a Silicon Valley veteran with twenty-five years in the semiconductor industry, as well as experience in venture capital. Today he's chief executive of Solexant, a thin film PV company that uses nanoparticle technology to bring down the cost of solar panels. Aside from running his company, one of Mattson's chief interests is to help a new generation of entrepreneurs. We met at Solexant's offices in Santa Clara, in one of the many low-slung buildings that stretch along the corridor of Highway 101, from San Jose to Redwood City. The names on the doors come and go, as ventures spring up and many fail, but as a whole the ecosystem remains vibrant and healthy.

Brad Mattson explained that starting a new business demands clear analysis with an ability to manage risk. "What I tell entrepreneurs is, 'Your job is risk management. If you can reduce or eliminate the key risk, you can succeed.'" New ventures face three kinds of risk: market, technical, and financial. Mattson commented: "The one I try to avoid is market risk. You can't control markets. You can't force customers to change. If your solution depends on the customer changing what they're doing, you're just adding risk."[21] It makes little sense to pursue a speculative market where demand doesn't already exist. Also beyond an entrepreneur's control are the actions of competitors and government policy.

Technical risk is a different matter. Not only is technology something we can influence, but improvements are very likely crucial for the new venture's success. Only with superior technology is there a chance to prevail. For this it was essential to take large risks. As Mattson put it: "You can't expect the market to adopt your product if it's 5 percent better; it needs to be 20 percent better." In a crowded market for new technology—whether semi-conductors or solar panels—only those who set their sights on very high performance will be in a position to succeed. It's very much what we saw earlier: when performance is relative and payoffs are highly skewed, an absolute advantage is necessary to achieve high relative performance.

The key to success is to set aggressive technical goals, then pursue them with confidence. The greatest danger is not to worry about an illusion of excessive control, but the reverse. It's to set sights too low. Mattson described one company that successfully created the product it set out to build, but failed as a business because the product wasn't ambitious enough. The company had reached its (absolute) target but ultimately collapsed because it fell short in relative terms. The moral: *"Don't fail because you succeed."*

Of course there is no point in attempting what is clearly impossible. "Don't try to invent *unobtanium*," was Brad Mattson's advice. "It can be demoralizing to find out something cannot be done." Yet he also said, "I've never yet been disappointed with a technical team, to be creative and to come up with amazing things."

Regarding the role of the leader in a start-up, with so many uncertainties it is essential to identify the critical success factors and provide a road map for success, and then to communicate it with confidence. Broad goals have to be broken into smaller goals, each of which is feasible. Mattson explained that the leader's job is to say, "There are the six to eight critical elements. If we do these things, we win. If you believe we can achieve these elements, then you can believe the total." Sounding much like Gene Kranz, Mattson commented that employees are constantly watching the boss. "They're reading your confidence of what's achievable. You have to have credibility."

The third kind of risk is financial. Raising money is only part of the challenge; spending it wisely is just as important. In his ventures, Mattson always tried to secure multiple sources of funds to avoid depending on just one. He sought funds from venture capitalists, from large companies that might want a stake in the technology, and sometimes from foreign investors. Just as crucial was spending money at the right time. Entrepreneurs often spend at the wrong time, either too soon or too late. "Don't spend lots of money in the first phase," Mattson warned, "because it doesn't help you. You have to know the technology linchpins. Those usually don't need lots of money. You *don't* need 200 people or large facilities. When we develop a technology, what we need is a small number of people." During the early phase it is vital to focus on the technical challenge while keeping costs down, very much the approach at VMware. Yes, some companies will be unable to develop the new technology and will go out of business, but if they have kept costs low, any losses will be small. Engineers will move on to other ventures, often better for the experience.

If the technical challenges can be solved and there is a viable product, the company enters a new phase. Now it is risky *not* to spend money. Many companies miss the transition point, Mattson said. Either they have too high a burn rate in the initial phase and run out of the money they'll need later, or else they're too slow to ramp up spending and fail to build a strong market presence. Managing a new venture is nothing like deciding to enter a game, with costs that are fixed and payoffs that are clearly stated. It's all about influencing outcomes to achieve success.

Even after a new venture is safely off the ground, success is not assured. The challenges facing a new business—exerting control over what we can, responding to what we cannot, while keeping an eye on competition—often continue for years. Many companies alter their products and adapt their business models in ways that would have been unimaginable at the outset.

In *Founders at Work*, Jessica Livingston reports that many entrepreneurs, far from exhibiting blind faith or bravado, were unsure their idea would succeed at all, much less produce a big hit. Evidence of overconfidence? Not at all. On the contrary, what characterized successful ventures was a willingness to keep at it, to improvise, and to adapt. As Livingston explains, rather than having superhuman confidence, many simply persisted and kept fixing what was broken. Managing a new venture often calls for a willingness to experiment, to try and see what works. Perseverance was crucial, she says, "not only because it takes a certain level of mental flexibility to understand what users want, but because the plan will probably change. People think startups grow out of some brilliant initial idea like a plant from a seed."[22] That view, so appealing to many, is wrong.

In fact, some of the best known high-tech companies began with entirely different products in mind. PayPal got its start writing encryption software and only later found an application in online payments. Excite started as a database search company, and Flickr began as an online game.[23] The same has often been the case for companies in traditional industries. It's not accurate to say that their initial efforts *failed*; rather, those early efforts opened doors that led in unexpected directions. Successful new ventures are less often those that insist on following a set vision or executing a precise business plan. They do well because they are able to adapt, learning from feedback to find new opportunities.

ANOTHER LOOK AT LABORATORY EVIDENCE

So far, we've called into question the common view that new venture failure is due to common decision errors. Not only should we question the premise that most new ventures fail, but many entrepreneurs are more adaptable, and less biased, than often imagined.

What, then, of the laboratory evidence mentioned above, that found a link between cognitive biases and excess entry?

That study was carefully devised to isolate a handful of variables, but in the process imposed a number of crucial constraints. It informed all players of a payoff distribution that was fixed and could not be changed. There was no way to change either the total payoff or the way it would be distributed. There was a clear end point. The number of competitors was visible to all. Finally, the entry fee was fixed and could not be changed.

Managing a new business, of course, is different on all counts. There's no fixed amount of profits to be distributed, nor is there a precise end-point when profits will be handed out. In fact, profits aren't distributed but created—and the better we perform, the more value we can create. Nor did this experiment allow players to influence one of the most basic factors of all—their costs. They had to pay a fixed fee to enter, with no way to lower or delay those costs. The result is an elegantly crafted experiment with statistically significant findings, but which does not provide a valid explanation of the phenomenon of interest, namely an entrepreneur's decision to start a business.

And there's more. In the aforementioned experiment, high performance came from doing well in a trivia contest about general knowledge or sports. That's significant because, as we saw in Chapter Five, people tend to overplace for easy tasks (like driving) but underplace for hard tasks (like drawing). A trivia contest is likely to appear easy, leading many people to think they will outperform rivals. No wonder they tended to enter in excess numbers.

What would happen if the contest was perceived to be very difficult? Would we still observe excess entry? To answer this question, a trio of researchers—Don Moore, John Oesch, and Charlene Zietsma—ran a similar experiment, but with one crucial difference: some industries were described as relatively easy, in which many companies could succeed, whereas others were said to be very difficult, with few likely to succeed. Their findings? In "easy" industries there was evidence of excess entry, as people imagined they would do very well and entered in large numbers. In "difficult" industries the reverse occurred. Now people imagined they would be *unlikely* to succeed, and fewer decided to play. Moore and his colleagues commented: "Contrary to the conclusions of some entrepreneurship researchers, our findings imply that entrepreneurs are not universally overconfident. . . . Entry decisions result from an information search that relies too heavily on the most easily accessible data: information about one's own and one's firm's capabilities. This tendency can lead to excess entry in some markets and insufficient entry in others."[24]

When we think about new venture failure, the examples that come to mind are in industries that are easy to enter, like restaurants, retail shops, and beauty salons. Capital costs are low, and there's little need for intellectual property. Many people think they have the skills to succeed and don't appreciate that other people have just as much chance as they do. We should expect to find excess entry in those industries, and we do.

In other industries success seems more difficult. Innovation is unpredictable, capital costs are high, and customer preferences change rapidly. Here, people may exaggerate the difficulties they expect to face and be reluctant to try their hand at a new business. Far from excess entry, the greater problem may be *insufficient* entry.

Once again a balanced experimental design is essential: balanced experiments lead to questionable conclusions.

THINKING ABOUT NEW VENTURES

Starting a new venture doesn't often grab headlines in the same way a multi-billion-dollar acquisition will, yet if we add up the numbers of all people involved in new venture creation, the total economic activity involved is vast. It is vital to understand how people make decisions to start and grow companies. Unfortunately, this process is often misunderstood. It's easy to look at the (alleged) high rate of start-up failure, connect that to (sometimes exaggerated) evidence of biases, and suggest that one is explained by the other. We can even construct laboratory simulations to provide supporting evidence.

Managing a new venture is not a one-time decision to enter a game costs and payoffs are known. It's nothing like buying a lottery ticket, in which the odds are against you and you can't influence outcomes.

People may suffer from an illusion of control when it comes to throwing dice or picking a lottery ticket, but as we saw with VMware, starting and managing a business is an entirely different matter. Managers can and do influence outcomes, not just once but repeatedly. They adjust and modify, sometimes shifting directions entirely, as they seek the upside while also limiting their losses.[25] As Saras Sarasvathy of the University of Virginia notes, "Entrepreneurs can mold, shape, transform and reconstitute current realities, including their own limited resources, into new opportunities."[26] These terms—*mold*, *shape*, *transform*, and *reconstitute*—all speak to the ability to exercise control. Far from suffering from an illusion of excessive control, we may fail to appreciate the control we have and underestimate our ability to shape and transform.

Starting a new business involves many of the same elements we have seen in other winning decisions: an ability to distinguish between what we can control and what we cannot; a sense of relative performance and the need to do better than rivals; the temporal dimension, in which decisions do not always produce immediate feedback; and an awareness that decisions are made in a social context, in which leaders sometimes need to inspire others to go beyond what may seem possible. Together, these elements help new ventures get off to a winning start

THE STUFF OF   12
WINNING DECISIONS

REVERE YOUR POWER OF JUDGMENT. ALL RESTS ON THIS TO MAKE
SURE THAT YOUR DIRECTING MIND NO LONGER ENTERTAINS ANY
JUDGMENT WHICH FAILS TO AGREE WITH THE NATURE OR CONSTI-
TUTION OF A RATIONAL BEING. AND THIS STATE GUARANTEES DE-
LIBERATE THOUGHT, AFFINITY WITH OTHER MEN, AND OBEDIENCE
TO THE GODS.

MARCUS AURELIUS, *MEDITATIONS*, BOOK 3.9

This book began with the story of Bill Flemming and his team at
Skanska USA Building deciding how much to bid for the Utah
Data Center. If they got it right, the prospects were bright; but if
they got it wrong, the results could be very costly.

On the night of August 12, 2010, after intense deliberations,
Flemming settled on a bid of $1.2107 billion, just $1.3 million under
the government's limit of $1.212 billion. "We had been struggling to
get to the number," he recalled, "but we did it. We felt good."

Five weeks later, on September 25, the Army Corps of Engineers
announced its decision: the UDC contract was awarded to a three-
way joint venture of DPR Construction, Balfour Beatty, and Big D

Construction. Their winning bid of $1.199 billion was about $12 million lower than Skanska's figure. A difference of just 1 percent, but enough to win the contract.[1]

At Skanska USA Building the news was met with deep disappointment. Months of work had been for naught. Skanska executives wondered what they might have done differently. Could they—*should they*—have lowered their bid by even more? Had they lost their nerve? Or had they simply been beaten by a rival with lower costs and a more efficient design? In that case, perhaps they had been wise to go no lower. It was difficult to know for sure.

After some reflection, Flemming said he had no regrets: "I don't think we missed anything, or that we could have taken a bigger chance. I felt we took as much risk as we could have. Maybe we could have found another $5 or $6 million, but never enough to get to [the] low bid. I said to my guys, 'If I had to find another $12 million, I don't think I could have gotten there.' We were struggling to get to the price we put in. We did a great job, but they were lower by $12 million." There was at least one silver lining: even without the UDC contract, Skanska USA Building posted excellent results for 2010, and 2011 looked strong, too.

Of course, to understand any competition we should consider more than one side of the story. Skanska USA Building's bid was good enough in absolute terms—it met the government's target—but came up short in relative terms. To learn more, I contacted one of the winners, DPR. How had *they* approached the same decision? Had they won because their costs were truly lower than Skanska's, or had they simply been willing to take a greater risk?

Some months later I visited DPR at its offices in Redwood City, California. DPR is a highly regarded construction company, with many schools, hospitals, and corporate offices to its credit. It's also one of the top technical builders in the country, having completed numerous data centers, including Facebook's immense complexes in Oregon and North Carolina. The following year, Facebook chose DPR to build its first European data center, in Sweden.[2]

I spoke with two executives who had been closely involved in the UDC bid process: David Ibarra, in charge of mission critical projects, and Gavin Keith, who oversaw the bid. Ibarra and Keith described a process that was similar in many ways to what I had heard at Skanska. When the NSA had first announced the UDC in the summer of 2009, DPR had been very eager. It had the experience and skills to make a strong bid. It had been one of twelve to submit an RFQ in February, and one of five invited to bid. From there, it assembled a strong team to prepare a winning proposal. Its first bid, in June 2010, was around $1.4 billion.

When DPR was given the NSA's new target of $1.212 billion, it devoted long hours to reach that limit. It worked with its subcontract partners to reduce costs. It went over the design in excruciating detail, looking for ways to simplify wherever possible while still meeting the technical specifications. Like Skanska, DPR reduced its risk contingency and looked for ways to shave its management fees. It was a very arduous process. By late July the company had made important progress, but still had further to go. Gavin Keith told me: "We had already pushed and cajoled our subcontractors. We had reduced our margins to a very tight number. And we were still over the number."[3]

By early August DPR's bid stood at $1.227 billion, now very close but still about $11 million over the target. At that point DPR also considered the likely bids of its rivals. Barely squeezing in under the limit wouldn't be enough; it wanted to make sure it would come in below the others. Keith recalled: "We wanted to be at 1.198.* That

---

* DPR's bid was $1,198,950,000. I rounded it to $1.199 on the previous page, although DPR referred to it in our interviews as $1.198.

wasn't scientific but strategic. We needed a bit of room off the 1.212." The desire to get to $1.198 billion was, as he put it, "a gut feeling based on experience." It was important to anticipate competitor moves and not lose at the finish line.

Reducing the bid to $1.198 billion would call for another $23 million in savings—$10 million to reach the target and another $13 million to provide a cushion. Where those savings would come from wasn't clear, but there were many possibilities. Gavin Keith described a methodical process: "We listed 10 or 12 things that might happen, and wrote them on white boards. We figured: maybe we'll buy better, or we'll design better, and so on. If some of these break our way, we'll recover our margin. . . . It's not an exact science. We knew we couldn't reduce by 30 million. Even 23 [million] was uncomfortable. We pushed the envelope, not like cowboys, but you have to push your comfort level."

During the course of the project, the joint venture team—DPR, Balfour Beatty, and Big D, working closely with their subcontractors—spent extensive time conducting a careful and objective analysis. Twenty-hour work days were common in the closing stretch. Eventually, satisfied that some combination of elements should let them find $23 million in further savings, they submitted a bid of $1,198,950,000. Even then they were far from certain of winning. "We were all nervous," Ibarra recalled. "We felt we had complied with everything and not left anything out. Still we felt jitters. We wondered if we had missed something."

In September, when DPR learned it had won, its first reaction was elation. Very soon that gave way to the sober realization of the immense task ahead. Quickly DPR moved on to the next phase. In January 2011 ground was broken at Camp Williams. Over the next two years construction proceeded on schedule, although not without challenges. By 2013 the project was on track and meeting its milestones for completion.

How did DPR's joint venture win the bid? What allowed it to come in $12 million lower than Skanska USA Building? One explanation is that DPR's experience with data centers gave it a slightly lower cost base. Furthermore, Balfour Beatty's successful experience with Army Corp of Engineers projects was vital in addressing key government requirements, and Big D, a Salt Lake City contractor, brought valuable insights about the local labor market. Together, these advantages provided a crucial edge, and allowed them to enter August needing only $10 million in further savings to reach the target, compared to $48 million for Skanska. That gap of $38 million would eventually make all the difference.

That's one view, but it's not shared by everyone. Another possibility is that DPR and its partners simply pushed a bit harder to win. They were willing to take more risk than Skanska was. Whether they will eventually earn a profit on the UDC or will fall short remains an open question and underscores the uncertainties inherent in large competitive bids, in which capabilities can improve and projects play out over years. Definitive explanations elude us; an element of uncertainty remains.

For our purposes, however, more important than the differences were the similarities in the ways that managers at Skanska USA Building and DPR approached a high-stakes decision. Describing the process, Bill Flemming had commented: "There's no science here. It's gut feel." Gavin Keith used a nearly identical term, noting that bidding was not "an exact science" but a "gut feeling based on experience." They're right, if by science we mean a precise way to calculate the correct figure. No formula, however carefully devised, could provide an answer that would lead to success every time. That's not the nature of decisions like this.

Yet neither did they make a blue sky guess, in which one number was as good as another. At Skanska a great deal of time and effort was devoted to careful and objective analysis. There was much to admire about the way Flemming and his team approached their task. They tried to separate what they could control from what they could not. They didn't get carried away with the optimistic inside view, but gave explicit consideration to the outside view. Flemming had learned that for a large project, another 3 percent in cost reductions was realistic, but expecting more was doubtful. At the same time, he knew that success comes to those who are willing to take a chance. He was prepared to make a bid that went beyond what could presently be justified. The ultimate bid was at the outside limit of what could reasonably be expected, but not beyond that. Flemming was also keenly aware of his role as a leader. He understood how his decision would reflect on him and his company, and he wanted to be seen as aggressive but not reckless, exhibiting healthy optimism not foolish optimism. Finally, he thought about the relative implications of Type I and Type II errors. Given Skanska USA Building's current performance, winning the UDC contract was desirable but not essential. It was better to make a strong effort but come up short than to take an outsize risk and lose money. That's why, although Skanska USA Building didn't prevail, there was no reason for regret. Flemming had pushed as far as was reasonable, but he knew his limits.

At DPR, too, David Ibarra and Gavin Keith conducted an exhaustive analysis over many months. They worked hard to minimize costs while meeting all technical standards. They looked to past experience to project future cost reductions. They gave explicit consideration to the way rivals were likely to bid and estimated (correctly, as it turned out) what it would take to win. They did their best to carry out a dispassionate analysis, but also saw the need to go beyond what was comfortable. DPR exhibited a combination of analysis and action, of calculation and courage, of left brain and right stuff.

BEYOND RATIONAL AND IRRATIONAL

At one level, the story of the Utah Data Center is a suspenseful tale, with several companies going down to the wire on a hot August night. At another level, it offers insights about the way managers approach complex decisions.

From the days of Adam Smith, economic theory has rested on a cornerstone belief in rational behavior. Human beings were assumed to make consistent decisions given their best interests. In the language of economics, consumers optimized their utility, producers maximized their profits, and the invisible hand of the free market worked effortlessly to allocate resources in the best way.

In the 1970s and 1980s, a series of path-breaking experiments, many of them ingenious in their simplicity, revealed that people often make judgments and choices in ways that run counter to the tenets of rationality. These were momentous findings that shook economic theory to its core. Yet to reach the other extreme, and to conclude that people are somehow *irrational*, is not quite right, either. As Daniel Kahneman has noted: "Irrational is a strong word, which connotes impulsivity, emotionality, and a stubborn resistance to reasonable argument. I often cringe when my work with Amos [Tversky] is credited with demonstrating that human choices are irrational, when in fact our research only showed that Humans are not well described by the rational-agent model."[3]

Some years ago, I attended a talk by another Nobel Prize–winning economist, George Stigler. It was 1987, the age of *perestroika* and *glasnost*, when Mikhail Gorbachev was leading the Soviet Union in a new direction. During the question-and-answer period, a member of the audience asked if Stigler thought the Soviets were rational. Stigler just shrugged. "Sure," he said. "If they want to go north, do they take out a compass and go south?" To Stigler, it wasn't a terribly interesting question. You may disagree with their motives and disapprove of their methods, he implied, but to dismiss the Soviets as irrational wasn't very helpful. I agree. Rather than use binary terms—rational or irrational—we would do better to employ Herbert Simon's phrase and recognize that people have *bounded rationality*. They may intend to be rational, and much of the time they meet the standards of rationality, but their abilities are limited. More accurate is to conclude that people often display systematic errors of judgment, or *biases*, a word with fewer negative connotations.[5]

By now a long and growing list of books has described many of the biases that affect our decisions. We have been told that our intuitions deceive us, that we suffer from blind spots, that we're predictably irrational, that we're not so smart, that we should learn the art of thinking clearly, and so forth. The appeal of such books is understandable. It's fascinating to read about common errors, and sobering to acknowledge that we, too, exhibit those same tendencies. It's useful to be aware when we're entering a cognitive minefield, and it makes good sense to look for ways to reduce the likelihood of error.

In many fields the contributions of decision research have been significant. But as noted, in other fields people seem not to heed the lessons. Business executives in particular seem not to have embraced the view that they suffer from common biases. In a recent article for the *McKinsey Quarterly*, "The Case for Behavioral Strategy," business professor Dan Lovallo and McKinsey director Olivier Sibony make this very point:

Once heretical, behavioral economics is now mainstream. Money managers employ its insights about the limits of rationality in understanding investor behavior. Policy makers use behavioral principles to boost participation in retirement savings plans. Marketers now understand why some promotions entice consumers and others don't. . . . Yet very few corporate strategists making important decisions consciously take into account the cognitive biases—systematic tendencies to deviate from rational calculations—revealed by behavioral economics."[6]

Lovallo and Sibony therefore urge managers to make a concerted effort to apply the lessons of behavioral research. They suggest that before making big decisions, corporate strategists should consider a range of biases and try to avoid them.

Yet if repeated admonitions have not been effective, we might wonder if one more attempt will make a difference. I suspect the answer is no.[7]

What's missing is the recognition that strategic decisions are fundamentally different from most decisions made by many managers, policy makers or marketers. Strategic decisions don't involve choices from a fixed set of options that cannot be altered, but allow us to influence outcomes. They aren't primarily about absolute performance, but usually involve a competitive dimension requiring that we do better than rivals. Strategic decisions are not made by individuals acting alone, but are taken by executives acting within an organizational setting, who must mobilize others to achieve goals. Take these points together, and we shouldn't be surprised that corporate strategists seem not to heed the lessons of decision research. Those lessons have not been adapted to address the realities that strategic decision makers face.

As a case in point, consider one of the most recent books about decision making, *Decisive: How to Make Better Choices in Life and*

Work, by Chip Heath and Dan Heath. Drawing on research that is by now well known, the authors recommend a four-step process to make better decisions: search for more alternatives, avoid the confirmation trap when evaluating alternatives, remove emotion, and avoid overconfidence.[8] That's a sound approach for many kinds of decisions, but it stops short of capturing the essential qualities of many complex decisions. In fact, it's largely notable for what it is missing. There's little sense that leaders in organizations face a different set of dynamics than individuals acting alone. There's little mention of competition, and no sense of the need to take risks in order to outperform rivals when payoffs are highly skewed. Perhaps most serious, they give little consideration to our ability to influence outcomes, in which case confidence is necessary for success. For all the attention that has been paid to avoiding common biases, much less effort has been spent on identifying how decisions differ, and how the lessons that make sense for some kinds of decisions are less relevant or even beside the point for others.

BETTER QUESTIONS FOR WINNING DECISIONS

In the opening chapter, I described a classroom episode in which a professor asked executives to provide ranges that they were 90 percent confident contained the correct figure. When the answers were revealed, and it was shown (yet again) that the ranges were far too narrow, the professor declared: "You see? You're overconfident!" And by extension: "You should avoid overconfidence to make better business decisions."

By now we know that this conclusion is flawed, and in more than one respect. At best the experiment provided evidence of overprecision, but said nothing about overestimation or overplacement. It hardly justifies the claim that people are overconfident. Moreover, judgments about things we cannot influence, made by individuals unconcerned with relative performance, are a world away from what business executives often face: judgments about things they *can* influence, and where they have to outperform rivals, made in an explicitly organizational setting.

Imploring a group of executives with a simple classroom demonstration may be good theater, but it tells us little about decisions in real-world settings. If anything, it distracts us from reaching a deeper level of understanding about what is really needed to make winning decisions.

In the opening chapter, I quoted Richard Feynman about the importance of asking questions. His example about the miracle at Lourdes was a humorous way to make a serious point: that any proposition, even one based on the existence of divine powers, can and should be investigated. The same logic applies here.

To make great decisions, we need above all to develop the capacity to question, to go beyond first-order observations and pose incisive second-order questions. An awareness of common errors and cognitive biases is only a start. Beyond that, we should ask:

Are we making a decision about something we cannot control, or are we able to influence outcomes? Often we have studied the way people make choices from options they cannot alter and judgments about things they cannot change. That's a fine way to isolate a single moment in time, as if captured by a strobe light. But many decisions—including some of the most important of all—are not choices made at a single moment in time. Furthermore, far from suffering from an illusion of excessive control, we often err in the other direction: we underestimate the amount of control we truly have. Overall, we're often better off acting as if we can effect change, rather than accepting that we cannot.

Are we seeking an absolute level of performance, or is performance relative? Do we need to do better than rivals, who themselves are trying to do better than us? If the latter, can we determine the way payoffs are distributed? Are they highly skewed or perhaps even winner-take-all? The level of risk we take will vary depending on answers to these questions. Furthermore, does competition have a clear end point, or is it open ended? Taking all of this into consideration, is it better to aim high and seek the aspiration point? Or is it better to play it safe and aim at the survival point, so we can stay in the game and try to do better in the future?

Are we making a decision that lends itself to rapid feedback, so we can make adjustments and improve a next effort? If so, the technique of deliberate practice can be a useful way to gain expertise. Or are we making a unique decision, or one the results of which will take longer to be known? In such a case, the benefits of deliberate practice are not available. The imperative may be to make sure this decision is sound, because there's little chance to make adjustments and improve for a next time.

Are we making a decision as an individual or as a leader in a social setting? Much of what has been studied looks at individuals, whether consumers or investors or voters. Decisions by leaders, by contrast, impose many additional complexities. Questions of consistency, reputation, and fairness are important. Furthermore, because leaders at times need to help others achieve more than is objectively justified, a series of questions arise. How should we reconcile the desire for transparency with the need to inspire others? How can we balance authenticity and sincerity? For all we know about decisions made by individuals, we face additional complications when it comes to decisions made by leaders.

Are we clear what we mean by overconfidence? The term is often used without sufficient clarity. Do we mean a level of confidence that seems to have been excessive given how things turned out? That's the most common usage, very often found in our everyday conversations and in the press, but it's problematic. Inferring overconfidence based on outcomes is little more than an ex-post rationalization. Or do we mean a level of confidence that's excessive based on some objective criteria, measured in the here and now? That's a step in the right direction, and is the way much decision research has used the term, but do we mean overprecision, overestimation, or overplacement? They are very different things, and evidence of one cannot be taken as evidence of another. As a third option, do we mean excessive confidence given competitive circumstances? When performance is relative and we have to do better than rivals, an elevated level of confidence may be necessary for success. At present, a single word is used to mean several entirely different things—and most people don't even know it. Anyone using the word *overconfidence* should have to indicate the point of comparison: *excessive compared to what?* Otherwise we run the risk, as George Orwell put it, that slovenly language leads to foolish thoughts.

Have we given careful thought to base rates, whether of the larger population at a point in time or historical rates of past events? We know that people often overlook information about the broader population and tend not to have an intuitive grasp of conditional probabilities, so an awareness of the base rate bias is useful. Just as important, however, is the ability to ask useful second-order questions. Where do base rates come from? Are they readily available, and if so, from a reliable source? Or must they be found? Next, are they steady over time or subject to change? If the latter, what causes them to change? Are we able to change them through our efforts? Furthermore, if we seek to go beyond what has been done before, can we break down a seemingly daunting base rate into components, each of which may be tractable? If so, what may seem impossible can sometimes be broken into manageable parts. Awareness of the tendancy to overlook base rates is only a first step. Thinking about them clearly, and recognizing how we can change them or overcome them is vital, too.

As for decision models, are we aware of their limits as well as strengths? Models can be very useful to overcome common biases and analyze large amounts of data, and they are becoming much more powerful and more widely used. That's all for the good. In our desire to embrace models, however, we have sometimes overlooked fundamental questions. Are we trying to predict things that are out of our control, or can we nudge the course of events? Do we recognize the third category of indirect influence, in which the findings of our model can indirectly change behavior? Decision models are a way to be smart, but even more important is to use them wisely.

When the best course of action remains uncertain, do we have a sense of on which side we should err? Is it better to commit a Type I error and take action, even if we may be wrong? Or are we better off not to act and run the risk of a Type II error? Toward the end of *Risk Taking: A Managerial Perspective*, Zur Shapira counsels: "It might be preferable to have managers imagine (sometimes falsely) that they can control their fates, rather than suffer the consequences of imagining (sometimes falsely) that they cannot."[9] When we recognize that management typically combines an ability to influence outcomes with a need to outperform rivals, we understand why this statement is correct. Not only *might* it be preferable to err on the side of action; as a general rule it is. In much of life, in management but also in so many other settings, the greater danger is not that we suffer from an illusion of excessive control, but that we fail to take action. A desire to reduce errors of one kind leads us to commit others that are potentially more serious.

In his profile of longtime St. Louis Cardinals manager Tony LaRussa, Buzz Bissinger wrote that a baseball manager requires "the combination of skills essential to the trade: part tactician, part psychologist, part river-boat gambler."[10] That's a good description for many kinds of strategic decision makers. The tactician plays a competitive game, anticipating the way a given move may lead to a countermove and planning the best response. The psychologist knows how to shape outcomes by inspiring others, perhaps by setting goals or by offering encouragement or maybe with direct criticism. The riverboat gambler knows that outcomes aren't just a matter of cold numbers and probabilities, but that it's important to read an opponent so as to know when to raise the stakes, when to bluff, and when to fold.

Winning decisions call for a combination of skills as well as the ability to shift among them. We may need to act first as a psychologist, then as a tactician, next as a riverboat gambler, and perhaps once again as a psychologist. In the real world, where we have to respond to challenges as they arise, one skill or another is insufficient; versatility is crucial.

Even then success is never assured, not in the competitive arenas of business or sports or politics. Performance is often relative and consequences of failure are harsh. A better understanding of decision making, however, and an appreciation for the role of analysis as well as action, can improve the odds of success. It can help us win.

ACKNOWLEDGMENTS

I am grateful to several colleagues who read this manuscript at various stages of development, and who generously offered their insights and comments. My greatest thanks go to Stuart Read, colleague and friend, for his steady encouragement and many incisive contributions. Thanks also to Joe Distefano, Enid Thompson, Michael Mauboussin, Zur Shapira, Paul Strebel, and Sunil Prabhune for reading and providing feedback. Pam Friedman and Michael Raynor read early versions of the manuscript and offered valuable comments.

This book has sought to extend the findings of cognitive psychologists into the world of management and leadership. Like so many others, I owe a great debt to Daniel Kahneman and Amos Tversky for their path-breaking work in the field of judgment and choice. I first encountered their work while a doctoral student at the University of Pennsylvania in 1986, and it has been a source of inspiration ever since. More recently, I have benefited greatly from discussions with Don Moore, first on the topic of overconfidence, and then regarding topics ranging from the illusion of control to new market entry.

Several people shared their personal experiences. Special thanks to Bill Flemming, Richard Kennedy, Bob Luckey, and Mike McNally at Skanska USA Building, and to David Ibarra and Gavin Keith at DPR, for their recollections about the Utah Data Center bidding process. My thanks, as well, to Edouard Bugnion and Mendel Rosenblum for their descriptions of VMware's early days, and to Brad Mattson for his insights on managing start-ups. I was fortunate to interview one of the bankers involved in the Cingular and Vodafone bidding for AT&T Wireless; he wished to remain unnamed, but my thanks are noted here. I'm grateful to Doug Glanville for his views about performance in baseball, and especially appreciative to Gene Kranz for answering my questions about Apollo 13.

My sister Suzanne Washburn offered comments on an early draft, and in the subsequent months never stopped asking how the book was coming along. My nephews made contributions that reflected their areas of expertise: David Washburn about cycling, gambling, and the mathematics of probability, and Greg Washburn about acting, sales, and the psychology of high performance.

For the past six years, I've had the privilege of directing IMD's Executive MBA Program. Several students provided expertise on technical matters: Frederik Smidth and Alexandre Grêt about petroleum drilling and extraction, Mads Dalsgaard about medical base rates, Stig Fjærli and Ragnvald Nærø about peak athletic performance, and John-Erik Horn about cloud computing. Kalev Reiljan and Greg Stark took particular interest in this project, and many others were supportive as well. They are far too numerous to mention individually but each class deserves recognition. My heartfelt thanks to the IMD classes of 2009, 2010, 2011, 2012, and 2013, and my best wishes for every success to each and every one.

Numerous colleagues at IMD helped in important ways. Thanks to Michael Sorell and Paul Bassett for running the Monte Carlo simulations described in Chapters Four and Ten, to William Milner for conducting searches on the use of overconfidence, to Sophie Pedgrift for gathering and tabulating data on decision surveys, to Matt Simmons for suggesting relevant articles, and to Patrick Saudan for printing copies of this work as it took shape. My thanks, as well, to the EMBA Program staff: Sophie Coughlan, Catherine Egli, and Rahel Mesple.

I owe a great deal to IMD faculty colleagues with related interests, notably Stuart Read, Arturo Bris, Didier Cossin, Albrecht Enders, and Stefan Michel. That this group includes people from five nationalities—American, Spanish, French, German, and Swiss, respectively—is a reflection of what makes IMD such a great place.

My agent, Max Brockman, was supportive of this project and worked hard on its behalf. At PublicAffairs, I extend warm thanks to John Mahaney for his many valuable ideas and comments, and to Melissa Raymond, Rachel King, Pauline Brown, and Sharon Langworthy for copyediting and production. At Profile Books, Daniel Crewe was highly supportive and also provided many helpful comments.

Most importantly I wish to thank my wife, Laura, and our children, Tom and Caroline, whose support and patience has been so greatly appreciated.

FOR FURTHER READING

The best single volume on behavioral decision theory is Daniel Kahneman's *Thinking, Fast and Slow*. Not only does Kahneman provide a comprehensive overview of the most important findings, including a review of common errors and cognitive biases, he also describes how the field evolved, drawing back the curtain to explain the genesis of many of the best-known experiments that he and Amos Tversky conducted. For brief but succinct texts, I recommend Reid Hastie and Robyn M. Dawes, *Rational Choice in an Uncertain World*, and Keith Stanovich's *Decision Making and Rationality in the Modern World*.

Decision research has made contributions to several fields and has produced a number of successful books. For consumer behavior, see Dan Ariely's *Predictably Irrational: The Hidden Forces That Shape Our Decisions*. For financial management, I recommend Jason Zweig's *Your Money & Your Brain*, and Gary Belsky and Thomas Gilovich's *Why Smart People Make Big Money Mistakes and How to Correct Them*. For public policy, see Richard Thaler and Cass Sunstein's *Nudge: Improving Decisions about Health, Wealth, and Happiness*. Each is excellent, although it is important to bear in mind what they address and what they do not. Ariely presents many insightful experiments in which individuals make discrete choices from options they cannot influence, and typically in situations that remove any consideration of competition. Zweig and Belsky and

Gilovich apply the lessons of decision research to personal investment management, which once again involves individual decisions about things that cannot be directly influenced—*The stock
doesn't know you own it*—in situations of absolute performance.
These approaches are fine for many kinds of decisions, but care
must be exercised when generalizing elsewhere, notably to managerial decisions.

A contrasting approach has been taken by Gary Klein, who studied decisions as they happen in the real world—by firefighters,
soldiers, pilots, and others. I particularly like two of Klein's works:
Sources of Power: How People Make Decisions and *Streetlights and
Shadows: Searching for the Keys to Adaptive Decision Making*. Klein
begins with decisions in which people can and must shape outcomes, often under pressure with high stakes, and thereby provides
a contrasting view of decision making than that obtained through
neatly controlled laboratory experiments. On the other hand, rarely
is the competitive dimension present; to cite one example, firefighters are trying to put out flames and save lives, not to compete
with other fire crews. Furthermore, studying decisions in their natural settings does not produce large amounts of reliable data, meaning that Gary Klein's research has tended not to be published in
academic journals to the same extent as experimental research.
Even so, I find Klein's research on decision making highly valuable
and an important complement to laboratory experiments.

For decision models and the science of prediction, the modern
classic is Philip Tetlock's *Expert Political Judgment: How Good Is It?
How Can We Know?* Also highly recommended, and covering fields
from sports to weather to politics, is Nate Silver's *The Signal and the
Noise: Why So Many Predictions Fail—But Some Don't*. Both show
how models often outperform humans, yet as I explain in Chapter
Nine, they generally focus on predictions about things we cannot

directly control. Once we can affect outcomes, either directly or indirectly, a different set of issues are present. Decision models are highly valuable for some kinds of decisions but less so for others.

At the opposite end of the continuum—not making predictions but getting things done—are several very good books. Here I recommend Martin Seligman's *Learned Optimism: How to Change Your Mind and Life*, as well as Carol Dweck's *Mindset: The New Psychology of Success*, and *Willpower: Rediscovering the Greatest Human Strength* by Roy F. Baumeister and John Tierney. Finally, a classic that everyone should read is Robert Cialdini's *Influence: The Psychology of Persuasion*.

For discussions about probability and risk, as well as a history of thinking about those topics, see Peter Bernstein's *Against the Gods: The Remarkable Story of Risk*. Also highly recommended are Nassim Nicholas Taleb's *Fooled by Randomness: The Hidden Role of Chance in Life and in the Markets* and *The Black Swan: The Impact of the Highly Improbable*. Both Bernstein and Taleb, coming from the world of financial markets, are mainly concerned about events that we may wish to predict but cannot directly influence.

Very few books combine an interest in decision making with an appreciation of the realities of managerial behavior. That's the gap I have tried to address in this book. Two that I especially like, and whose perspective is perhaps closest to mine, are by academics: Zur Shapira's *Risk Taking: A Managerial Perspective* and Richard Rumelt's *Good Strategy, Bad Strategy: The Difference and Why It Matters*. Last but certainly not least is the single volume that perhaps best captures the need to shape outcomes, the intensity of competition, and what all of that means for leaders: Andy Grove's *Only the Paranoid Survive: How to Exploit Crisis Points That Challenge Every Company*. Technology has moved on since Grove wrote this landmark book, but the fundamental challenges that managers face remain largely the same.

FULL LIST, IN ORDER CITED

Kahneman, Daniel. *Thinking, Fast and Slow*. New York: Farrar, Straus, and Giroux, 2011.

Hastie, Reid, and Robyn M. Dawes. *Rational Choice in an Uncertain World: The Psychology of Judgment and Decision Making*. 2nd ed. Thousand Oaks, CA: Sage Publications, 2010.

Stanovich, Keith E. *Decision Making and Rationality in the Modern World*. New York: Oxford University Press, 2009.

Ariely, Dan. *Predictably Irrational: The Hidden Forces That Shape Our Decisions*. New York: HarperCollins, 2008; revised and expanded, 2010.

Zweig, Jason. *Your Money and Your Brain: How the New Science of Neuroeconomics Can Help Make You Rich*. New York: Simon & Schuster, 2007.

Belsky, Gary, and Thomas Gilovich. *Why Smart People Make Big Money Mistakes and How to Correct Them: Lessons from the Life-Changing Science of Behavioral Economics*. New York: Simon & Schuster, 2010.

Thaler, Richard H., and Cass Sunstein. *Nudge: Improving Decisions about Health, Wealth, and Happiness*. New Haven, CT: Yale University Press, 2008.

Klein, Gary. *Sources of Power: How People Make Decisions*. Cambridge, MA: MIT Press, 1998.

Klein, Gary. *Streetlights and Shadows: Searching for the Keys to Adaptive Decision Making*. Cambridge, MA: MIT Press, 2009.

Tetlock, Philip E. *Expert Political Judgment: How Good Is It? How Can We Know?* Princeton, NJ: Princeton University Press, 2005.

Silver, Nate. *The Signal and the Noise: Why So Many Predictions Fail—But Some Don't*. New York: Penguin, 2012.

Seligman, Martin E. P. *Learned Optimism: How to Change Your Mind and Life*. New York: Vintage Books, 2006.

Dweck, Carol. *Mindset: The New Psychology of Success*. New York: Random House, 2007.

Baumeister, Roy F., and John Tierney. *Willpower: Rediscovering the Greatest Human Strength*. New York: Penguin, 2011.

Cialdini, Robert B. *Influence: The Psychology of Persuasion*. New York: HarperCollins, 2007.

Bernstein, Peter L. *Against the Gods: The Remarkable Story of Risk*. New York: John Wiley & Sons, 1996.

Taleb, Nassim Nicholas. *Fooled by Randomness: The Hidden Role of Chance in Life and in the Markets*. New York: Random House, 2004.

Taleb, Nassim Nicholas. *The Black Swan: The Impact of the Highly Improbable*. New York: Random House, 2007.

Shapira, Zur. *Risk Taking: A Managerial Perspective*. New York: Russell Sage Foundation, 1995.

Rumelt, Richard. *Good Strategy, Bad Strategy: The Difference and Why It Matters*. New York: Crown Business, 2011.

Grove, Andrew S. *Only the Paranoid Survive: How to Exploit Crisis Points That Challenge Every Company*. New York: Currency, 1999.

NOTES

Chapter 1: Crunch Time on a Hot August Night

1. All quotations from Bill Flemming are from interviews with the author in September and October 2010, January 2011, and January 2013.

2. Patrick McGeehan, "It's Official—This Is New York's Hottest Summer," *New York Times,* September 1, 2010, A16.

3. Skanska's costs eventually exceeded $998 million, because the owner added some features, but compared to the basic project, Skanska was profitable at $998 million.

4. Itamar Simonson and Amos Tversky, "Choice in Context: Tradeoff Contrast and Extremeness Aversion," *Journal of Marketing Research* 29, no. 3 (August 1992): 281–295.

5. I ran this experiment on four occasions with a total of 126 managers. The figures for the first question were S1, 42 and S2, 27; for the second the answers were S1, fourteen; S2, 40; and S3, three.

6. Dan Ariely, *The Upside of Irrationality: Defying Logic at Home and at Work* (New York: HarperCollins, 2010), 10.

7. When Daniel Kahneman was awarded the 2002 Nobel Prize in Economics, the Nobel Committee noted that Kahneman and his longtime research partner, the late Amos Tversky, had "inspired a new generation of researchers in economics and finance to enrich economic theory using insights from cognitive psychology into intrinsic human motivation."

8. Dan Ariely offers many such examples in *Predictably Irrational: The Hidden Forces that Shape Our Decisions* (New York: HarperCollins, 2008).

9. Examples about public policy are discussed by Richard H. Thaler and Cass Sunstein in *Nudge: Improving Decisions about Health, Wealth, and Happiness* (New Haven, CT: Yale University Press, 2008). Thaler has been a forceful advocate on policy issues such as retirement savings: Richard H. Thaler, "Shifting Our Retirement Savings into Automatic," *New York Times,* April 6, 2013.

10. Many excellent examples are provided by Jason Zweig in *Your Money and Your Brain: How the New Science of Neuroeconomics Can Help Make You Rich* (New York: Simon & Schuster, 2007) and by Michael J. Mauboussin in *More Than You Know: Finding Financial Wisdom in Unconventional Places* (Boston: Harvard Business School Press, 2007).

11. Adam Smith, *The Money Game* (New York: Vintage Books, 1976), 72.

12. Some kinds of investments allow for direct control. Private equity investments involve buying enough of a company to shape its performance, and activist investors like William Ackman seek to change the direction of companies in which they invest.

But for most people investing means buying and selling assets the value of which cannot be directly influenced. We hunt for bargains, looking for undervalued assets that we think may rise faster than the market, or perhaps overvalued assets that we will sell short. Even investors with deep pockets rarely influence directly the performance of their holdings. Warren Buffett is occasionally an exception, able to buy enough of a stock to move the market, as he did with a $10 billion purchase of IBM in late 2011, but even Buffett is mainly a value investor.

13. Philip E. Tetlock, *Expert Political Judgment* (Princeton, NJ: Princeton University Press, 2005), 41.

14. Daniel Kahneman, *Thinking, Fast and Slow* (New York: Farrar, Straus and Giroux, 2011), 417.

15. Tom Wolfe, *The Right Stuff* (New York: Farrar, Straus and Giroux, 1979), 186.

16. Richard P. Feynman, "What Is and What Should Be the Role of Scientific Culture in Modern Society" (address to the Galileo Symposium, Italy, 1964), in *The Pleasure of Findings Things Out: The Best Short Works of Richard P. Feynman* (London: Penguin 1999), 106–107.

Chapter 2: The Question of Control

1. Ian Poulter, "Opinion," *Golf World*, January 2011, 25.

2. Jon Feinstein, *The Majors: In Pursuit of Golf's Holy Grail* (New York: Little, Brown, 1999), 119.

3. Jaime Diaz, "Perils of Putting: Duffers, Take Heart. A New Study by the PGA Tour Reveals That When It Comes to Putting, the Pros Aren't So Hot Either," *Sports Illustrated*, April 3, 1989, http://sportsillustrated.cnn.com/vault/article/magazine/MAG 1068219/3/index.htm.

4. Diaz, "Perils of Putting." Of the putts studied, 272 were measured at six feet in length, of which 54.8 percent were made successfully. For five-footers, the success rate was 58.9 percent for 353 putts, and for seven-footers, 53.1 percent of 256.

5. Jessica K. Witt, Sally A. Linkenauger, and Dennis R. Proffitt, "Get Me Out of This Slump! Visual Illusions Improve Sports Performance," *Psychological Science* 23 (2012): 397–399. Whereas previous experiments had shown that successful performance leads to changes in perception, this experiment offered evidence of the reverse: changing perceptions can lead to improved performance.

6. Mark Robert Stone, Kevin Thomas, Michael Wilkinson, Andrew M. Jones, Alan St. Clair Gibson, and Kevin G. Thompson. "Effects of Deception on Exercise Performance: Implications for Determinants of Fatigue in Humans," *Medicine & Science in Sports & Exercise* 44 (2012): 534–541.

7. Xan Rice, "Finish Line: An Olympic Marathon Champion's Tragic Weakness," *New Yorker*, May 21, 2012, 54.

8. Karl Kuehl, John Kuehl, and Casey Tefertiller, *Mental Toughness: Baseball's Winning Edge* (Chicago: Ivan R. Dee, 2005), 90.

9. Ron Kroichick, "Giants' Wilson Hopes Hitters Fear the Beard," *San Francisco Chronicle*, October 7, 2010, http://www.sfgate.com/sports/kroichick/article/Giants-Wilson-hopes-hitters-fear-the-beard-3171420.php.

10. Tommy Lasorda and David Fisher, *The Artful Dodger* (New York: Arbor House, 1985), 165.

11. Lasorda and Fisher, *Artful Dodger*, 166.

12. Shelley E. Taylor and Jonathan D. Brown, "Illusion and Well-Being: A Social Psychological Perspective on Mental Health," *Psychological Bulletin* 103, no 2 (March 1988): 193–210.

13. Taylor and Brown, "Illusion and Well-Being," 204.

14. See also Elizabeth King Humphrey, "Be Sad and Succeed," *Scientific American*, March 3, 2010, http://www.scientificamerican.com/article.cfm?id=be-sad-and-succeed.

15. Niebuhr's authorship, for many years questioned, appears to have been validated. See Laurie Goodstein, "Serenity Prayer Skeptic Now Credits Niebuhr," *New York Times*, November 28, 2009, A11.

16. A book published in 2009 uses this exact phrase for its title; see Eileen Flanagan, *The Wisdom to Know the Difference: When to Make a Change—and When to Let Go* (New York: Tarcher, 2009).

17. If we think people shouldn't care, it's because we imagine the goal is to win the prize. But if people are driven by something else, namely the joy of taking part, it makes sense. Whether you are playing because you actually think you can control the dice, or whether what you are getting is the thrill of participation, is a different matter. If it's all about the experience, not the outcome, then of course it makes sense that people would rather do the rolling than watch someone else.

18. Langer defined the illusion of control as "an expectancy of a personal success probability inappropriately higher than the objective probability would warrant." Ellen J. Langer, "The Illusion of Control," *Journal of Personality and Social Psychology* 32 (1975): 311–328.

19. Francesca Gino, Zachariah Sharek, and Don A. Moore, "Keeping the Illusion of Control Under Control: Ceilings, Floors, and Imperfect Calibration," *Organizational Behavior and Human Decision Processes* 114, no. 2 (March 2011): 104–114.

20. Atul Gawande, *Better: A Surgeon's Notes on Performance* (London: Profile, 2007), 154.

21. Groopman, Jerome. *How Doctors Think.* New York: Houghton Mifflin, 2007. See also Daylian M. Cain and Allan S. Detsky, "Everyone's a Little Bit Biased (Even Physicians)," *JAMA* 299, no. 24 (June 25, 2008): 2893–2895.

22. Rasmussen, Heather N., Michael F. Scheier, and Joel B. Greenhouse, Optimism and Physical Health: A Meta-analytic Review," *Annals of Behavioral Medicine*, 37(3) (June 2009): 239–256.

23. Jerome Groopman, *The Anatomy of Hope: How People Prevail in the Face of Illness* (New York: Random House, 2003).

24. Barbara Ehrenreich, *Bright-Sided: How Positive Thinking Is Undermining America* (New York: Holt, 2009).

25. "[M]anagerial risk taking is an endeavor where a manager can use his judgment, exert control, and utilize skills." Zur Shapira, *Risk Taking: A Managerial Perspective* (New York: Russell Sage Foundation, 1995), 48.

26. Shapira, *Risk Taking*, 80.

27. A few more kinds of errors have been suggested, sometimes tongue-in-cheek: Type III is to make the right decision but for the wrong reasons, and Type IV is to make the right decision but at the wrong time.

Chapter 3: Performance, Absolute and Relative

1. Advice of this nature goes back to the very first book I read on the topic, *A Random Walk Down Wall Street*, by Burton Malkiel, in 1976. A more recent example in the same vein is *The Investment Answer: Learn to Manage Your Money and Protect Your Financial Future*, by Daniel C. Goldie and Gordon S. Murray (New York: Business Plus, 2011).

2. Geoff McMaster, "School of Business Wins National Stock Market Contest," *ExpressNews*, December 19, 2001, http://www.expressnews.ualberta.ca/article.cfm?id=1615.

3. McMaster, "School of Business Wins National Stock Market Contest."

4. The fact that the students were playing with fictitious money also made them willing to take outsize bets, because they wouldn't have to bear any losses.

5. Avinash K. Dixit and Barry J. Nalebuff, *The Art of Strategy: A Game Theorist's Guide to Success in Life and Business* (New York: Norton, 2008), xvi.

6. Dixit and Nalebuff, *The Art of Strategy*, 271.

7. For such small stakes, some of us were no doubt prepared to bet on our favorite teams even if we didn't think they would win. I would have been willing to lose a few dollars rather than experience the cognitive dissonance of cheering against a favorite. Viewed that way, a pool has both a financial and an emotional payoff.

8. The game in question was the AFC wild card game on December 22, 1984.

9. There is also the chance, in a contest like this with no money invested and relatively small payoffs for the university, that some teams will prefer to go for broke and risk everything, seeing the contest more as an exercise in fun than one in which the objective is to win something. There are psychic payoffs as well as monetary ones, and the interests of the team may not coincide entirely with those of their university; indeed, different team members may feel differently about their objectives and aims.

10. See *The Red Queen in Organizations: How Competitiveness Evolves* (Princeton, NJ: Princeton University Press, 2008) by William P. Barnett, a professor at Stanford's Graduate School of Business.

11. Robert R. Wiggins and Timothy W. Ruefli, "Schumpeter's Ghost: Is Hypercompetition Making the Best of Times Shorter?" *Strategic Management Journal* 26, no. 10 (2005): 887–911.

12. James G. March and Zur Shapira, "Variable Risk Preference and the Focus of Attention," *Psychological Science* 99, no 1 (1992): 172–183; Elizabeth Boyle and Zur Shapira, "The Liability of Leading: Battling Aspiration and Survival Goals in Jeopardy's Tournament of Champions," *Organization Science* 23, no.4, (2012):1110–1113.

13. Jonathan Haidt, *The Happiness Hypothesis: Putting Ancient Wisdom and Philosophy to the Test of Modern Science* (London: Arrow Books, 2006).

14. Demonstration effects notwithstanding, there are examples in which the recovery of one patient helps another.

15. Thomas B. Newman and Michael A. Kohn, *Evidence-Based Diagnosis* (New York: Cambridge University Press, 2009).

16. David Bornstein, "The Dawn of Evidence-Based Budget," *New York Times*, May 30, 2012, http://opinionator.blogs.nytimes.com/2012/05/30/worthy-of-government-funding -prove-it.

17. Jeffrey Pfeffer and Robert I Sutton, "Evidence-Based Management," *Harvard Busi-*

ness Review (January 2006): 63–74.

18. John Gapper, "McKinsey's Model Springs a Leak," *Financial Times*, March 10, 2011, 9.

19. Behavioral game theory is concerned precisely with competitive games and often relies on laboratory studies. See, for example, Colin Camerer's *Behavioral Game Theory: Experiments in Strategic Interaction* (Princeton, NJ: Princeton University Press, 2003) or research by scholars such as Amnon Rapoport. Studies of judgment and choice, however, typically do not involve competition or relative performance.

Chapter 4: What It Takes to Win

1. Tyler Hamilton and Daniel Coyle, *The Secret Race: Inside the Hidden World of the Tour de France: Doping, Cover-Ups, and Winning at All Costs* (New York: Bantam Books, 2012); Ian Austen, "Bicycle Thieves: World-Class Cycling's Drug Trade," *New York Times*, September 12, 2012, C7.

2. Austin Murphy, "Guide to a Broken Tour: Tyler Hamilton Shines a Revealing Light on Cycling's Drug Era," *Sports Illustrated*, September 24, 2012, 18.

3. Ian Lovett, "'Tattooed Guy' Pivotal in Armstrong Case," *New York Times*, October 18, 2012, B11.

4. Armstrong was explicit on the eve of the 2013 Tour de France. *Le Monde* asked, "When you raced, was it possible to perform without doping?" Armstrong replied, "That depends on which races you wanted to win. The Tour de France? No. Impossible to win without doping. Because the Tour is a test of endurance where oxygen is decisive." "Lance Armstrong: 'Impossible to Win Without Doping'," *USA Today*, June 28, 2013, http://www.usatoday.com/story/sports/cycling/2013/06/28/lance-armstrong-impossible -win-tour-de-france-doping/2471413/. (*Le Monde*: "Était-il possible de réaliser des performance sans se doper?" Armstrong: "Cela dépend des courses que tu voulais gagner. Le Tour de France? Non. Impossible de gagner sans doper. Car le Tour est une épreuve d'endurance où l'oxygène est déterminent. Pour ne prendre qu'un exemple, l'EPO ne va pas aider un sprinteur à remporter un 100m, mais elle sera déterminante pour un coureur de 10,000 m. C'est évident." Stéphane Mandard, "Lance Armstrong: Le Tour de France? Impossible de gagner sans dopage," *Le Monde*, June 29, 2013, Sport & Forme, 5.)

5. A good description of the origins of Monte Carlo simulations in physics was provided by Professor David Spiegelhalter on *Tails You Win: The Science of Chance* (BBC4, December 20, 2012). See also Roger Eckhardt, "Stan Ulam, John von Neumann, and the Monte Carlo Method," *Los Alamos Science* Special Issue 15 (1987): 131–137.

6. Michael E. Raynor, *The Strategy Paradox: Why Committing to Success Leads to Failure (and What to Do About It)* (New York: Currency Doubleday, 2007), 1.

7. Thomas J. Peters and Robert H. Waterman Jr., *In Search of Excellence: Lessons from America's Best Managed Companies* (New York: Warner Books, 1982).

8. Robert I. Sutton, *Weird Ideas That Work: 11½ ways to Promote, Manage, and Sustain Innovation* (New York: Penguin, 2001).

9. Heike Bruch and Sumantra Ghoshal, *A Bias for Action: How Effective Managers Harness Their Willpower, Achieve Results, and Stop Wasting Time* (Boston: Harvard Business School Press, 2004), 9.

10. Robert R. Wiggins and Timothy W. Ruefli, "Schumpeter's Ghost: Is Hypercompetition Making the Best of Times Shorter?" *Strategic Management Journal* 26, no. 10

(2005), 887–911.

11. Quentin Hardy, "Intel Tries to Secure Its Footing Beyond PCs," *New York Times*, April 15, 2013, B1.

12. Dan Lovallo, Carmina Clarke, and Colin Camerer, "Robust Analogizing and the Outside View: Two Empirical Tests of Case-based Decision Making," *Strategic Management Journal* 33, no. 5 (May 2012): 496–512.

Chapter 5: Confidence . . . and Overconfidence

1. Walter F. DeBondt and Richard Thaler, "Financial Decision-making in Markets and Firms: A Behavioral Perspective," *Handbooks in OR & MS* 9 (1995): 385–410.

2. Scott Plous, *The Psychology of Judgment and Decision Making* (New York: McGraw-Hill, 1993), 217.

3. Joseph T. Hallinan, *Why We Make Mistakes: How We Look Without Seeing, Forget Things in Seconds, and Are All Pretty Sure We Are Way Above Average* (New York: Broadway Books, 2009), 9.

4. David Brooks, *The Social Animal: A Story of How Success Happens* (London: Short Books, 2011), 218.

5. Kenneth L. Fisher, "The Eight Biggest Mistakes Investors Make," *UT Today*, no. 1 (2007): 50–53, http://www.fimm.com.my/pdf/investment%20strategies/3_June2007_8Biggestmistakesinv.pdf.

6. Nate Silver, *The Signal and the Noise: The Art and Science of Prediction* (London: Allen Lane, 2012), 359.

7. George Orwell, "Politics and the English Language," *A Collection of Essays*. San Diego, CA: Harvest, 1981. 156-157.

8. Callie Moran, "Overconfident Romney Was So Sure of Victory That He Spent 25 Grand on Victory Fireworks," *Capitol Hill Blue*, November 9, 2012, http://www.capitolhillblue.com/node/45630.

9. Peter Baker and Jim Rutemberg, "The Long Road to a Clinton Exit," *New York Times*, June 8, 2008.

10. John Heilemann and Mark Halperin, *Game Change: Obama and the Clintons, McCain and Palin, and the Race of a Lifetime* (New York: HarperCollins, 2010), 223–224.

11. "Former FEMA Chief Says Bush Was Engaged but Overconfident," *Associated Press*, March 1, 2006, http://www.foxnews.com/story/0,2933,186546,00.html.

12. Greg Bishop, "Pacquiao Stunned in Sixth Round," *New York Times*, December 9, 2012, http://www.nytimes.com/2012/12/09/sports/juan-manuel-marquez-knocks-out-manny-pacquiao-in-sixth-round.html.

13. "Manny Pacquiao Will Not Give up Boxing, Despite Pleas from Family," BBC, December 10, 2012, http://www.bbc.co.uk/sport/0/boxing/20666106.

14. Nick Wingfield and Brian Stelter, "A Juggernaut Stumbles," *New York Times*, October 25, 2011, B1.

15. Dawn Kopecki, Clea Benson, and Phil Mattingly, "Dimon Says Overconfidence Fueled Loss He Can't Defend," *Bloomberg News*, June 14, 2012, http://www.bloomberg.com/news/2012-06-14/dimon-says-overconfidence-fueled-loss-he-can-t-defend.html.

16. Peter Wonacott, "Path to India's Market Dotted with Potholes—Savvy Cola Giants Stumble over local agendas; KFC climbs back from the abyss," *The Wall Street Journal*, September 12, 2006.

17. Chad Terhune, "Home Depot, Seeking Growth, Knocks on Contractors' Doors—CEO looks to stave off critics and gain new customers with building supply unit," *The Wall Street Journal*, August 7, 2006.

18. J. Lynn Lunsford and Daniel Michaels, "Bet on Huge Plane Trips up Airbus," *Wall Street Journal*, June 15, 2006, http://online.wsj.com/article/SB115027552490479926.html.

19. Chip Heath and Dan Heath. *Decisive: How to Make Better Choices in Life and Work*. New York: Crown Business, 2013.

20. Ola Svenson, "Are We all Less Risky and More Skillful Than Our Fellow Drivers?" *Acta Psychologica* 47 (1981): 143–148. It is possible (although very unlikely) that more than 50 percent of drivers can be above the mean, although not above the median.

21. College Board, *Student Descriptive Questionnaire* (Princeton, NJ: Educational Testing Service, 1976–1977).

22. Todd R. Zenger, "Why Do Employers Only Reward Extreme Performance? Examining the Relationship Among Pay, Performance, and Turnover," *Administrative Science Quarterly* 37, no. 2 (1992): 198–219.

23. Neil D. Weinstein, "Unrealistic Optimism about Future Life Events," *Journal of Personality and Social Psychology* 39, no. 5 (1980): 806–820; Shelley E. Taylor and Jonathan D. Brown, "Illusion and Well-Being: A Social Psychological Perspective on Mental Health," *Psychological Bulletin* 103, no 2 (March 1988): 193–210.

24. Marc Alpert, and Howard Raiffa, "A Progress Report on the Training of Probability Assessors" (unpublished manuscript, 1969), in *Judgment Under Uncertainty: Heuristics and Biases*, ed. Daniel Kahneman, Paul Slovic, and Amos Tversky (Cambridge, UK: Cambridge University Press, 1982).

25. Don Moore and Paul J. Healy, "The Trouble with Overconfidence," *Psychological Review* 115, no. 2 (April 2008): 502–517.

26. Silver, *Signal and the Noise*, 183.

27. Tali Sharot, *The Optimism Bias: A Tour of the Irrationally Positive Brain* (New York: Pantheon Books, 2011), 15.

28. "NTSB Suggests Alcohol Detection Systems on All New Cars," CBS Local, December 17, 2012, http://dfw.cbslocal.com/2012/12/17/ntsb-suggests-alcohol-detection-systems-on-all-new-cars/.

29. In an essay for the *New Yorker*, in which he described his effort as an adult learning to draw, Adam Gopnik began with an admission: "I hadn't learned to draw because I had never been any good at drawing." But then he offered an intriguing perspective on why people tend to overestimate and overplace, noting that as we grow up and choose our paths in life, we gravitate toward those things that we do well and no longer have to do those things at which we're less competent. We can avoid the small humiliations of our school days, when the less gifted of us were called on to do long division, or act in a school play, or perform gymnastics, or do some other task we came to dread. As adults many of us go about our lives without the worry of being asked to do what we do poorly. The result is an illusion of competence. Gopnik observed: "Whatever sense of accomplishment we feel in adult life is less the sum of accomplishment than the absence of impossibility: it's really our relief at no longer having to do things we were never good at doing in the first place—relief at never again having to dissect a frog or memorize the periodic table. Or having to make a drawing that looks like the thing we're drawing."

Adam Gopnik, "Life Studies: What I Learned When I Learned to Draw," *New Yorker*, June 27, 2011, 58.

30. J. Kruger, "Lake Wobegon Be Gone! The 'Below-Average' Effect and the Egocentric Nature of Comparative Ability Judgments," *Journal of Personality and Social Psychology* 77 (1999): 221–232.

31. P. D. Windschitl, J. Kruger, and E. Simms, "The Influence of Egocentrism and Focalism on People's Optimism in Competitions: When What Affects Us Equally Affects Me More," *Journal of Personality and Social Psychology* 85 (2003): 389–408.

32. These findings are related to the Dunning-Kruger effect, in which unskilled people are unaware of their deficiencies and believe they are better than they really are, leading to illusory superiority, whereas highly skilled people are aware of their deficiencies and underestimate their (relative) abilities. Kruger and Dunning authors note that "the miscalibration of the incompetent stems from an error about the self, whereas the miscalibration of the highly competent stems from an error about others." The questions about driving and drawing say nothing about the accuracy of ratings of absolute abilities (overestimation or underestimation), but only relative abilities (overplacement or underplacement). In both directions, people imagine that others are less extreme than they believe themselves to be. Kruger, Justin and David Dunning. "Unskilled and Unaware of It: How Difficulties in Recognizing One's Own Incompetence Lead to Inflated Self-Assessments," *Journal of Personality and Social Psychology* 77 (6), 1999, 1121–34.

33. Now and then a respondent seems to be immune to myopia. In one of my classes I had a respondent who rated himself as an excellent driver, but placed himself in the middle quintile, no better or worse than average, and also rated himself poor at drawing, yet again he placed himself in the middle of the pack, no better or worse than average. This response suggested that he understood that an extreme level of absolute skill was entirely ordinary in a relative sense. Of course, in a large sample we can probably find one respondent who says just about anything, so we should never make too much of a single answer. Yet the ability to see that a very high or low absolute ranking doesn't mean much about relative placement seems to be very perceptive, as well as unusual.

34. David Brooks, "The Fatal Conceit," *New York Times*, October 27, 2009, A31.

35. Samuel Clemens may have been thinking about his own life, growing up in Missouri, working at various jobs but never amounting to much until he joined his brother in Nevada, where he invented himself as a writer and chronicler of the American West. He became an American original, a writer, storyteller, humorist, and mordant observer of the human experience. He showed a willingness to try what had never been done before and was both confident in his abilities and ignorant enough to believe he could succeed. To set aside those limits and believe we can go beyond them may seem foolish, but if that's what it takes to succeed, it may not be ignorance after all.

36. Paul McGee, *Self-Confidence: The Remarkable Truth of Why a Small Change Can Make a Big Difference*, 2nd ed. (Chichester, UK: Capstone, 2012); Mike McClement, *Brilliant Confidence: What Confident People Know, Say and Do* (Harlow, UK: Prentice Hall, 2010); Dr. Rob Yeung, *Confidence: The Power to Take Control and Live the Life You Want* (Harlow, UK: Pearson Life, 2011); and Paul McKenna, *Instant Confidence: The Power to Go for Anything You Want* (London: Transworld Publishers, 2006). The last of these, said to be a number one best seller, is by an author whose other titles include

I Can Make You Happy, I Can Make You Smarter, I Can Make You Rich, and *I Can Make You Thin.*

37. Jeremy Eichler, "String Theorist: Christian Tetzlaff Rethinks How a Violin Should Sound," *New Yorker,* August 27, 2012, 34.

Chapter 6: Base Rates and Breaking Barriers

1. Amos Tversky and Daniel Kahneman, "Judgment under Uncertainty: Heuristics and Biases," *Science* 185, no. 4157 (1974): 1124–1131. See also Daniel Kahneman and Amos Tversky, "On the Psychology of Prediction," *Psychological Review* 80 (1973): 237–257.

2. "An Essay Toward Solving a Problem in the Doctrine of Chances" first laid out the idea in *Philosophical Transactions of the Royal Society of London* 53 (1763): 370–418, http://www.socsci.uci.edu/~bskyrms/bio/readings/bayes_essay.pdf. Stephen E. Fienberg, "When Did Bayesian Inference Become Bayesian?" *Bayesian Analysis* 1, no. 1 (2006): 1–40.

3. In the extreme case that the population was said to be 100 percent lawyers, it should be obvious that anyone drawn from the sample has to be a lawyer, no matter what his or her hobbies or personal inclinations are. But when the ratios are .3/.7, or .7/.3, the likelihoods are scarcely affected.

4. Amos Tversky and Daniel Kahneman, "Evidential Impact of Base Rates," in *Judgment Under Uncertainty: Heuristics and Biases,* ed. Daniel Kahneman, Paul Slovic, and Amos Tversky (Cambridge, UK: Cambridge University Press, 1982).

5. Ward Casscells, Arno Schoenberger, and Thomas Graboys "Interpretation by physicians of clinical laboratory results." *New England Journal of Medicine,* 299: 18 (1978) 999–1001. Of the 999 healthy people, 95 percent accuracy means we will have 49.95 false positive results. Of the 1 afflicted, 95 percent accuracy means we will have 0.95 positive result. Out of 50.90 positive results (49.95 + 0.95), only 0.95/50.90, or 1.9 percent, have the disease. The other 49.95 out of 50.90, or 98.1 percent, are false positives.

6. Even so, articles continue to appear that describe the base rate bias as if it were something new. Although it was identified many years ago, much of the general public remains unaware of it, and in any event pointing out errors makes for a good story. See, for example, Tim Harford, "Screening: It's All in the Numbers," *Financial Times, FT.com Magazine,* December 10/11, 2011.

7. *The Black Swan: The Impact of the Highly Improbable* (New York: Random House, 2007).

8. If all the Blue Cabs but only three-fifths of the Green Cabs were on the road, we would have 15 Blue Cabs and (.6 × 85) = 51 Green Cabs. The true positive would still be 12 but the false positive only 10.2, and the chance that a car identified as a Blue Cab was in fact blue would be [12/(12+10.2)] = 54.1 percent, up from 41.4 percent.

9. Zhen-Xin Zhang, Gustavo C. Roman, Zhen Hong, Cheng-Bing Wu, Qui-Ming Qu, Jue-Bing Huang, Bing Zhou, Zhi-Ping Geng, Ji-Zing Wu, Hong-Bo Wen, Heng Zhao, and Gwendolyn E. P. Zahner, "Parkinson's Disease in China: Prevalence in Beijing, Xian, and Shanghai," *Lancet* 365 (February 12, 2005): 595–597. I am grateful to Mads Dalsgaard for this example and the reference.

10. National Center for Health Statistics, http://www.cdc.gov/nchs/pressroom/05facts /moreboys.htm. There are some variations by year, by age of the mother, and by eth-

nic group: "The highest sex birth ratio occurred in 1946 (1,059 male births per 1,000 females) while the lowest occurred in 1991 and again in 2001 (1,046 male births per 1,000 females). Combining all the years studied, older mothers (40 to 44 years of age and 45 years and over) have the lowest total sex birth ratios (1,038 and 1,039, respectively) and mothers 15 to 19 years of age had the highest sex birth ratio (1,054). For all available years combined, Chinese mothers (1,074) and Filipino mothers (1,072) had the highest differences between the number of boys born compared with girls, whereas non-Hispanic black mothers (1,031) and American Indian mothers (1,031) had the lowest." "Trend Analysis of the Sex Ratio at Birth in the United States." *National Vital Statistics Reports* 53, no. 20 (June 14, 2005).

11. Sharon Bertsch McGrayne, *The Theory That Would Not Die: How Bayes' Rule Cracked the Enigma Code, Hunted Down Russian Submarines, and Emerged Triumphant from Two Centuries of Controversy* (New Haven, CT: Yale University Press, 2011), 26–28.

12. Atul Gawande, "The Bell Curve: What Happens When Patients Find Out How Good Their Doctors Really Are?" *New Yorker*, December 6, 2004, 82–91.

13. Daniel Kahneman, *Thinking, Fast and Slow* (New York: Farrar, Straus and Giroux, 2011), 241–247.

14. Project planning expert Bent Flyvbjerg has conducted extensive research about project planning and offers a three-step approach to warding off the planning fallacy: identify the relevant reference class, establish a base line for that class, and make adjustments to that baseline to the extent warranted. Bent Flyvbjerg, Mette K. Skamris Holm, and Søren L. Buhl, "How (In)Accurate Are Demand Forecasts in Public Works Projects?" *Journal of the American Planning Association* 71 (2005):131–146.

15. Dan Lovallo and Daniel Kahneman, "Delusions of Success: How Optimism Undermines Executives' Decisions," *Harvard Business Review* (July 2003): 63.

16. Thomas L. Friedman, "Obama's Best-Kept Secrets," *New York Times*, October 21, 2012, SR1.

17. George Bernard Shaw, Maxim 124, "Maxims for Revolutionists," in *Man and Superman: A Comedy and Philosophy* (London: Penguin Books, 2000).

18. H. Guyford Stever and James J Haggerty, *Flight* (New York: Time Inc., 1965), 23.

19. Chuck Yeager and Leo Janos, *Yeager: An Autobiography* (New York: Bantam Books, 1985), 103.

20. Yeager and Janos, *Yeager*, 117–118.

21. Yeager and Janos, *Yeager*, 118.

22. Yeager and Janos, *Yeager*, 137.

23. Yeager and Janos, *Yeager*, 121.

24. Yeager and Janos, *Yeager*, 132.

25. Yeager and Janos, *Yeager*, 150.

26. Chuck Yeager, Bob Cardenas, Bob Hoover, Jack Russell, and James Young, *The Quest for Mach One: A First-Person Account of Breaking the Sound Barrier* (New York: Penguin, 1997), 99.

27. Michael Walsh, "Solar-Paneled Plane Completes First Leg of Historic Cross-Country Flight from San Francisco to New York," *New York Daily News*, May 4, 2013, http://www.nydailynews.com/news/national/all-solar-airplane-making-jfk-article-1 .1335172.

28. "No Sun, No Problem for Plane," Associated Press in *Shanghai Daily*, May 4, 2013, A3.

29. Valérie Lion, "L'Entretien: Bertrand Piccard 'Explorer, c'est aller au-delà des évidences,'" *L'Express* 3187 (August 1, 2012): 8–11 (author's translation). "Mon but n'est pas de dépasser les limites extérieurs, physiques. C'est de dépasser les limites qu'on s'inflige à soi-même. L'être humain s'empêche de sortir de ce qu'il connaît, de se mettre dans des situations où il risquerait de perdre le contrôle. Ce sont justement ces situations-là qui m'intéressent, quand on entre dans l'inconnu."

Chapter 7: Better Decisions over Time

1. http://www.basketball-reference.com/leagues/NBA_2012_leaders.html.

2. Michael Austin, "Building the Perfect Arc: Research Shows Players Need to Keep Shot Arc around 45 Degrees," *Winning Hoops*, May/June 2010, 20–27. See also www .noahbasketball.com.

3. Benjamin S. Bloom, ed., *Developing Talent in Young People* (New York: Ballantine Books, 1985).

4. Stephen J. Dubner and Steven D. Levitt, "A Star Is Made," *New York Times*, May 7, 2006, http://www.nytimes.com/2006/05/07/magazine/07wwln_freak.html?pagewanted=all.

5. See K. Anders Ericsson, Ralf Th. Krampe, and Clemens Tesch-Römer, "The Role of Deliberate Practice in the Acquisition of Expert Performance," *Psychological Review* 100, no. 3 (1993): 363–406.

6. Ericsson, K. Anders, Michael J. Prietula, and Edward T. Cokely, "The Making of an Expert," *Harvard Business Review*, July–August 2007, 114–121.

7. "We observed that the deliberative mindset leads to an accurate and impartial analysis of information that speaks to the feasibility and desirability of possible goals, whereas the implemental mindset promotes an optimistic and partial analysis of such information. Moreover, the deliberative mindset is associated with open-mindedness, whereas the implemental mindset is characterized by closed-mindedness." Quotation from Professor Gollwitzer's Web site, http://www.psych.nyu.edu/gollwitzer/.

8. Peter M. Gollwitzer and Ronald F. Kinney, "Effects of Deliberative and Implemental Mind-sets on Illusion of Control," *Journal of Personality and Social Psychology* 56, no. 4 (1989): 531–542.

9. One of many examples comes from Carl Richard, in a blog in the *New York Times*: "Viewing the Glass as Half Full, but Not Too Full," March 18, 2013. Richard discussed the pros and cons of positive thinking, but like most people did not add the temporal dimension and ask when it is best to take an optimistic view and when it is best to insist on a detached and realistic view. http://bucks.blogs.nytimes.com/2013/03/18 /viewing-the-glass-as-half-full-but-not-too-full/?src=recg.

10. This dramatic incident has already become the stuff of legend. It has been cited by Gary Klein as an example of "recognition primed decision making." As Klein tells it, Captain Chesley Sullenberger went with the first option that could work, rather than following a classical decision model approach of evaluating all options at once. It has also been mentioned by Dr. Atul Gawande as an example of the power of checklists, with Sullenberger proceeding in a logical sequence to determine the cause of the problem and identify the best action.

11. If you're wondering why golfers overestimate their ability to sink a six-foot putt, described in Chapter Two, it may be because a short putt involves little deliberation. Unlike shots that call for assessment and choices of club, a six-foot putt is often just a straight shot.

12. Dr. Bob Rotella, *Golf Is a Game of Confidence* (New York: Simon & Schuster, 1996), 18.

13. "Harrington using electrodes in battle with the left side of his brain," *The Independent*, March 6, 2013, http://www.independent.ie/sport/golf/harrington-using-electrodes-in-battle-with-the-left-side-of-his-brain-29113728.html.

14. Brian Keogh, "Harrington and the Man with Two Brains," *Irish Golf News*, March 6, 2013, http://www.irishgolfdesk.com/news-files/2013/3/6/harrington-and-the-man-with-two-brains.html.

15. http://sports.espn.go.com/golf/masters10/news/story?id=5075606. The Associated Press reported: "The signature moment came on the 13th, a hole Mickelson has dominated like no other at Augusta. With a 2-shot lead, he was stuck between two Georgia pines and had just over 200 yards to the hole. He never considered anything but a shot at the green. 'I was going to have to go through that gap if I laid up or went for the green,' Mickelson said. 'I was going to have to hit a decent shot. The gap . . . it wasn't huge, but it was big enough, you know, for a ball to fit through. I just felt like at that time, I needed to trust my swing and hit a shot,' he said. 'And it came off perfect.'"

16. Mickelson's historic shot can be seen on YouTube at http://www.youtube.com/watch?v=Gh1ZVLuZdvE.

17. http://sports.espn.go.com/golf/masters10/news/story?id=5075606.

18. http://www.golf.com/tour-and-news/mickelsons-guts-talent-came-together-shot-defined-masters#ixzz2LSUceD00.

19. Ericsson, Prietula, and Cokely, "Making of an Expert," 115.

20. Daniel Coyle, *The Talent Code: Greatness Isn't Born. It's Grown. Here's How* (New York: Bantam, 2009); David Shenk, *The Genius in All of Us: Why Everything You've Been Told About Genetics, Talent, and IQ Is Wrong* (New York: Anchor, 2011); Matthew Syed, *Bounce: The Myth of Talent and the Power of Practice: Beckham, Serena, Mozart, and the Science of Success* (New York: Harper, 2011).

22. Joshua Foer, *Moonwalking with Einstein: The Art and Science of Remembering Everything*, New York: Penguin, 2012.

22. In fact, not even Anders Ericsson makes the claim that ten thousand hours of practice leads predictably to success. A twenty-nine-year-old named Dan McLaughlin, who had never played golf before, decided in 2010 to devote himself to playing golf for ten thousand hours, essentially full time for six and a half years, with the goal of qualifying for the PGA Tour, which would make him one of the top 250 or so golfers in the world. Can he do it? Ericsson isn't sure: "Nobody has done it, which means nobody knows how it's going to wind up. He's like Columbus." *Businessweek* comments that McLaughlin may never become an excellent golfer, but he's talented at self-promotion. Joel Stein, "From Doofus to Genius?" *Bloomberg Businessweek*, November 29–December 4, 2011, 101.

23. Vanderbilt University researchers David Lubinski and Camilla Benbow tracked more than two thousand people who had scored in the top 1 percent of an intelligence test at age thirteen. They found that of those who were at the very top—the 99.9th per-

centile, or the "profoundly gifted"—were three to five times as likely to eventually earn a doctorate, register a patent, or publish a scientific article, as those who were only in the top 99.1th percentile. Among the top students, outstanding talent at an early age proved to be an important predictor of the very highest levels of success. Very high intellectual ability confers an enormous real-world advantage for the most demanding accomplishments. In further research, this time with pianists, Lubinski and Benbow confirmed a strong positive correlation between practice habits and sight-reading performance, but also determined that an innate mental talent, known as working memory capacity, was important as well. David Z. Hambrick and Elizabeth J. Meinz, "Sorry, Strivers: Talent Matters," *New York Times*, November 20, 2011, SR12.

24. Steven Pinker, "Malcolm Gladwell, Eclectic Detective," *New York Times*, November 15, 2009, BR1.

25. Geoff Colvin. *Talent Is Overrated: What Really Separates World-Class Performers from Everybody Else*, New York: Portfolio Trade, 2010, 1–2 and 199.

26. Ericsson, Prietula, and Cokely, "Making of an Expert," 118.

27. Ericsson, Prietula, and Cokely, "Making of an Expert," 119.

Chapter 8: Decisions of a Leader

1. Joseph S. Nye Jr., *The Powers to Lead* (Oxford: Oxford University Press, 2008), 18.

2. Jack Welch and Suzy Welch, "How Not to Succeed in Business," *Business Week*, March 2, 2009, 74.

3. In *A Force for Change: How Leadership Differs from Management* (New York: Free Press, 1990), John Kotter argues that leadership is a force for change, but management emphasizes the status quo. In my view the distinction between leaders and managers is not only a false dichotomy, but one that does a disservice to managers; because leadership is often an aspirational term, management suffers by comparison. Henry Mintzberg takes an opposing and wise view in "We're Overled and Undermanaged," *Business Week*, August 17, 2009, 68.

4. Nye, *Powers to Lead*, 70. "If emotional intelligence is not authentic, others will likely find out in the long run, but successful management of personal impressions requires some of the same emotional discipline and skills possessed by good actors." A similar mention of acting is made by Warren Bennis: "Like great actors, great leaders create and sell an alternative vision of the world, a better one in which we are are an essential part." "Acting the Part of a Leader," *Business Week*, September 14, 2009, 80.

5. Speech presented at Rice University, September 12, 1962. The exact quote was: "We choose to go to the moon in this decade and do the other things, not because they are easy, but because they are hard."

6. Chris Kraft, *Flight: My Life in Mission Control* (New York: Dutton, 2001), 82.

7. Kraft, *Flight*, 229.

8. Stephen B. Johnson, *The Secret of Apollo: Systems Management in American and European Space Programs* (Baltimore, MD: Johns Hopkins University Press, 2002), 146.

9. Sy Liebergot, *Apollo EECOM: Journey of a Lifetime* (Burlington, ON: Apogee Books, 2003), 138.

10. According to Liebergot, it was Swigert who radioed: "Okay, Houston, we've had a problem here."

11. Liebergot, *Apollo EECOM*, 140.

12. Gene Kranz, *Failure Is Not an Option: Mission Control from Mercury to Apollo 13 and Beyond* (New York: Berkley Books, 2000), 314.

13. Miles O'Brien, CNN Anchor interview, "Veteran NASA Flight Director Discusses Book About Race to the Moon," *CNN Sunday Morning News*, May 7, 2000.

14. Kranz, *Failure Is Not an Option*, 321.

15. It is not clear whether Kranz said the memorable line, "Failure is not an option." Some claim it was written by the screenwriters. But it summed up Kranz's attitude, and he used the phrase for the title of his 2000 autobiography.

16. Gary Klein has used the crisis aboard Apollo 13 as an example of organizational problem solving, with examples of six distinct purposes: generating new actions, providing forecasts, formulating plans, deriving diagnoses, making decisions, and revising goals. I have looked at the same story from the perspective of confidence and leadership. Gary Klein, *Sources of Power: How People Make Decisions* (Cambridge, MA: MIT Press, 1998).

17. Kranz, *Failure Is Not an Option*, 12. When the mission was over, NASA's deliberative mind-set returned to the fore. Expressions of certainty—"Failure is not an option" and "This crew is coming home"—were set aside as NASA reverted to rational analysis. A special panel, the Cortright Commission, examined every major component, from cryogenic tanks to computers, at every moment in its history, from design to manufacture to safety testing to deployment. The Cortright Commission found that the explosion was caused by the confluence of two earlier faults. Thermostat switches on the Apollo fuel tanks had originally been designed for the spacecraft's 28-volt power grid, but were not modified when new 65-volt heaters were installed, leaving 28-volt switches on a 65-volt tank. That was serious, but not sufficient to cause the explosion until combined with a second error. A fuel tank had been dropped after its use on Apollo 7 in October 1968, then installed in slightly damaged condition on Apollo 13. That damage, although small and undetected, meant that a thermostat was fused shut while 65 volts surged through the tanks, creating an enormous buildup of pressure and eventually an explosion. The report concluded: "While the exact point of initiation of combustion and the specific propagation path involved may never be known with certainty, the nature of the occurrence is sufficiently well understood to permit taking corrective steps to prevent its recurrence." The tone of the report, consistent with NASA culture, was fact based and unemotional. NASA was once again in a supremely analytical mode, sparing no cost to identify the root cause of failure and to eliminate problems from future missions. Yet in three days when it had mattered most, from the first frantic moments when the extent of the explosion was clear until the final splashdown, an implemental mind-set had prevailed.

18. Gene Kranz, correspondence with author, March 2010.

19. Chris Kraft, *Flight: My Life in Mission Control* (New York: Dutton, 2001), 337.

20. Kranz, correspondence.

21. We tell the story of Apollo 13 because everything turned out well, which is an example of the survivor bias. We'll never know if Mission Control would have performed as brilliantly for the *Challenger* space shuttle mission in January 1986, because the explosion seventy seconds after launch destroyed the vehicle. Lost amid the cheering about Apollo 13 is an uncomfortable fact: if the explosion had taken place at a slightly different time, even the best leadership, teamwork, and tenacity would not have gotten

Lovell, Haise, and Swigert home safely. The explosion in Apollo 13's service module took place fifty-five hours into the mission. Had it taken place a few hours *earlier*, there wouldn't have been enough oxygen left to support three men for the time needed to get back to Earth. Had the explosion taken place a day *later*, after the lunar module had descended to the moon's surface and the command module was orbiting the moon, all would have been lost. And had the explosion been slightly more powerful, tearing away additional life-support systems, there would have been no chance for a safe return. Under only slightly different conditions, we would never have had a chance to marvel at the brilliant dedication and grace under pressure of Mission Control and the crew. *Apollo 13: The NASA Mission Reports* (Burlington, ON: Apogee Books, 2000), 4.

22. Welch and Welch, "How Not to Succeed in Business," 74.

23. Walter Isaacson, *Steve Jobs* (New York: Little, Brown, 2011); Murad Ahmed, "Jobs: The Special One," *The Times, Saturday Review*, October 29, 2011, 16.

24. Typical of recent treatments of authenticity is the mention by Rob Goffee and Gareth Jones in "Managing Authenticity: The Great Paradox of Leadership," *Harvard Business Review* (December 2005): 87–94: "Leaders and followers both associate authenticity with sincerity, honesty, and integrity. It's the real thing—the attribute that uniquely defines great leaders." One must ask, however, if authenticity, objectively defined, leads to great leadership, or if those considered to be great leaders are perceived to be authentic. The latter, in common speech, seems more likely than the former.

25. Apollo 13 called for a very high level of performance, but an absolute level, not one with relative performance as in competition.

26. "Sincerity, he said, requires us to act and really be the way that we present ourselves to others. Authenticity involves finding and expressing the true inner self and judging all relationships in terms of it." Orlando Patterson, "Our Overrated Inner Self," *New York Times*, December 26, 2006, A35. Patterson refers to Lionel Trilling, *Sincerity and Authenticity* (Cambridge, MA: Harvard University Press, 1971).

27. "'Duty, Honor, Country'—those three hallowed words reverently dictate what you ought to be, what you can be, what you will be. They are your rallying point to build courage when courage seems to fail, to regain faith when there seems to be little cause for faith, to create hope when hope becomes forlorn." Gen. Douglas MacArthur, speech to the Corps of Cadets at the U.S. Military Academy at West Point, New York, May 12, 1962.

28. Patterson, "Our Overrated Inner Self."

29. Others are even more scathing about the current emphasis on authenticity. Simon Critchley, a professor of philosophy, and Jamieson Webster, a psychoanalyst, write: "In the gospel of authenticity, well-being has become the primary goal of human life. Rather than being the by-product of some collective project, some upbuilding of the New Jerusalem, well-being is an end in itself. . . . Authenticity, needing no reference to anything outside itself, is an evacuation of history. The power of now. At the heart of the ethic of authenticity is a profound selfishness and callous disregard of others. This ideology functions prominently in the contemporary workplace, where the classical distinction between work and nonwork has broken down." Simon Critchley and Jamieson Webster, "The Gospel According to 'Me,'" *New York Times*, June 30, 2013, SR8.

30. Patterson, "Our Overrated Inner Self."

31. "Depend upon it, sir, when a man knows he is to be hanged in a fortnight, it

concentrates his mind wonderfully." Thomas Boswell, *Life of Johnson* (Oxford: Oxford University Press, 2008), 849.

32. Carol J. Loomis, "Why Carly's Bet Is Failing," *Fortune*, February 7, 2005, 50–64.

33. Rakesh Khurana, *Searching for a Corporate Savior: The Irrational Quest for Charismatic CEOs* (Princeton, NJ: Princeton University Press, 2002).

34. James G. March and Zur Shapira, "Managerial Perceptions on Risk and Risk-Taking," *Management Science* 33 (1987): 1404–1418.

35. Barry M. Staw, "Leadership and Persistence," in *Leadership and Organizational Culture: New Perspectives on Administrative Theory and Practice*, ed. Thomas J. Sergiovanni and John E. Corbally (Champaign: University of Illinois Press, 1986), 72–84.

36. Staw, "Leadership and Persistence," 82.

37. For a review, see Barry M. Staw, "The Escalation of Commitment to a Course of Action," *Academy of Management Review* 6, no. 4 (1981): 577–587.

38. Staw, "Leadership and Persistence," 80.

39. Nye, *The Powers to Lead*, 124.

Chapter 9: Where Models Fear to Tread

1. Ashlee Vance, "Algorithms on the Prairie," *Bloomberg Businessweek*, March 26, 2012, 37–39.

2. John Tierney, "From Tinseltown to Splitsville: Just Do the Math," *New York Times*, September 19, 2006, A25.

3. They included the circuit court of origin, the issue area, the type of petitioner, and the ideological direction of the lower court ruling.

4. Ian Ayres, *Super Crunchers: Why Thinking-By-Numbers Is the New Way to Be Smart* (New York: Bantam Dell Books, 2007). The original citation is Andrew D. Martin et al., "Competing Approaches to Predicting Supreme Court Decision Making," *Perspectives on Policy* 2 (2004): 763; Theodore W. Ruger et al., "The Supreme Court Forecasting Project: Legal and Political Science Approaches to Predicting Supreme Court Decisionmaking," *Columbia Law Review* 104 (2004): 1150.

5. Orley Ashenfelter, "Predicting the Quality and Prices of Bordeaux Wine," *Economic Journal* 118, no. 529 (June 2008): F174–F184; Ayres, *Super Crunchers*, 1–6.

6. Orley Ashenfelter's model for predicting the quality of wine has by now been reported many times, not only by Ian Ayres but also by Michael Mauboussin in *Think Twice* (Boston: Harvard Business Press, 2009) and by Daniel Kahneman in *Thinking, Fast and Slow* (New York: Farrar, Straus and Giroux, 2011).

7. Ayres, *Super Crunchers*, 114.

8. Bill James. *Solid Fool's Gold: Detours on the Way to Conventional Wisdom* (Chicago: ACTA Sports, 2011), 185.

9. Adapted from Joseph Adler, *Baseball Hacks: Tips & Tools for Analyzing and Winning with Statistics* (Sebastapol, CA: O'Reilly, 2006), 313. I have left this example at a fairly broad level, considering only whether runs are scored in the inning. The analysis could be more sophisticated, examining particular pitchers and batters, the innings, the number of runs ahead or behind, whether home or visitor, and more. Nor have I considered attempted bunts that either led to the batter reaching base safely—beating it out for a hit, or the fielders making an error—or bunts that led to the runner being forced out at second. But as a first cut, as a way to show how analysis of a large data set can show overall effectiveness, the insights are compelling.

10. James, *Solid Fool's Gold*, 186.

11. Tim Adams, "How a Book about Baseball Statistics Changed the Way We Think about Football—Forever," *Esquire*, September 2011, 201.

12. Jonah Keri, *The Extra 2%: How Wall Street Strategies Took a Major League Team from Worst to First* (New York: Ballantine Books, 2011), 188.

13. Keri, *Extra 2%*, 192.

14. Jon Swartz, "San Francisco Giants Ride Techball to the Top," *USAToday*, March 31, 2013, http://www.usatoday.com/story/tech/2013/03/31/giants-social-media-world-series-technologh/2013497/.

15. Susan Slusser, "Can't Keep Beane Down: No More Talk of Moneyball, Please," *San Francisco Chronicle*, July 12, 2009, B1–B7.

16. Michael Lewis, "Out of Their Tree," *Sports Illustrated*, March 1, 2004, http://sports illustrated.cnn.com/vault/article/magazine/MAG1031308/index.htm.

17. Paul White, "'Moneyball' Principles Have Become Old Hat," *USA Today*, September 21, 2011, 6C.

18. Bill James rates Morgan the best second baseman of all time, ahead of Eddie Collins and Rogers Hornsby. *Bill James Historical Baseball Abstract* (New York: The Free Press, 2001), 479.

19. Tommy Craggs, "Say-It-Ain't-So Joe," *SF Weekly*, July 6, 2005, http://www.sfweekly.com/2005-07-06/news/say-it-ain-t-so-joe.

20. The phrase comes from Theodore Roosevelt's speech, "Citizenship in a Republic," on April 23, 1910. "It is not the critic who counts; not the man who points out how the strong man stumbles, or where the doer of deeds could have done them better. The credit belongs to the man who is actually in the arena, whose face is marred by dust and sweat and blood; who strives valiantly; who errs, who comes short again and again, because there is no effort without error and shortcoming." http://www.theodore-roosevelt.com/trsorbonnespeech.html.

21. Joe Morgan and David Falkner, *Joe Morgan: A Life in Baseball* (New York: W.W. Norton & Co., 1993), 39.

22. Pete Rose could serve equally well as an example, achieving outstanding results through hard work and a strong mental attitude, but Rose is neither in the Hall of Fame nor a member of baseball's "club." A teammate, Merv Rettenmund, observed: "Peter's confidence was at such a high level that if he had a bad week, he figured that was more hits he had coming to him the next week. He turned it into a positive. Good hitters learn from their failures, but they don't dwell on them. Pete was the ultimate example of that." Quoted in Michael Sokolove, *Hustle: The Myth, Life, and Lies of Pete Rose* (New York: Simon & Schuster, 1990), 90.

23. David Leonhardt, "Science and Art at Odds on the Field of Dreams," *New York Times*, August 28, 2005, http://www.nytimes.com/2005/08/28/sports/28iht-THEORIES.html.

24. Philip E. Tetlock, *Expert Political Judgment: How Good Is It? How Can We Know?* Princeton, NJ: Princeton University Press, 2005. Daniel Kahneman remarked that "Tetlock has set the terms for any future discus¬sion of this topic." *Thinking, Fast and Slow*, 218. Daniel Kahneman remarked that "Tetlock has set the terms for any future discussion of this topic." *Thinking, Fast and Slow*, 218.

25. Joan Hoff, *Nixon Reconsidered* (New York: Basic Books, 1995), 6, quoted in Margaret MacMillan, *Nixon and Mao: The Week That Changed the World* (New York:

Random House, 2007).

26. Felicia Sonmez, "Vice President Biden Predicts Supreme Court Won't Rule Health Care Law Unconstitutional," *Washington Post*, April 1, 2012, http://www.washington post.com/blogs/post-politics/post/vice-president-biden-predicts-supreme-court-wont -rule-health-care-law-unconstitutional/2012/04/01/gIQADBE8oS_blog.html.

27. Jennifer Bendery, "Nancy Pelosi Predicts 6–3 Supreme Court Vote in Favor of Health Care Law," *Huffington Post*, April 4, 2012, http://www.huffingtonpost.com /2012/04/04/nancy-pelosi-health-care-law_n_1402908.html.

28. Dylan Byers, "Dick Morris Fesses Up," *Politico.com*, November 13, 2012, http://www.politico.com/blogs/media/2012/11/dick-morris-fesses-up-149453.html.

29. In July 2013, Nate Silver announced he was leaving the New York Times for a new role at ESPN that would let him combine sports and also report on politics for ABC News. ESPN and ABC are both owned by Disney, leading the Drudge Report to offer a parting shot: "Nate Silver joins Mickey Mouse media empire." Stelter, Brian."Blogger for Times Is to Join ESPN Staff," *New York Times*, July 20, 2013, B6.

30. Nate Silver, *The Signal and the Noise: Why So Many Predictions Fail—but Some Don't* (New York: Penguin, 2012), 243–245. In *Thinking Statistically*, Uri Bram uses a similar example, this time asking whether your girlfriend who told you she was going home because she wasn't feeling well but snuck off to have dinner with a former boyfriend is cheating on you. Perhaps these are just meant as ways to make statistics compelling to a wide audience, or maybe these are the questions that statisticians tend to think about?

31. The taxicab and medical test examples were slightly simpler, in that the false positive and false negative rates were the same. We were simply told the witness was accurate 80 percent of the time, with no difference between false negatives and false positives—she was equally likely to call a Green Cab blue as she was to call a Blue Cab green. The same applied to the medical test, which was said to have a false positive of 5 percent, but no mention was made of false negatives.

32. Nate Silver explained this probability of .5 as follows: "If he's cheating on you, it's cer¬tainly easy enough to imagine how the panties got there. Then again, even (and perhaps especially) if he is cheating on you, you might expect him to be more careful." Silver seems to be saying: maybe he's cheating on you and maybe he isn't, so let's call it 50/50. But that's not what 50 percent means here. This base rate means that if he is having an affair, 50 percent of the time mysterious underwear will wind up in the dresser, and 50 percent it won't. This figure seems much too high (although I don't claim to be an expert). I suspect Silver really meant that 50 percent was the chance of an affair given that you found the underwear, which is the question we're trying to solve.

33. Jeremy Fox: "One unfortunate side effect of the increasing popularity of technically-sophisticated, computationally-intensive statistical approaches in ecology has been to make ecologists even more reluctant to engage with philosophical issues—i.e. less fluent, or else less likely to care about fluency. It seems like there's a 'shut up and calculate the numbers' ethos developing, as if technical proficiency with programming could substitute for thinking about what the numbers mean." http://oikosjournal.word press.com/2011/10/11/frequentist-vs-bayesian-statistics-resources-to-help-you-choose/.

Chapter 10: When Are Winners Cursed?

1. Edward C. Capen, Robert V. Clapp, and William M. Campbell, "Competitive Bidding in High-Risk Situations," *Journal of Petroleum Technology* 23 (1971): 641.

2. Capen, Clapp, and Campbell, "Competitive Bidding in High-Risk Situations," 644.

3. "The Tale of the 'Winner's Curse,' Bidding Science Saved $$," http://www.aapg.org/explorer/2004/12dec/capen.cfm.

4. Capen, Clapp, and Campbell, "Competitive Bidding in High-Risk Situations," 647.

5. Capen, Clapp, and Campbell, "Competitive Bidding in High-Risk Situations," 641–653.

6. Max H. Bazerman and William F. Samuelson, "I Won the Auction but I Don't Want the Prize," *Journal of Conflict Resolution* 27 (1983): 618–634.

7. Richard H. Thaler, "The Winner's Curse," *Journal of Economic Perspectives* 2, no. 1 (1988): 191–202.

8. Nate Silver, *The Signal and the Noise: Why So Many Predictions Fail—but Some Don't* (New York: Penguin, 2012), 359.

9. In *Think Twice: Harnessing the Power of Counterintuition* (Boston: Harvard Business Press, 2009), Michael Mauboussin explains that he runs similar experiments with his class on financial investments, and financial markets, to teach the dangers of competitive auctions.

10. It's also an example of a *sealed first-price auction*, as each party places a bid without knowing the bids of others, and the winner pays the full amount bid. Sealed first-price auctions often result in very high winning bids, because bidders can't see what others are willing to pay. Other auction formats lessen the tendency to overpay. In *sealed second-price auctions*, also known as Vickrey auctions after Nobel Prize–winning economist William Vickrey, the top bidder pays the amount bid by the runner-up, or second-price. That way the winner is protected from his excesses, although not from those of the second-place bidder. In *open ascending price auctions*, also called English auctions, participants bid openly with full knowledge of one another's bids. Finally, in *open descending price auctions*, also known as Dutch auctions, the auctioneer begins with a high asking price and then lowers the price until a bidder is willing to buy. Each kind of auction has somewhat different bidding dynamics and lends itself to different tactics, but the winner's curse can occur in all of them.

11. Daniel Kreps, "Lennon's 'A Day in the Life' Lyrics Sell for $1.2 Million," *Rolling Stone*, June 18, 2010, http://www.rollingstone.com/music/news/lennons-a-day-in-the-life-lyrics-sell-for-1-2-million-20100618.

12. J. J. Taber, F. D. Martin, and R. S. Seright, "EOR Screening Criteria Revisited-Part 1: Introduction to Screening Criteria and Enhanced Recovery Field Projects," *SPE Reservoir Engineering*, 12, no. 3 (August 1997): 189–198.

13. Keith Schaefer, "Natural Gas: Costs Go Down as Learning Curve Goes Up," www.oilandgas-investments.com, June 6, 2009. "That learning curve is still happening. Production out of these long horizontal wells is getting better in all the unconventional gas (and oil) plays in North America.. . . . And as I wrote in an earlier article, the energy producers are learning how to frac these plays much better, using special mixes of chemicals and water to get the most oil or gas out of these new, very tight reservoirs. It can sometimes take some expensive trial and error on how to get that frac formula right. Tristone estimates the average break even level of these new shale plays is now

hovering around $5/mcf, with the best plays already at $4, and as the learning curve goes up, the cost curve will continue to go down, taking the break-even price for natural gas production down with it."

14. "Greater Prudhoe Bay," BP Fact Sheet, http://www.bp.com/liveassets/bp_internet/globalbp/STAGING/global_assets/downloads/A/abp_wwd_alaska_prudhoe_bay_fact_sheet.pdf.

15. I assumed that companies get better at exploration, drilling, and extraction at between 0 and 2 percent each year, with an average of 1 percent. That means a company would improve its productivity between 0 and 6 percent per year, but 3 percent on average. To keep things simple, I assumed that improvements in exploration, drilling, and extraction are independent not only of one another in any given year but also across years, such that there's no carryover from one year to the next.

16. Max H. Bazerman, *Judgment in Managerial Decision Making*, 2nd ed. (New York: Wiley, 1990), 143. Despite the book's title, many examples have little to do with the decisions that real managers face; indeed, there is no consideration of what makes a managerial decision different from other kinds.

17. One of the first explanations in terms of chief executive hubris came from Richard Roll, "The Hubris Theory of Corporate Takeovers," *Journal of Business* 59, no. 2 (1986): 197–216.

18. The evidence is based on financial markets' immediate responses to the announcement of an acquisition. If financial markets are efficient, or at least efficient most of the time, then all that's publicly known is factored in at the time of acquisition. When the announcement is made that Company A will pay a given sum to acquire Company B, the change in their share prices reflects the market's expectation of changes in financial performance. We expect the share price of the acquired firm to go up, for otherwise there would be no sale, but what about the price of the acquiring firm? If the deal is expected to be a good move for the acquiring firm, we would expect its share price to go up as well. But that's not what usually happens. The market usually sends the shares of the acquiring company lower, reflecting a sense that benefits will not be as great as the amount paid.

19. Mark L. Sirower and Sumit Sahni, "Avoiding the 'Synergy Trap': Practical Guidance on M&A Decisions for CEOs and Boards," *Journal of Applied Corporate Finance* 18, no. 3 (Summer 2006): 83–95. Recently there has been evidence of a change. JP Morgan reported in 2012 that investor responses to acquisitions have moved from slightly negative on average to somewhat positive. One explanation, however, is that as markets learned to be skeptical of most deals, fewer were attempted, leaving only the most credible and likely to succeed to go through. Thus, the average improves because the mix of deals changes. See Corporate Finance Advisory and Mergers & Acquisitions, *Uncorking M&A: The 2013 Vintage* (J.P. Morgan, December 2012), https://www.jpmorgan.com/cm/BlobServer/JPMorgan_CorporateFinanceAdvisory_MA.pdf.

20. Edward E. Whitacre Jr., *Corporate Acquisitions Can Create Winners: A Case in Point*, The CEO Series, Business Leaders, Thought and Action, (St. Louis, MO: Washington University, Center for the Study of American Business, 1998).

21. Almar Latour and Shawn Young, "Two Who May Pop the Question to AT&T Wireless—Intent on Wireless Expansion, SBC Communications' Whitacre Takes Risks Seeking Acquisitions," *Wall Street Journal*, February 10, 2004, B1.

22. Wachtell Lipton was again in the news, on September 12, 2008, when the sale of Merrill Lynch to Bank of America was hammered out at its offices. James B. Stewart, "Eight Days: The Battle to Save the American Financial System," *New Yorker*, September 21, 2009, 69.

23. Matt Richtel, "List of Suitors Said to Narrow for Mobile Giant," *New York Times*, February 11, 2004, http://www.nytimes.com/2004/02/11/business/list-of-suitors-said-to-narrow-for-mobile-giant.html.

24. Ed Whitacre, *American Turnaround: Reinventing AT&T and GM and the Way We Do Business in the USA* (New York: Business Plus, 2013), 129.

25. Latour and Young, "Two Who May Pop the Question to AT&T Wireless."

26. AT&T Wireless Services, Inc., Proxy Statement Pursuant to Section 14(a) of the Securities Exchange Act of 1934, March 22, 2004.

27. "Vodafone Bids for AT&T Wireless: Vodafone and Cingular Square off in Bids for No. 3 U.S. Wireless Firm at about $35 Billion," New York (*CNN/Money*), February 15, 2004, http://money.cnn.com/2004/02/15/technology/att_bids/.

28. Dan Sabbagh, "Vodafone in $35bn Fight for AT&T Wireless," *The Times*, February 16, 2004, http://www.thetimes.co.uk/tto/business/article2103013.ece.

29. Vodafone was engaged in two sets of calculations, determining what to bid for AT&T Wireless while also negotiating a sale price for its 45 percent stake in Verizon Wireless. The more it could get for Verizon Wireless, the more it would be able to pay for AT&T Wireless. Rumors suggested that Verizon Communications had agreed to buy Vodafone's share for $23 billion, which would have given it plenty of ready cash for an aggressive bid.

30. Anita Raghavan, Almar Latour, and Jesse Drucker, "Battle Intensifies for AT&T Wireless—Vodafone and Cingular Submit Revised Offers as Others Decline to Bid," *Wall Street Journal Europe*, February 16, 2004, A1.

31. Maija Pesola, James Politi, Dan Roberts, and Peter Thal Larsen, "Vodafone Edges Ahead in AT&TW Bidding," *Financial Times*, February 17, 2004, 24.

32. Andrew Ross Sorkin and Matt Richtel, "Cingular Wins AT&T Wireless in an Early-Morning Drama," *New York Times*, February 19, 2004, http://www.nytimes.com/learning/teachers/featured_articles/20040219thursday.html.

33. Whitacre, *American Turnaround*, 131.

34. Whitacre, *American Turnaround*, 131.

35. Sorkin and Richtel, "Cingular Wins AT&T Wireless."

36. Maija Pesola, James Politi, Dan Roberts, and Peter Thal Larsen, "Cingular Grabs AT&TW from Sleeping Vodafone," *Financial Times*, February 18, 2004, 44.

37. Pesola, Politi, Roberts, and Larsen, "Cingular Grabs AT&TW," 44.

38. Richard Wray, "Cingular's $41bn Forces Vodafone out of AT&T Race," *The Guardian*, February 18, 2004, 19.

39. When trading opened on Tuesday, news of the record bid helped push the Standard & Poor's 500 stock index up by 11 points, or about 1 percent, while the Dow Jones industrial average was up 87 points, or 0.8 percent. As for the two principals, shares of Vodafone rose 7 percent on the London FTSE. Investors seemed relieved it had missed out. Meanwhile, shares in Cingular's parent, Ed Whitacre's SBC, fell 18 cents to $24.87, a loss of 0.7 percent, and BellSouth dropped 49 cents to $29.06, a loss of 1.7 percent. Financial markets often punish the stock of an acquirer, assuming that if it bid enough to win the auction, it may have paid too much.

40. Dominic White, "Vodafone Looks to Next Target," *Daily Telegraph*, February 25, 2004, http://www.telegraph.co.uk/finance/2878078/Vodafone-looks-to-next-target.html. Vodafone released this statement: "On 17 February 2004, Vodafone withdrew from the auction when it concluded that it was no longer in its shareholders' best interests to continue discussions. Vodafone remains committed to its existing position in the U.S. market with its successful partnership in Verizon Wireless."

41. When Dow Chemical bought Rohm & Haas in July 2008, the company's CEO justified the high price by describing the target as "a high quality beachfront property." That disastrous deal is one of many in a very good general treatment of optimism in mergers and acquisitions. Mauboussin, *Think Twice*.

42. Whitacre, *American Turnaround*, 133.

43. Whitacre, *American Turnaround*, 131.

44. Whitacre, *American Turnaround*, 129.

45. Chairman's Letter, 2005 AT&T Annual Report [at that time SBC], http://www.att.com/Investor/ATT_Annual/2005/chairletter.html.

46. Leslie Cauley, "BellSouth Likes to Go It Alone," *USA Today*, October 31, 2005, http://www.usatoday.com/tech/news/techpolicy/business/2005-10-31-bellsouth-mergers_x.htm.

47. A year later Whitacre retired from AT&T Wireless and subsequently was called into government service as chairman of General Motors, which he led from 2009 until 2011. Yet the powerhouse he built continued to grow. In March 2011 AT&T Wireless agreed to pay $39 billion to acquire T-Mobile, which would have made it the largest wireless carrier, with 42 percent of US subscribers, vaulting it past Verizon. "From AT&T's perspective, this is a huge win," said one market analyst. "It's about being No. 1 and having economy of scale." Andrew Ross Sorkin, Michael J. De La Merced, and Jenna Wortham, "AT&T to Buy T-Mobile USA for $39 Billion," *New York Times*, March 20, 2011, http://dealbook.nytimes.com/2011/03/20/att-to-buy-t-mobile-usa-for-39-billion/. Eventually, however, that proposed acquisition fell through.

48. Whitacre, *American Turnaround*, 129.

49. Aditya Chakrabortty, "Haven't the Politicians Desperately Scrambling to Form a Government Heard of the Winner's Curse?" *The Guardian*, November 5, 2010, 5.

Chapter 11: Starting Up, Starting Out

1. US Dept. of Commerce, Bureau of the Census, *Business Dynamics Statistics*, http://weblog.sba.gov/blog-advo/?p=1037.

2. Timothy Dunne, Mark J. Roberts, and Larry Samuelson, "Patterns of Firm Entry and Exit in U.S. Manufacturing Industries," *Rand Journal of Economics* 19, no 4 (Winter 1988): 233–271; Daniel Kahneman, *Thinking, Fast and Slow* (New York: Farrar, Straus, and Giroux, 2011), 256.

3. This view is captured as follows: "An individual's decision whether to become an entrepreneur will be based upon a comparison of the expected reward to entrepreneurship and the reward to the best alternative use of his time." C. A. Campbell, "A Decision Theory Model of Entrepreneurial Acts," *Entrepreneurship Theory and Practice* 17, no. 1 (1992): 21–27.

4. If we're not careful, subjective expected utility can be used to justify anything, even the most pernicious addictions. It can become a tautology and therefore offer little explanatory power.

5. Mathew L. A. Hayward, Dean A. Shepherd, and Dale Griffin, "A Hubris Theory of Entrepreneurship," *Management Science* 52, no. 2 (2006): 160–172.

6. Colin Camerer and Dan Lovallo "Overconfidence and Excess Entry: An Experimental Approach," *American Economic Review* 89, no 1 (1999): 313.

7. Camerer and Lovallo, "Overconfidence and Excess Entry," 306–318.

8. "Cognitive and decision biases are likely to be intrinsic ingredients of technological development and corporate strategies, including those concerning new start-up firms." Giovanni Dosi and Dan Lovallo, "Rational Entrepreneurs or Optimistic Martyrs? Some Considerations on Technological Regimes, Corporate Entries, and the Evolutional Role of Decision Biases," in *Technological Innovation: Oversights and Foresights,* ed. Raghu Garud, Praveen Nattar Nayyar, and Zur Baruch Shapira (New York: Cambridge University Press, 1997), 41–68.

9. Kahneman, *Thinking, Fast and Slow,* 255–257.

10. Barry J. Moltz, *You Need to Be a Little Crazy: The Truth About Starting and Growing Your Business* (Chicago: Dearborn Trade Publishing, 2003).

11. Michael Lewis, "In Defense of the Boom," *New York Times Magazine,* October 27, 2002, http://www.nytimes.com/2002/10/27/magazine/27DEFENSE.html.

12. Martha Lane Fox, interview on *HARDtalk,* BBC, December 11, 2003.

13. We need not even conclude that entrepreneurs suffer from overestimation to observe excess entry. As long as people have fallible judgment and will vary around the mean, those who are most confident will go on to found a new company. This phenomenon is analogous to the winner's curse: even if on average people are risk averse, with some variation around the mean, it is those who stand at an extreme point on the distribution who will pay the most. Robin M. Hogarth and Natalia Karelaia, "Entrepreneurial Success and Failure: Confidence and Fallible Judgment," *Organization Science* 23 (2012): 1733–1747.

14. See, for example: Brian Headd, "Redefining Business Success: Distinguishing Between Closure and Failure." *Journal Small Business Economics.* 1(1) (2004): 51–61; Knaup, Amy E. "Survival and Longevity in the Business Employment Dynamics data." *Monthly Labor Review.* Vol. 128, Iss. 5, (May 2005): 50-56; US Small Business Administration, "Frequently Asked Questions About Small Business," (2009) http://www.sba .gov/ADVO/stats/sbfaq.txt.

15. David B. Yoffie, Ward Bullard, Nikhil Raj, and Suja Vaidyanathan, "VMware Inc. (A)," *Harvard Business School Case* 9-707-013 (2007).

16. Mendel Rosenblum, interview with author, September 2012.

17. Ed Bugnion, interview with author, September 2011.

18. Bugnion interview.

19. Rosenblum interview.

20. Rosenblum interview.

21. Brad Mattson, interview with author, September 2012.

22. Jessica Livingston, *Founders at Work: Stories of Startups' Early Days* (Berkeley, CA: Apress, 2008), xviii.

23. Livingston, *Founders at Work,* xviii.

24. Don A. Moore, John M. Oesch, and Charlene Zietsma, "What Competition? Myopic Self-Focus in Market-Entry Decisions," *Organization Science* 18, no. 3 (May–June 2007): 440–454.

25. Nicholas Dew, Saras Sarasvathy, Stuart Read, and Robert Wiltbank, "Affordable Loss: Behavioral Aspects of the Plunge Decision," *Strategic Entrepreneurship Journal* 3 (2009): 105–126.

26. Saras D. Sarasvathy, "The Affordable Loss Principle" (technical note, University of Virginia Darden School Foundation, Charlottesville, VA, 2006).

Chapter 12: The Stuff of Winning Decisions

1. The NSA identified several factors for success: schedule, drawings, past performance, technical approach, subcontractor experience, and price. If bidders were similar on the rest, price would be definitive. In its final report, Skanska was rated equal to DPR and Balfour Beatty in three, superior in two, and behind in one. Ultimately the contract appeared to have been awarded on price.

2. http://finance.yahoo.com/news/DPR-Construction-Build-iw-1500962679.html?x=0DPR. "Construction to Build Facebook's Sweden Data Center: Construction to Commence This Month on Social Networking Giant's First Data Center Outside the U.S" (press release, DPR Construction, October 27, 2011).

3. Interviews with David Ibarra, September 2012, and with Gavin Keith, January 2013.

4. Daniel Kahneman, *Thinking, Fast and Slow* (New York: Farrar, Straus, and Giroux, 2011), 419.

5. Bruce Bueno de Mesquita comments that aside from two-year-olds and schizophrenics, most people are able to state their preferences and act in reasonably consistent ways to achieve them. *The Predictioneer's Game: Using the Logic of Brazen Self-Interest to See and Shape the Future* (New York: Random House, 2009), 19.

6. Dan Lovallo and Olivier Sibony. "The Case for Behavioral Strategy," *McKinsey Quarterly* 2 (Spring 2010): 30-43.

7. The need for strategic decision makers to avoid cognitive biases was explained by Dan P. Lovallo and Olivier Sibony in "Distortions and Deceptions in Strategic Decisions," *McKinsey Quarterly* (February 2006): 19–29, and also by Daniel Kahneman, Dan Lovallo, and Olivier Sibony in "Before You Make that Big Decision . . . " *Harvard Business Review* (June 2011): 51–60.

8. Chip Heath and Dan Heath. *Decisive: How to Make Better Choices in Life and Work*. New York: Crown Business, 2013.

9. Zur Shapira, *Risk Taking: A Managerial Perspective* (New York: Russell Sage Foundation, 1995), 132.

10. Buzz Bissinger, *Three Nights in August: Strategy, Heartbreak, and Joy Inside the Mind of a Manager* (Boston and New York: Mariner, Houghton Mifflin and Company, 2005), 17.

BIBLIOGRAPHY

BOOKS

Adler, Joseph. *Baseball Hacks: Tips & Tools for Analyzing and Winning with Statistics.* Sebastapool, CA: O'Reilly, 2006.

Apollo 13: The NASA Mission Reports. Burlington, ON: Apogee Books, 2000.

Ariely, Dan. *Predictably Irrational: The Hidden Forces that Shape Our Decisions.* New York: HarperCollins, 2008.

———. *The Upside of Irrationality: Defying Logic at Home and at Work.* New York: HarperCollins, 2010.

Ayres, Ian. *Super Crunchers: Why Thinking-by-Numbers Is the New Way to Be Smart.* New York: Bantam Dell Books, 2007.

Barnett, William P. *The Red Queen among Organizations: How Competitiveness Evolves.* Princeton, NJ: Princeton University Press, 2008.

Bazerman, Max H. *Judgment in Managerial Decision Making.* 2nd ed. New York: Wiley, 1990.

Bazerman, Max H., and Don A. Moore. *Judgment in Managerial Decision Making.* 7th ed. New York: Wiley, 2008.

Bloom, Benjamin S., ed. *Developing Talent in Young People.* New York: Ballantine Books, 1985.

Boswell, James. *Life of Johnson.* Oxford: Oxford University Press, 2008.

Bram, Uri. *Thinking Statistically.* N.p.: Kuri Books, 2012.

Brooks, David. *The Social Animal: A Story of How Success Happens,* London: Short Books, 2011

Bruch, Heike, and Sumantra Ghoshal. *A Bias for Action: How Effective Managers Harness Their Willpower, Achieve Results, and Stop Wasting Time.* Boston: Harvard Business School Press, 2004.

Bueno de Mesquita, Bruce. *The Predictioneer's Game: Using the Logic of Brazen Self-Interest to See and Shape the Future.* New York: Random House, 2009.

College Board. *Student Descriptive Questionnaire.* Princeton, NJ: Educational Testing Service, 1976–1977.

Colvin, Geoff. *Talent Is Overrated: What Really Separates World-Class Performers from Everybody Else*, New York: Portfolio Trade, 2010.

Coyle, Daniel. *The Talent Code: Greatness Isn't Born. It's Grown. Here's How.* New York: Bantam, 2009.

Dixit, Avinash K., and Barry J. Nalebuff. *The Art of Strategy: A Game Theorist's Guide to Success in Life and Business.* New York: Norton, 2008.

Ehrenreich, Barbara. *Bright-Sided: How the Relentless Promotion of Positive Thinking Has Undermined America.* New York: Holt, 2009.

Feinstein, Jon. *The Majors: In Pursuit of Golf's Holy Grail.* New York: Little, Brown, 1999.

Feynman, Richard P. *The Pleasure of Findings Things Out: The Best Short Works of Richard P. Feynman.* London: Penguin, 1999.

Flanagan, Eileen. *The Wisdom to Know the Difference: When to Make a Change—and When to Let Go.* New York: Tarcher, 2009.

Foer, Joshua. *Moonwalking with Einstein: The Art and Science of Remembering Everything,* New York: Penguin, 2012.

Garud, Raghu, Praveen Nattar Nayyar, and Zur Baruch Shapira, eds. *Technological Innovation: Oversights and Foresights.* New York: Cambridge University Press, 1997.

Gawande, Atul. *Better: A Surgeon's Notes on Performance.* London: Profile, 2007.

George, Bill. *Authentic Leadership: Rediscovering the Secrets to Creating Lasting Value.* San Francisco: Jossey-Bass, 2004.

Goldie, Daniel C., and Gordon S. Murray. *The Investment Answer: Learn to Manage Your Money and Protect Your Financial Future.* New York: Business Plus, 2011.

Groopman, Jerome. *The Anatomy of Hope: How People Prevail in the Face of Illness.* New York: Random House, 2003.

———. *How Doctors Think.* New York: Houghton Mifflin, 2007.

Haidt, Jonathan. *The Happiness Hypothesis: Putting Ancient Wisdom and Philosophy to the Test of Modern Science.* London: Arrow Books, 2006.

Hallinan, Joseph T. *Why We Make Mistakes: How We Look Without Seeing, Forget Things in Seconds, and Are All Pretty Sure We Are Way Above Average.* New York: Broadway Books, 2009.

Hamilton, Tyler, and Daniel Coyle. *The Secret Race: Inside the Hidden World of the Tour de France: Doping, Cover-Ups, and Winning at All Costs.* New York: Bantam Books, 2012.

Heath, Chip, and Dan Heath. *Decisive: How to Make Better Choices in Life and Work.* New York: Crown Business, 2013.

Heilemann, John, and Mark Halperin. *Game Change: Obama and the Clintons, McCain and Palin, and the Race of a Lifetime.* New York: HarperCollins, 2010.

Hoff, Joan. *Nixon Reconsidered.* New York: Basic Books, 1995.

Isaacson, Walter. *Steve Jobs*. New York: Little, Brown, 2011.

James, Bill. *Bill James Historical Baseball Abstract*. New York: Free Press, 2001.

———. *Solid Fool's Gold: Detours on the Way to Conventional Wisdom*. Chicago: ACTA Sports, 2011.

Johnson, Stephen B. *The Secret of Apollo: Systems Management in American and European Space Programs*. Baltimore, MD: Johns Hopkins University Press, 2002.

Kahneman, Daniel. *Thinking, Fast and Slow*. New York: Farrar, Straus, and Giroux, 2011.

Keri, Jonah. *The Extra 2%: How Wall Street Strategies Took a Major League Team from Worst to First*. New York: Ballantine Books, 2011.

Khurana, Rakesh. *Searching for a Corporate Savior: The Irrational Quest for Charismatic CEOs*. Princeton, NJ: Princeton University Press, 2002.

Klein, Gary. *Sources of Power: How People Make Decisions*. Cambridge, MA: MIT Press, 1998.

———. *Streetlights and Shadows: Searching for the Keys to Adaptive Decision Making*. Cambridge, MA: MIT Press, 2009.

Kotter, John. *A Force for Change: How Leadership Differs from Management*. New York: Free Press, 1990.

Kraft, Chris. *Flight: My Life in Mission Control*. New York: Dutton, 2001.

Kranz, Gene. *Failure Is Not an Option: Mission Control from Mercury to Apollo 13 and Beyond*. New York: Berkley Books, 2000.

Kuehl, Karl, John Kuehl, and Casey Tefertiller. *Mental Toughness: Baseball's Winning Edge*. Chicago: Ivan R. Dee, 2005.

Lasorda, Tommy, and David Fisher. *The Artful Dodger*. New York: Arbor House, 1985.

Lewis, Michael. *Moneyball: The Art of Winning an Unfair Game*. New York: Norton, 2003.

Liebergot, Sy. *Apollo EECOM: Journey of a Lifetime*. Burlington, ON: Apogee Books, 2003.

Livingston, Jessica. *Founders at Work: Stories of Startups' Early Days*. Berkeley, CA: Apress, 2008.

MacMillan, Margaret. *Nixon and Mao: The Week That Changed the World*. New York: Random House, 2007.

Malkiel, Burton G. *A Random Walk Down Wall Street: The Time-Tested Strategy for Successful Investing.* 10th ed. New York: W.W. Norton, 2012.

Marks, Howard. *The Most Important Thing: Uncommon Sense for the Thoughtful Investor*. New York: Columbia University Press, 2011.

Mauboussin, Michael J. *More Than You Know: Finding Financial Wisdom in Unconventional Places*. Boston: Harvard Business School Press, 2007.

———. *Think Twice: Harnessing the Power of Counterintuition*. Boston: Harvard Business Press, 2009.

McClement, Mike. *Brilliant Confidence: What Confident People Know, Say and Do.* Harlow, UK: Pearson Education, 2010.

McGee, Paul. *Self-Confidence: The Remarkable Truth of Why a Small Change Can Make a Big Difference.* 2nd ed. Chichester, UK: Capstone Publishing Ltd., 2012.

McGrayne, Sharon Bertsch. *The Theory That Would not Die: How Bayes' Rule Cracked the Enigma Code, Hunted Down Russian Submarines, and Emerged Triumphant from Two Centuries of Controversy.* New Haven, CT: Yale University Press, 2011.

McKenna, Paul. *Instant Confidence: The Power to Go for Anything You Want.* London: Transworld Publishers, 2006.

Moltz, Barry J. *You Need to Be a Little Crazy: The Truth About Starting and Growing Your Business.* Chicago: Dearborn Trade Publishing, 2003.

Morgan, Joe, and David Falkner. *Joe Morgan: A Life in Baseball.* New York: W.W. Norton & Co., 1993.

Newman, Thomas B., and Michael A. Kohn. *Evidence-Based Diagnosis.* New York: Cambridge University Press, 2009.

Nye, Joseph S., Jr. *The Powers to Lead.* Oxford: Oxford University Press, 2008.

Orwell, George. *A Collection of Essays.* San Diego, CA: Harvest, 1981.

Peters, Thomas J., and Robert H. Waterman Jr. *In Search of Excellence: Lessons from America's Best Managed Companies.* New York: Warner Books, 1982.

Plous, Scott. *The Psychology of Judgment and Decision Making.* New York: McGraw-Hill, 1993.

Raynor, Michael E. *The Strategy Paradox: Why Committing to Success Leads to Failure (and What to Do About It).* New York: Currency Doubleday, 2007.

Rotella, Dr. Bob. *Golf Is a Game of Confidence.* New York: Simon & Schuster, 1996.

———. *Learned Optimism: How to Change Your Mind and Your Life.* New York: Vintage Books, 2006.

Shapira, Zur. *Risk Taking: A Managerial Perspective.* New York: Russell Sage Foundation, 1995.

Sharot, Tali. *The Optimism Bias: A Tour of the Irrationally Positive Brain.* New York: Pantheon Books, 2011.

Shaw, George Bernard. "Maxims for Revolutionists." In *Man and Superman: A Comedy and Philosophy.* London: Penguin Books, 2000.

Shenk, David. *The Genius in All of Us: Why Everything You've Been Told About Genetics, Talent, and IQ Is Wrong.* New York: Anchor, 2011.

Silver, Nate. *The Signal and the Noise: Why So Many Predictions Fail—But Some Don't.* New York: Penguin, 2012.

Smith, Adam. *The Money Game.* New York: Vintage Books, 1976.

Sokolove, Michael. *Hustle: The Myth, Life, and Lies of Pete Rose.* New York: Simon & Schuster, 1990.

Stever, H. Guyford, and James J. Haggerty. *Flight*. New York: Time Inc., 1965.

Sutton, Robert I. *Weird Ideas That Work: 11½ Ways to Promote, Manage, and Sustain Innovation*. New York: Penguin, 2001.

Syed, Matthew. *Bounce: The Myth of Talent and the Power of Practice: Beckham, Serena, Mozart, and the Science of Success*. New York: Harper, 2011.

Taleb, Nassim Nicholas. *The Black Swan: The Impact of the Highly Improbable*. New York: Random House, 2007.

Tetlock, Philip E. *Expert Political Judgment: How Good Is It? How Can We Know?* Princeton, NJ: Princeton University Press, 2005.

Thaler, Richard H., *The Winner's Curse: Paradoxes and Anomalies of Economic Life*. Princeton, NJ: Princeton University Press, 1992.

Thaler, Richard H., and Cass Sunstein. *Nudge: Improving Decisions about Health, Wealth, and Happiness*. New Haven, CT: Yale University Press, 2008.

Trilling, Lionel. *Sincerity and Authenticity*. Cambridge, MA: Harvard University Press, 1971.

Whitacre, Ed, with Leslie Cauley. *American Turnaround: Reinventing AT&T and GM and the Way We Do Business in the USA*. New York: Business Plus, 2013.

Wolfe, Tom. *The Right Stuff*. New York: Farrar, Straus, and Giroux, 1979.

Yeager, Chuck, Bob Cardenas, Bob Hoover, Jack Russell, and James Young. *The Quest for Mach One: A First-Person Account of Breaking the Sound Barrier*. New York: Penguin, 1997.

Yeager, Chuck, and Leo Janos. *Yeager: An Autobiography*. New York: Bantam Books, 1985.

Yeung, Dr. Rob. *Confidence: The Power to Take Control and Live the Life You Want*. Harlow, UK: Pearson Education Ltd., 2011.

Zweig, Jason. *Your Money and Your Brain: How the New Science of Neuroeconomics Can Help Make You Rich*. New York: Simon & Schuster, 2007.

ARTICLES

Adams, Tim. "How a Book about Baseball Statistics Changed the Way We Think about Football." *Esquire*, September 2011, 198–203.

Ahmed, Murad. "Jobs: The Special One." *The Times*, October 29, 2011, 16.

Alpert, Marc, and Howard Raiffa. "A Progress Report on the Training of Probability Assessors." Unpublished manuscript, 1969. In *Judgment Under Uncertainty: Heuristics and Biases*, edited by Daniel Kahneman, Paul Slovic, and Amos Tversky. Cambridge, UK: Cambridge University Press, 1982.

Ashenfelter, Orley. "Predicting the Quality and Prices of Bordeaux Wine." *Economic Journal* 118, no. 529 (June 2008): F174–F184.

AT&T Wireless Services, Inc. Proxy Statement Pursuant to Section 14(a) of the Securities Exchange Act of 1934, March 22, 2004.

Austen, Ian. "Bicycle Thieves: World-Class Cycling's Drug Trade." *New York Times*, September 12, 2012, C7.

Austin, Michael. "Building the Perfect Arc: Research Shows Players Need to Keep Shot Arc around 45 Degrees." *Winning Hoops*, May/June 2010, 20–27.

Baker, Peter, and Jim Rutemberg. "The Long Road to a Clinton Exit." *New York Times*, June 8, 2008, A1.

Bazerman, Max H., and William F. Samuelson. "I Won the Auction but I Don't Want the Prize." *Journal of Conflict Resolution* 27 (1983): 618–634.

Bendery, Jennifer. "Nancy Pelosi Predicts 6–3 Supreme Court Vote in Favor of Health Care Law." *Huffington Post*, April 4, 2012, http://www.huffington post.com/2012/04/04/nancy-pelosi-health-care-law_n_1402908.html.

Bennis, Warren. "Acting the Part of a Leader." *Businessweek*, September 14, 2009, 80.

Bishop, Greg. "Pacquiao Stunned in Sixth Round." *New York Times*, December 9, 2012, http://www.nytimes.com/2012/12/09/sports/juan-manuel -marquez-knocks-out-manny-pacquiao-in-sixth-round.html.

Bornstein, David. "The Dawn of Evidence-Based Budget." *New York Times*, May 30, 2012, http://opinionator.blogs.nytimes.com/2012/05/30/worthy-of-govern ment-funding-prove-it.

Boyle, Elizabeth, and Zur Shapira. "The Liability of Leading: Battling Aspiration and Survival Goals in *Jeopardy*'s Tournament of Champions." *Organization Science* 23, no.4, (2012): 1110–1113.

Brooks, David. "The Fatal Conceit." *New York Times*, October 26, 2009, A31.

Byers, Dylan. "Dick Morris Fesses Up." *Politico.com*, November 13, 2012, http://www.politico.com/blogs/media/2012/11/dick-morris-fesses-up -149453.html.

Cain, Daylian M., and Allan S. Detsky, "Everyone's a Little Bit Biased (Even Physicians)." *JAMA* 299, no.24 (June 25, 2008): 2893–2895.

Camerer, Colin, and Dan Lovallo. "Overconfidence and Excess Entry: An Experimental Approach." *American Economic Review* 89, no 1 (1999): 306–318.

Campbell, Charles A. "A Decision Theory Model of Entrepreneurial Acts." *Entrepreneurship Theory and Practice* 17, no. 1 (1992): 21–27.

Capen, Edward C., Robert V. Clapp, and William M. Campbell. "Competitive Bidding in High Risk Situations." *Journal of Petroleum Technology* 23 (1971): 641–653.

Casscells, Ward, Arno Schoenberger, and Thomas Graboys "Interpretation by physicians of clinical laboratory results." *New England Journal of Medicine* 299: 18 (1978) 999–1001.

Cauley, Leslie. "BellSouth Likes to Go It Alone." *USA Today*, October 31, 2005, http://usatoday30.usatoday.com/tech/news/techpolicy/business/2005 -10-31-bellsouth-mergers_x.htm?POE=TECISVA.

Chakrabortty, Aditya. "Haven't the Politicians Desperately Scrambling to Form a Government Heard of the Winner's Curse?" *The Guardian*, November 5, 2010, 5.

College Board. *Student Descriptive Questionnaire*. Princeton, NJ: Educational Testing Service, 1976–1977.

Corporate Finance Advisory and Mergers & Acquisitions. "Uncorking M&A: The 2013 Vintage." *J.P. Morgan*, December 2012.

Craggs, Tommy. "Say-It-Ain't-So Joe." *SF Weekly*, July 6, 2005, http://www.sfweekly.com/2005-07-06/news/say-it-ain-t-so-joe.

Critchley, Simon, and Jamieson Webster. "The Gospel According to 'Me'." *New York Times*, June 30, 2013, SR8.

DeBondt, Walter F., and Richard H. Thaler. "Financial Decision-Making in Markets and Firms: A Behavioral Perspective." *Handbooks in OR & MS 9* (1995): 385–410.

Dew, Nicholas, Saras Sarasvathy, Stuart Read, and Robert Wiltbank. "Affordable Loss: Behavioral Aspects of the Plunge Decision." *Strategic Entrepreneurship Journal* 3 (2009): 105–126.

Diaz, Jaime. "Perils of Putting: Duffers, Take Heart. A New Study by the PGA Tour Reveals That When It Comes to Putting, the Pros Aren't So Hot Either." *Sports Illustrated*, April 3, 1989.

Dosi, Giovanni, and Dan Lovallo, "Rational Entrepreneurs or Optimistic Martyrs? Some Considerations on Technological Regimes, Corporate Entries, and the Evolutional Role of Decision Biases." In *Technological Innovation: Oversights and Foresights*, edited by Raghu Garud, Praveen Nattar Nayyar, and Zur Baruch Shapira, 41–68. New York: Cambridge University Press, 1997.

Dubner, Stephen J., and Steven D. Levitt. "A Star Is Made." *New York Times*, May 7, 2006, http://www.nytimes.com/2006/05/07/magazine/07wwln_freak.html?pagewanted=all.

Dunne, Timothy, Mark J. Roberts, and Larry Samuelson. "Patterns of Firm Entry and Exit U.S. Manufacturing Industries." *Rand Journal of Economics* 19, no. 4 (Winter 1988): 233–271.

Eckhardt, Roger. "Stan Ulam, John von Neumann, and the Monte Carlo Method." *Los Alamos Science* 15, Special Issue (1987): 131–137.

Eichler, Jeremy. "String Theorist: Christian Tetzlaff Rethinks How a Violin Should Sound." *New Yorker*, August 27, 2012, 34–39.

Ericsson, K. Anders, Ralf Th. Krampe, and Clemens Tesch-Römer. "The Role of Deliberate Practice in the Acquisition of Expert Performance." *Psychological Review* 100, no. 3 (1993): 363–406.

Ericsson, K. Anders, Michael J. Prietula, and Edward T. Cokely, "The Making of an Expert," *Harvard Business Review*, July–August 2007, 114–121.

Feynman, Richard P. "What Is and What Should Be the Role of Scientific

Culture in Modern Society." Address to the Galileo Symposium, Italy, 1964. In *The Pleasure of Findings Things Out: The Best Short Works of Richard P. Feynman*, 106–107. London: Penguin, 1999.

Fienberg, Stephen E. "When Did Bayesian Inference Become Bayesian?" *Bayesian Analysis* 1, no. 1 (2006): 1–40.

Fisher, Kenneth L. "The Eight Biggest Mistakes Investors Make." *UT Today* 1 (2007): 50–53.

Flyvbjerg, Bent, Mette K. Skamris Holm, and Søren L. Buhl. "How (In)Accurate Are Demand Forecasts in Public Works Projects?" *Journal of the American Planning Association* 71 (2005): 131–146.

"Former FEMA Chief Says Bush Was Engaged but Overconfident." *Associated Press*, March 1, 2006, http://www.foxnews.com/story/0,2933,186546,00.html.

Fox, Jeremy. "Frequentist vs. Bayesian Statistics: Resources to Help You Choose," http://oikosjournal.wordpress.com/2011/10/11/frequentist-vs-bayesian-statistics-resources-to-help-you-choose/.

Friedman, Thomas L. "Obama's Best-Kept Secrets." *New York Times*, October 21, 2012, SR1.

Gapper, John. "McKinsey's Model Springs a Leak." *Financial Times*, March 10, 2011, 9.

Gawande, Atul. "The Bell Curve: What Happens When Patients Find out How Good Their Doctors Really Are?" *New Yorker*, December 6, 2004, 82–91.

Gino, Francesca, Zachariah Sharek, and Don A. Moore. "Keeping the Illusion of Control Under Control: Ceilings, Floors, and Imperfect Calibration." *Organizational Behavior and Human Decision Processes* 114, no. 2 (March 2011), 104–114.

Goffee, Robert, and Gareth Jones. "Managing Authenticity: The Great Paradox of Leadership." *Harvard Business Review* (December 2005): 87–94.

Gollwitzer, Peter M., and Ronald F. Kinney. "Effects of Deliberative and Implemental Mind-sets on Illusion of Control." *Journal of Personality and Social Psychology* 56, no. 4 (1989): 531–542.

Goodstein, Laurie. "Serenity Prayer Skeptic Now Credits Niebuhr." *New York Times*, November 28, 2009, A11.

Gopnik, Adam. "Life Studies: What I Learned When I Learned to Draw." *New Yorker*, June 27, 2011, 56–63.

"Greater Prudhoe Bay," BP Fact Sheet, http://www.bp.com/liveassets/bp_internet/globalbp/STAGING/global_assets/downloads/A/abp_wwd_alaska_prudhoe_bay_fact_sheet.pdf.

Hambrick, David Z., and Elizabeth J. Meinz. "Sorry, Strivers: Talent Matters." *New York Times*, November 20, 2011, SR12.

Hardy, Quentin. "Intel Tries to Secure Its Footing Beyond PCs," *New York Times*, April 15, 2013, B1.

Harford, Tim. "Screening: It's All in the Numbers." *Financial Times/FT.com Magazine*, December 10/11, 2011.

Hayward, Mathew L. A., Dean A. Shepherd, and Dale Griffin. "A Hubris Theory of Entrepreneurship." *Management Science* 52, no. 2 (2006): 160–172.

Headd, Brian. "Redefining Business Success: Distinguishing Between Closure and Failure." *Journal Small Business Economics*. 1(1) (2004): 51–61.

Hogarth, Robin M., and Natalia Karelaia. "Entrepreneurial Success and Failure: Confidence and Fallible Judgment." *Organization Science* 23 (2012): 1733–1747.

Humphrey, Elizabeth King. "Be Sad and Succeed." *Scientific American*, March 3, 2010, http://www.scientificamerican.com/article.cfm?id=be-sad-and-succeed.

Kahneman, Daniel, and Amos Tversky. "On the Psychology of Prediction." *Psychological Review* 80 (1973): 237–257.

Kahneman, Daniel, Dan Lovallo, and Olivier Sibony. "Before You Make that Big Decision. . . ." *Harvard Business Review* (June 2011): 51–60.

Keogh, Brian. "Harrington and the Man with Two Brains." *Irish Golf News*, March 6, 2013, http://www.irishgolfdesk.com/news-files/2013/3/6/harrington-and -the-man-with-two-brains.html.

Knaup, Amy E. "Survival and Longevity in the Business Employment Dynamics data." *Monthly Labor Review*. Vol. 128, Iss. 5, (May 2005): 50–56.

Kopecki, Dawn, Clea Benson, and Phil Mattingly. "Dimon Says Overconfidence Fueled Loss He Can't Defend." *Bloomberg News*, June 14, 2012, http:// www.bloomberg.com/news/2012-06-14/dimon-says-overconfidence -fueled-loss-he-can-t-defend.html.

Kreps, Daniel. "Lennon's 'A Day in the Life' Lyrics Sell for $1.2 Million." *Rolling Stone*, June 18, 2010, http://www.rollingstone.com/music/news /lennons-a-day-in-the-life-lyrics-sell-for-1-2-million-20100618.

Kroichick, Ron. "Giants' Wilson Hopes Hitters Fear the Beard." *San Francisco Chronicle*, October 7, 2010, http://www.sfgate.com/sports/kroichick /article/Giants-Wilson-hopes-hitters-fear-the-beard-3171420.php.

Kruger, J. "Lake Wobegone Be Gone! The 'Below-average' Effect and the Egocentric Nature of Comparative Ability Judgments." *Journal of Personality and Social Psychology* 77 (1999): 221–232.

"Lance Armstrong: 'Impossible to Win Without Doping'." *USA Today*, June 28, 2013, http://www.usatoday.com/story/sports/cycling/2013/06/28/lance -armstrong-impossible-win-tour-de-france-doping/2471413/.

Langer, Ellen J. "The Illusion of Control." *Journal of Personality and Social Psychology* 32 (1975): 311–328.

Latour, Almar, and Shawn Young. "Two Who May Pop the Question to AT&T Wireless—Intent on Wireless Expansion, SBC Communications' Whitacre Takes Risks Seeking Acquisitions." *Wall Street Journal*, February 10, 2004, B1.

Leonhardt, David. "Science and Art at Odds on the Field of Dreams." *New York Times*, August 29, 2005, http://www.nytimes.com/2005/08/28/sports/28iht-THEORIES.html.

Lewis, Michael. "In Defense of the Boom." *New York Times Magazine*, October 27, 2002, http://www.nytimes.com/2002/10/27/magazine/27DEFENSE.html.

———. "Out of Their Tree." *Sports Illustrated*, March 1, 2004, http://sportsillustrated.cnn.com/vault/article/magazine/MAG1031308/index.htm.

Lion, Valérie. "L'Entretien: Bertrand Piccard 'Explorer, c'est aller au-delà des évidences'." *L'Express* no. 3187, August 1, 2012, 8–11.

Loomis, Carol J. "Why Carly's Bet Is Failing." *Fortune*, February 7, 2005, 50–64.

Lovallo, Dan, Carmina Clarke, and Colin Camerer. "Robust Analogizing and the Outside View: Two Empirical Tests of Case-based Decision Making." *Strategic Management Journal* 33, no. 5 (May 2012): 496–512.

Lovallo, Dan, and Daniel Kahneman. "Delusions of Success: How Optimism Undermines Executives' Decisions." *Harvard Business Review* (July 2003): 56–63.

Lovallo, Dan, and Olivier Sibony. "The Case for Behavioral Strategy," *McKinsey Quarterly* 2 (Spring 2010): 30–43.

Lovallo, Dan P., and Olivier Sibony. "Distortions and Deceptions in Strategic Decisions." *McKinsey Quarterly* 1 (February 2006): 19–29.

Lovett, Ian. "Tatooed Guy Pivotal in Armstrong Case," *New York Times*, October 18, 2012, B11.

Lunsford, J. Lynn, and Daniel Michaels. "Bet on Huge Plane Trips up Airbus." *Wall Street Journal*, June 15, 2006, http://online.wsj.com/article/SB115027552490479926.html.

Mandard, Stéphane. "Lance Armstrong: Le Tour de France? Impossible de gagner sans dopage." *Le Monde*, June 29, 2013, Sport & Forme, 5.

"Manny Pacquiao Will Not Give Up Boxing, Despite Pleas From Family." BBC, December 10, 2012, http://www.bbc.co.uk/sport/0/boxing/20666106.

March, James G., and Zur Shapira. "Managerial Perceptions on Risk and Risk-Taking." *Management Science* 33 (1987): 1404–1418.

———. "Variable Risk Preference and the Focus of Attention." *Psychological Science* 99, no. 1 (1992): 172–183.

Martin, Andrew D., et al. "Competing Approaches to Predicting Supreme Court Decision Making." *Perspectives on Politics* 2 (2004): 763.

McGeehan, Patrick. "It's Official—This Is New York's Hottest Summer." *New York Times*, September 1, 2010, A16.

McMaster, Geoff. "School of Business Wins National Stock Market Contest." *ExpressNews*, December 19, 2001, http://www.expressnews.ualberta.ca/article.cfm?id=1615.

Mintzberg, Henry. "We're Overled and Undermanaged." *Business Week*, August 17, 2009, 68.

Moore, Don, and Paul J. Healy. "The Trouble with Overconfidence." *Psychological Review* 115, no. 2 (April 2008): 502–517.

Moore, Don A., John M. Oesch, and Charlene Zietsma. "What Competition? Myopic Self-Focus in Market-Entry Decisions." *Organization Science* 18, no. 3 (May–June 2007): 440–454.

Moran, Callie. "Overconfident Romney Was So Sure of Victory That He Spent 25 Grand on Victory Fireworks." *Capitol Hill Blue*, November 9, 2012, http://www.capitolhillblue.com/node/45630.

Murphy, Austin. "Guide to a Broken Tour: Tyler Hamilton Shines a Revealing Light on Cycling's Drug Era." *Sports Illustrated*, September 24, 2012, 18.

"No Sun, No Problem for Plane." Associated Press in *Shanghai Daily*, May 4, 2013, A3.

"NTSB Suggests Alcohol Detection Systems on All New Cars." *CBS Local*, December 17, 2012, http://dfw.cbslocal.com/2012/12/17/ntsb-suggests-alcohol-detection-systems-on-all-new-cars/.

O'Brien, Miles CNN Anchor Interview, "Veteran NASA Flight Director Discusses Book About Race to the Moon," *CNN Sunday Morning News*, May 7, 2000.

Patterson, Orlando. "Our Overrated Inner Self." *New York Times*, December 26, 2006, A35.

Pesola, Maija, James Politi, Dan Roberts, and Peter Thal Larsen. "Cingular Grabs AT&TW from Sleeping Vodafone." *Financial Times*, February 18, 2004, 44.

———. "Vodafone Edges Ahead in AT&TW Bidding." *Financial Times*, February 17, 2004, 24.

Pfeffer, Jeffrey, and Robert I. Sutton. "Evidence-Based Management." *Harvard Business Review* (January 2006): 63–74.

Pinker, Steven. "Malcolm Gladwell, Eclectic Detective." *New York Times*, November 15, 2009, BR1.

Poulter, Ian. "Opinion." *Golf World* (January 2011): 25.

Price, Richard. "An Essay Toward Solving a Problem in the Doctrine of Chances." *Philosophical Transactions of the Royal Society of London* 53 (1763): 370–418.

Raghavan, Anita, Almar Latour, and Jesse Drucker. "Battle Intensifies for AT&T Wireless—Vodafone and Cingular Submit Revised Offers as Others Decline to Bid." *Wall Street Journal Europe*, February 16, 2004, A1.

Raiffa, Howard. "Decision Analysis: A Personal Account of How It All Got Started and Evolved." *Operations Research* 50, no. 1 (January–February 2002): 179–185.

Rasmussen, Heather N., Michael F. Scheier, and Joel B. Greenhouse, Optimism and Physical Health: A Meta-analytic Review," *Annals of Behavioral Medicine*, 37(3) (June 2009): 239–256.

Richards, Carl. "Viewing the Glass as Half Full, but Not Too Full." *New York Times*, March 18, 2013, http://bucks.blogs.nytimes.com/2013/03/18/viewing -the-glass-as-half-full-but-not-too-full/.

Richtel, Matt. "List of Suitors Said to Narrow for Mobile Giant." *New York Times*, February 11, 2004, http://www.nytimes.com/2004/02/11/business /list-of-suitors-said-to-narrow-for-mobile-giant.html.

Roll, Richard. "The Hubris Theory of Corporate Takeovers." *Journal of Business* 59, no. 2 (1986): 197–216.

Ruger, Theodore W., P. Kim, A. Martin, and K. Quinn. "The Supreme Court Forecasting Project: Legal and Political Science Approaches to Predicting Supreme Court Decisionmaking." *Columbia Law Review* 104 (2004): 1150.

Rice, Xan. "Finish Line: An Olympic Marathon Champion's Tragic Weakness." *New Yorker*, May 21, 2012, 48–57.

Sabbagh, Dan. "Vodafone in $35bn fight for AT&T Wireless." *The Times*, February 16, 2004, http://www.thetimes.co.uk/tto/business/article2103013.ece.

Sarasvathy, Saras D. "The Affordable Loss Principle." Technical Note. Charlottesville, VA: University of Virginia Darden School Foundation, 2006.

Schaefer, Keith. "Natural Gas: Costs Go Down as Learning Curve Goes Up." June 6, 2009. www.oilandgas-investments.com.

Simonson, Itamar, and Amos Tversky. "Choice in Context: Tradeoff Contrast and Extremeness Aversion." *Journal of Marketing Research* 29, no. 3 (1992): 281–295.

Sirower, Mark L., and Sumit Sahni. "Avoiding the 'Synergy Trap': Practical Guidance on M&A Decisions for CEOs and Boards." *Journal of Applied Corporate Finance* 18, no. 3 (Summer 2006): 83–95.

Slusser, Susan. "Can't Keep Beane Down: No More Talk of Moneyball, Please." *San Francisco Chronicle*, July 12, 2009, B1–B7.

Sonmez, Felicia. "Biden Says Supreme Court Will Uphold Health-care Law." *Washington Post*, April 1, 2012, http://www.washingtonpost.com/blogs /post-politics/post/vice-president-biden-predicts-supreme-court-wont -rule-health-care-law-unconstitutional/2012/04/01/gIQADBE8oS_blog .html.

Sorkin, Andrew Ross, Michael J. de la Merced, and Jenna Wortham. "AT&T to Buy T-Mobile USA for $39 Billion." *New York Times*, March 20, 2011, http://dealbook.nytimes.com/2011/03/20/att-to-buy-t-mobile-usa-for -39-billion.

Sorkin, Andrew Ross, and Matt Richtel. "Cingular Wins AT&T Wireless in an Early-Morning Drama." *New York Times*, February 19, 2004, http://www

.nytimes.com/learning/teachers/featured_articles/20040219thursday .html.

Spiegelhalter, David. "Tails You Win: The Science of Chance." *BBC4*, December 20, 2012.

Staw, Barry M. "Leadership and Persistence." In *Leadership and Organizational Culture: New Perspectives on Administrative Theory and Practice*, edited by Thomas J. Sergiovanni and John E. Corbally, 72–84. Champaign: University of Illinois Press, 1986.

Staw, Barry M. "The Escalation of Commitment to a Course of Action." *Academy of Management Review* 6, no. 4 (1981): 577–587.

Stein, Joel. "From Doofus to Genius?" *Bloomberg Businessweek*, November 29–December 4, 2011, 101.

Stewart, James B. "Eight Days: The Battle to Save the American Financial System." *New Yorker*, September 21, 2009, 69.

Stone, Mark Robert, Kevin Thomas, Michael Wilkinson, Andrew M. Jones, Alan St. Clair Gibson, and Kevin G. Thompson. "Effects of Deception on Exercise Performance: Implications for Determinants of Fatigue in Humans." *Medicine & Science in Sports & Exercise* 44, (2012): 534–541.

Svenson, Ola. "Are We All Less Risky and More Skillful Than Our Fellow Drivers?" *Acta Psychologica* 47 (1981): 143–148.

Swartz, Jon. "San Francisco Giants Ride Techball to the Top." *USAToday*, March 31, 2013, http://www.usatoday.com/story/tech/2013/03/31/giants -social-media-world-series-technologh/2013497.

Taber, Joseph John, F. D. Martin, and R. S. Seright. "EOR Screening Criteria Revisited—Part 1: Introduction to Screening Criteria and Enhanced Recovery Field Projects." *SPE Reservoir Engineering* 12, no. 3 (August 1997): 189–198.

"The Tale of the 'Winner's Curse,' Bidding Science Saved $$." http://www .aapg.org/explorer/2004/12dec/capen.cfm.

Taylor, Shelley E., and Jonathan D. Brown. "Illusion and Well-Being: A Social Psychological Perspective on Mental Health." *Psychological Bulletin* 103, no. 2 (March 1988): 193–210.

Terhune, Chad. "Home Depot, Seeking Growth, Knocks on Contractors' Doors—CEO looks to stave off critics and gain new customers with building supply unit," The Wall Street Journal, August 7, 2006 http://online.wsj .com/article/SB115491714152328447.html.

Thaler, Richard H. "Shifting Our Retirement Savings into Automatic." *New York Times*, April 7, 2013, BU6.

———. "The Winner's Curse." *Journal of Economic Perspectives* 2, no. 1 (1988): 191–202.

Tierney, John. "From Tinseltown to Splitsville: Just Do the Math." *New York Times*, September 19, 2006, A25.

"Trend Analysis of the Sex Ratio at Birth in the United States." *National Vital Statistics Reports* 53, no. 20 (June 14, 2005).

Tversky, Amos, and Daniel Kahneman. "Evidential Impact of Base Rates." In *Judgment Under Uncertainty: Heuristics and Biases*, edited by Daniel Kahneman, Paul Slovic, and Amos Tversky. Cambridge, UK: Cambridge University Press, 1982.

Tversky, Amos, and Daniel Kahneman. "Judgment under Uncertainty: Heuristics and Biases." *Science* 185, no. 4157 (1974): 1124–1131.

US Small Business Administration, "Frequently Asked Questions About Small Business," (2009) http://www.sba.gov/ADVO/stats/sbfaq.txt.

Vance, Ashlee. "Algorithms on the Prairie." *Bloomberg Businessweek*, March 26, 2012, 37–39.

"Vodafone bids for AT&T Wireless: Vodafone and Cingular Square Off in Bids for No. 3 U.S. Wireless Firm at About $35 billion," New York (CNN/Money), February 15, 2004, http://money.cnn.com/2004/02/15 /technology/att_bids/.

Walsh, Michael. "Solar-Paneled Plane Completes First Leg of Historic Cross-Country Flight from San Francisco to New York." *New York Daily News*, May 4, 2013, http://www.nydailynews.com/news/national/all-solar-airplane -making-jfk-article-1.1335172.

Weinstein, Neil D. "Unrealistic Optimism about Future Life Events." *Journal of Personality and Social Psychology* 39, no. 5 (1980): 806–820.

Welch, Jack, and Suzy Welch. "How Not to Succeed in Business." *Business Week*, March 2, 2009, 74.

Whitacre, Edward E., Jr. *Corporate Acquisitions Can Create Winners: A Case in Point*. The CEO Series, Business Leaders, Thought and Action. St. Louis, MO: Washington University, Center for the Study of American Business, 1998.

White, Dominic. "Vodafone Looks to Next Target." *Daily Telegraph*, February 25, 2004, http://www.telegraph.co.uk/finance/2878078/Vodafone-looks-to -next-target.html.

White, Paul. "'Moneyball' Principles Have Become Old Hat." *USA Today*, September 21, 2011, 6C.

Wiggins, Robert R., and Timothy W. Ruefli. "Schumpeter's Ghost: Is Hyper-competition Making the Best of Times Shorter?" *Strategic Management Journal* 26, no. 10 (2005): 887–911.

Windschitl, P. D., J. Kruger, and E. Simms. "The Influence of Egocentrism and Focalism on People's Optimism in Competitions: When What Affects Us Equally Affects Me More." *Journal of Personality and Social Psychology* 85 (2003): 389–408.

Wingfield, Nick, and Brian Stelter. "A Juggernaut Stumbles." *New York Times*, October 25, 2011, B1.

Witt, Jessica K., Sally A. Linkenauger, and Dennis R. Proffitt, "Get Me Out of This Slump! Visual Illusions Improve Sports Performance." *Psychological Science* 23 (2012): 397–399.

Wonacott, Peter. "Path to India's Market Dotted with Potholes—Savvy Cola Giants Stumble over local agendas; KFC climbs back from the abyss," *The Wall Street Journal*, September 12, 2006 http://online.wsj.com/article/SB115 801500763459902.html.

Wray, Richard. "Cingular's $41bn Forces Vodafone out of AT&T Race." *The Guardian*, February 18, 2004, 19.

Yoffie, David B., Ward Bullard, Nikhil Raj, and Suja Vaidyanathan. "VMware Inc. (A)." *Harvard Business School Case* 9-707-013 (2007).

Zenger, Todd R. "Why Do Employers Only Reward Extreme Performance? Examining the Relationship Among Pay, Performance, and Turnover." *Administrative Science Quarterly* 37, no. 2 (1992):198–219.

Zhang, Zhen-Xin, Gustavo C. Roman, Zhen Hong, Cheng-Bing Wu, Qui-Ming Qu, Jue-Bing Huang, Bing Zhou, Zhi-Ping Geng, Ji-Zing Wu, Hong-Bo Wen, Heng Zhao, and Gwendolyn E P Zahner. "Parkinson's Disease in China: Prevalence in Beijing, Xian, and Shanghai." *The Lancet* 365 (February 12, 2005): 595–597.

INDEX

Pierre-Antoine Grisoni

PHIL ROSENZWEIG is a professor at IMD in Lausanne, Switzerland, where he works with executives from leading companies on questions of strategy and organization. He is a native of Northern California, where he worked for six years at Hewlett-Packard. Prior to joining IMD, he was an assistant professor at Harvard Business School. Rosenzweig's PhD is from the Wharton School, University of Pennsylvania. He is the author of numerous case studies and has published articles in journals including *Harvard Business Review, California Management Review, Management Science* and *Strategic Management Journal*. His 2007 book, *The Halo Effect . . . and the Eight Other Business Delusions that Deceive Managers*, was described by the *Wall Street Journal* as "a trenchant view of business and business advice" and lauded by Nassim Nicholas Taleb as "one of the most important management books of all time."

PublicAffairs is a publishing house founded in 1997. It is a tribute to the standards, values, and flair of three persons who have served as mentors to countless reporters, writers, editors, and book people of all kinds, including me.

I. F. STONE, proprietor of *I. F. Stone's Weekly*, combined a commitment to the First Amendment with entrepreneurial zeal and reporting skill and became one of the great independent journalists in American history. At the age of eighty, Izzy published *The Trial of Socrates*, which was a national bestseller. He wrote the book after he taught himself ancient Greek.

BENJAMIN C. BRADLEE was for nearly thirty years the charismatic editorial leader of *The Washington Post*. It was Ben who gave the *Post* the range and courage to pursue such historic issues as Watergate. He supported his reporters with a tenacity that made them fearless and it is no accident that so many became authors of influential, best-selling books.

ROBERT L. BERNSTEIN, the chief executive of Random House for more than a quarter century, guided one of the nation's premier publishing houses. Bob was personally responsible for many books of political dissent and argument that challenged tyranny around the globe. He is also the founder and longtime chair of Human Rights Watch, one of the most respected human rights organizations in the world.

·　　·　　·

For fifty years, the banner of Public Affairs Press was carried by its owner Morris B. Schnapper, who published Gandhi, Nasser, Toynbee, Truman, and about 1,500 other authors. In 1983, Schnapper was described by *The Washington Post* as "a redoubtable gadfly." His legacy will endure in the books to come.

Peter Osnos, *Founder and Editor-at-Large*